SPEEDWAY

IN THE SOUTH-EAST

SPEEDWAY
IN THE SOUTH-EAST

Norman Jacobs

TEMPUS

First published 2003

Published in the United Kingdom by:
Tempus Publishing Ltd
The Mill, Brimscombe Port
Stroud, Gloucestershire GL5 2QG

Published in the United States of America by:
Tempus Publishing Inc.
2 Cumberland Street
Charleston, SC 29401

British Library Cataloguing in Publication Data.
A catalogue record for this book is available from the British Library.

ISBN 0 7524 2725 3

Typesetting and origination by Tempus Publishing.
Printed in Great Britain by Midway Colour Print, Wiltshire.

CONTENTS

PART III – OTHER TRACKS

ACKNOWLEDGEMENTS

I am indebted to many people for making this book possible. Amongst those who have willingly spent hours talking to me about their involvement in the sport in the South-East and those who have lent me photographs, programmes and other ephemera for inclusion in this book are Len Silver, Peter Lipscombe, Bryn Williams, Wally Green, Archie Windmill, Robert Andrews, Bill Mathieson, Pete Sampson, David Valentine, Bob Miller, Ghillean Bates-Salter, Ken Taylor, Mike Kemp, Ian Moultray and Ian Hawkins. I would also like to thank Robert Bamford for giving me permission to quote from his and John Jarvis's invaluable reference book, *Homes of British Speedway* (Tempus Publishing, 2001) and Graham Fraser for allowing me to use the information from his *History of Speedway in the Portsmouth Area* printed in the September and December 1999 editions of the *Speedway Researcher*. A special thank you also goes to Tom's shoes.

INTRODUCTION

Although there are various claimants to the title of 'first speedway meeting in Great Britain,' it is now generally accepted that speedway as we know it today first saw the light of day in this country on 19 February 1928 at High Beech in Essex. Since that day, the area around London has continued to make a major contribution to the progress of speedway in this country. Even today, there are still four major tracks operating five teams within the area generally known as the South-East.

With London being the main centre for speedway in the pre-war and immediate post-war boom years, it is probably only natural that the surrounding area should have played a major part in the training of riders for the 'big time'. Tracks at High Beech, Dagenham, Barnet, Smallford, Luton, Rye House, Eastbourne and Iwade have all played their part in finding the stars of tomorrow. But the South-East's contribution to speedway has not just been confined to training tracks. Teams at Eastbourne, Hastings, Rye House, Crayford, Canterbury, Romford, Sittingbourne, Arena Essex and Isle of Wight have all taken part in the country's major leagues.

This book is the story of those tracks, both as training tracks and as league teams, from that very first meeting in 1928 up to the present day.

Dedicated to the Memory of
Bill Mathieson

PART I
MAJOR LEAGUE TRACKS

1

HIGH BEECH

Perhaps the best known date in the history of speedway is 19 February 1928 as it was on that day that the first speedway meeting took place in this country at the back of the King's Oak public house at High Beech in Essex. This is not the place to go into the claims of Camberley and Droylsden to have held prior meetings, except to say that the major contemporary motorcycling magazine, *The Motor Cycle*, recognised High Beech as the first meeting. Its editorial for 16 February 1928 said that, 'For many months *The Motor Cycle* has urged clubs to organise dirt-track races – events which have proved so successful overseas that they attract thousands of the general public in addition to motorcyclists – and a number of schemes with this end in view are already nearing completion. That such a meeting is to be held at a time when those interested in the new sport are only just forming their plans comes as a welcome surprise, and we wish to extend to the Ilford Motor Cycle Club our congratulations on its achievement in being the first in the field.' (Its congratulations were however tempered by the fact that they 'deprecated' the club for choosing a Sunday as the day for its opening meeting!)

Speedway had been popular in Australia and America since the early 1920s but it was Lionel Wills, a Cambridge undergraduate and keen motorcyclist, who first created an interest in the sport in Great Britain. Whilst visiting Australia in 1926, Wills visited Sydney Royale speedway and could not believe his eyes. This speedway was nothing like anything he had ever witnessed before and riders like Charlie Datson were hurtling round the track, broadsiding round bends in a way he would not have thought possible until he saw it with his own eyes. So enthused was he with what he saw, that he knew he had to try out this new sport for himself. Johnnie Hoskins, the promoter at the Royale Stadium, agreed to give him a trial and so, when he pushed out his trusty Rudge Whitworth onto the Sydney track later that year, he became the first Englishman to take up the sport. He immediately wrote home to the technical press in this country describing his own riding experiences and describing the hair-raising exploits of riders like Paddy Dean, 'Cyclone' Billy Lamont and 'Sprouts' Elder and urging motorcycle clubs to take up this new sport.

Following this, in 1927, another Briton, Stanley Glanfield, also arrived in Australia and had his first sight of speedway at Mr A.J. Hunting's Brisbane circuit. He convinced

KING'S OAK SPEEDWAY, HIGH BEECH, LOUGHTON, ESSEX
(By kind permission of L. W. E. MARDEN, Esq.)

PROGRAMME of . .

DIRT TRACK RACING

Organised by the ILFORD MOTOR CYCLE & LIGHT CAR CLUB under A.C.U Permit. Restricted to the following Clubs :
Ilford M.C. & L.C.C. and Colchester Motor Club.

SUNDAY, FEBRUARY 19th, 1928, at 10.30 a.m.

Officials :

Eastern Centre Stend.—M. R.W.Fison, Esq. *Judges*—E. J. Bass, Esq. (Essex M.C.). C. Baxter, Esq. (Ilford), P. Cox, Esq. (Ilford).
Timekeeper and Starter—Ray Abbot, Esq. (Essex M.C.).
Lap Scorers—O. Verrall, Esq. (Ilford), P. Clifton, Esq. (Colchester). *Finance*—D. Page, Esq. (Ilford).
Marshals—Members of Clubs. *Marshal in Charge*—A. Bellamy, Esq. (Ilford).

Spectators must keep to the inner portion of the track behind ropes.	If Competitors fall they must be left to the Marshals. On no account must the public invade the track.
No dogs allowed inside under any consideration.	These rules are laid down by the Governing Body, the Auto-Cycle Union and unless strictly adhered to the
Spectators will only be allowed to cross track between events and at one place only.	Stewards of the Meeting have power to stop this event and also further events.

Please help all you can. *Thank you !*

ADMISSION SIXPENCE   **PROGRAMME TWOPENCE**
CAR PARK under supervision. Cars 6d., Cycles and Three-wheelers 3d.
LUNCHEONS : 4/- (Table d'Hote), 3/-   Hon. Organising Secretary :
TEAS, 1/6   R. J. HILL-BAILEY,
These must be booked from the Hotel if wanted.   41, Hickling Road, Ilford.

Programme cover for the opening meeting at High Beech on 19 February 1928.

Hunting that he should send a contingent of Australian riders over to Britain and start the sport there.

On his return to Britain, Lionel Wills immediately set about obtaining support for his idea of introducing speedway into this country. Amongst those he contacted were Fred Mockford and Cecil Smith, who were operating path racing at Crystal Palace, but it was Jack Hill-Bailey, honorary secretary of the Ilford Motor Cycle and Light Car Club (Ilford MC and LCC), who was first off the mark. After some long discussions with Lionel Wills and the Australian rider, Keith MacKay, who arrived in England in October 1927, Hill-Bailey decided to take the plunge and organise a speedway meeting.

His first proposed venue was a half-mile trotting track in Ilford called Parsloes Park. This was owned by the London County Council (LCC) and Hill-Bailey thought it prudent to ask the Ilford MC and LCC's club president, Sir Frederick Wise, MP for Ilford, to conduct the negotiations with the LCC. Unfortunately just as negotiations started, Sir Frederick died and the discussions were put on hold.

Jack Hill-Bailey continued to look around for a suitable site and discovered a disused cycle track at the back of the King's Oak public house in Epping Forest near Loughton at a place called High Beech. He immediately sought and was granted permission to convert the track into a speedway track. He then applied to the Auto Cycle Union (ACU) for permission to run a meeting on 9 November 1927, but he was turned down as the ACU would not grant an open licence for racing on a Sunday (they must have 'deprecated' it as well!). However, they told Hill-Bailey that if he came back and asked for permission to run a closed meeting, that is one restricted to club members only, they would grant it. Hill-Bailey therefore reapplied for permission to run a closed meeting on 19 February 1928, restricted to members of the Ilford Club and the

Colchester Motor Cycle Club, which had decided to come in with Ilford on the venture.

On a bleak and snowy day in January, three ACU stewards came down to inspect the track. After three hours of discussion with Hill-Bailey, they agreed to grant permission for the meeting to take place. Permission to hold the first speedway meeting in this country on 19 February 1928 was given wide publicity through the trade press and even national newspapers. Since it was to be a closed meeting, the Ilford Club began to receive applications from motor cyclists all over the country to join so they could take part. Within a couple of weeks, letters were pouring in at the rate of a hundred a day from would-be participants. Some came from novice motorcyclists, others from top trials riders and road racers such as Colin Watson, Alf Foulds, Reg Pointer, Ivor Creek and Jack Barnett.

At last the big day arrived. Fortunately for a February morning, it dawned fine and sunny and Mr and Mrs Hill-Bailey set out from their Ilford home to High Beech armed with 2,000 admission tickets for the general public and 500 programmes. The meeting was due to start at 10 a.m. By the time the Hill-Baileys arrived at 8 a.m., a crowd of 2,000 people was already waiting. As soon as the entrance gate was opened the crowd surged in, paying their 6d admission. By 9.30 a.m. all the tickets and programmes were gone as more and more people began arriving. In the end Jack Hill-Bailey gave up trying to collect any more money as barriers were pushed over and the barbed wire fence surrounding the ground was cut down. The Ilford Club had reckoned on a crowd of 2,000 people turning up, certainly no more than 3,000. By the advertised starting time of 10.30 a.m. the crowd was estimated at between 12 and 15,000 with large numbers still arriving. Every police station within a radius of ten miles had been asked for reinforcements to help control the crowds and direct the traffic which was now blocking all roads between Epping and East London.

Spectators at the first meeting. Note the spectators viewing from the inside of the track.

Part of the ACU's permission for agreeing to the meeting was that all spectators were to be kept behind the rope barrier inside the track on the centre green. It was obvious to everyone that this could not be done and thousands of spectators were swarming all around the track, some even taking vantage points up in the beech trees which overlooked the venue. One of these was a young man by the name of Wal Phillips, who was later to become one of England's leading riders. In all, it was estimated that between 20 and 30,000 people attended that first speedway meeting.

A final entry list contained forty-two riders who were to compete in eight main events consisting of over fifty races with heats, semi-finals and finals. However, the very first speedway race in this country, heat one of the novice event, turned out to be a bit of an anti-climax as only one rider took part. Mr A. Barker was the name that was to go down to posterity as the first ever winner as he rode his Ariel in a sedate fashion taking no chances to take that first heat in a walk-over.

After that however, things started to warm up and by the time of the first semi-final the riders had begun to get the hang of this new style of riding. On lap one, Fred Ralph and Ivor Creek had a 'rare tussle' as they roared round side by side. Eventually Ralph's Coventry Eagle began to get the better of Creek's camshaft Norton and he squeezed home the winner. The second semi-final is said to have had the crowd rocking with laughter as L.P. Wilson on his tiny 172 cc Francis-Barnett had the temerity to challenge H.M. Smythe on his much bigger 493 cc ohv Sunbeam. 'With the little Villiers engine screaming over, Wilson poked his front wheel alongside the tail of Smyth's machine and dusted up the latter for the whole of the race – one more pony and he would have won in spite of being on the outside', was how *The Motor Cycle* colourfully described the race.

The final of the novice event was even more exciting. For two laps, Creek, Smythe and Ralph raced round neck and neck. As they entered the third lap, Creek managed to get the advantage but on the fifth and final lap he skidded wildly and Ralph, seizing his opportunity, passed Creek on the outside and romped home to become the first event winner of the day.

It was, of course, the case that none of the British riders had actually seen any real speedway, Australian or American style, and so had no idea how to broadside. In fact, it was considered unethical to put your foot on the track whilst racing, so all the riders kept their foot glued to the footrest. Hill-Bailey was hoping that the two Australians he had signed up to race that day would show the home-grown riders the way, but it was not to turn out that way. The first Australian to appear was Billy Galloway, who took on Colin Watson in heat three of event two. Getting off to a bad start he found himself last on lap one, but gradually his greater experience told and he carved his way through the field, finally passing Watson to take first place. However he discovered that the hard cinder track at High Beech was not suitable for sliding. He and McKay, the other Australian rider to appear that day, had been used to the continuous loose surfaces of the Australian dirt tracks and they were unable to adapt sufficiently to put on a display of broadsiding. Galloway was also using a totally unsuitable bike as he had had to borrow Freddie Dixon's Isle of Man TT machine with road-race gearing and never got out of bottom gear.

One of the sidecar events from the opening day.

Probably the most exciting race of the day came in heat seven of event two. Colchester rider Alf Medcalf, the first Briton to ride a Duggie, took the lead with C.M. Harley hot on his heels. J. Barrett got a poor start but set out in pursuit of the other two. He eventually caught up Harley on lap three and passed him. Still screaming round the track he caught up Medcalf and, side by side, they plunged into the bends, neither of them giving an inch. For over half a lap they hurtled round as if locked together and then the inevitable happened. Their machines touched and both went down leaving Harley to finish the race alone.

Further spectacular racing followed until the final of the open solo event saw the two Australians up against two British boys in Alf Foulds and Reg Pointer. It was expected to be a foregone conclusion for the two Australians, but Galloway crashed and McKay lost a tyre leaving Foulds the winner.

Event three was a sidecar event which was won by C.M. Harley. By now it was 12.30 p.m. and time for lunch. The King's Oak found it impossible to cater for the 20-30,000 crowd and some spectators took themselves off to the nearby towns of Epping and Loughton for refreshments.

All the morning events had been run over five laps, but, in the afternoon, these were cut down to three laps, owing to the lack of time. Racing continued until 5 p.m.; the last event of the day being the one-lap standing start races for solo machines and sidecars. Alf Medcalf turned in the fastest time of the day with 26.8 seconds.

And so the day's racing came to a successful conclusion. Racing had taken place from 10 a.m. to 5 p.m. between dense masses of spectators, twenty-five deep on the inside

Colin Watson, who rode at High Beech on that historic first day. He went on to become one of England's best riders before the war, captaining Wembley and riding for England.

of the track and thirty deep round the outside with only a white line and a slender rope between them. Yet there had not been one single casualty to either riders or spectators. In fact, just about the worst casualty at the first meeting occurred when a rider by the name of Dicky Bird swallowed a wasp while racing.

Of the riders to race on that historic day, some were to go on to great success in British speedway. These included Fred Ralph, who became a member of the Stamford Bridge team that won the very first League championship. Ivor Creek who went on to become a hero at West Ham. Alf Foulds, who later rode for Lea Bridge and, perhaps the best of them all, Colin Watson, who later rode for the famous Wembley Lions and captained England against Australia. He continued riding until 1946 when a bad crash at Odsal (Bradford) finally put an end to his career.

There is no doubt that the day had been an unqualified success that had far exceeded the expectations of its organiser, the Ilford club secretary, Jack Hill-Bailey, and of another man, who had modestly taken on the role of raker for the day, Lionel Wills. It laid the foundations for the sport in this country and very soon tracks were cropping up at every conceivable venue. As a perspiring, exhausted Hill-Bailey told reporters at the end of the day, 'It looks as though we've started something.'

The ACU steward sent to oversee the day was generally favourable in his report but he did make a number of recommendations. These included widening the track by a further 16 feet and he added that, 'certain parts of the track be rolled at intervals, and then raked over to a depth of two inches in order to retain sufficient looseness to permit skidding.' He also recommended that stands be built for the public.

Another spectator present that day was the famous Australian promoter, A.J. Hunting. He was a bit more forthright in his criticism of the meeting. Finding Mr Hill-Bailey, he said to him, 'My boy, you're all wrong – this isn't the way to run a dirt-track meeting.' He continued to explain to Hill-Bailey how the track should be redesigned and to suggest several other improvements such as the need for a good wire safety fence. The Ilford Club knew that Hunting was right but they did not have the money to make the necessary improvements, so they made a financial appeal to two known supporters of motorcycle racing, Alderman F.D. Smith and W.J. (Bill) Cearns of Wanstead, vice-president of the club. Both agreed to give the necessary financial backing and so, work could begin on altering the track.

Bill Cearns was, in fact, head of The Structural Engineering Company, a large engineering firm in Stratford, u.c. East London. He agreed to carry out the work for nothing and by 29 March, *The Motor Cycle* was able to report, 'Considerable strides have been made in the reconstruction of the King's Oak Speedway in High Beech, Loughton and the track will be ready for practising on Saturday. The width of the track has been increased to 40ft on the bends and 30ft on the straights, and later there are to be concrete terraces and a grandstand for spectators. Three meetings have been arranged.'

The newly created Track Licensing Committee of the ACU inspected the track and gave it their approval. The first two meetings were held on Easter Monday, 9 April 1928, one in the morning and one in the afternoon. These two meetings were the first licensed speedway meetings to be run in this country. *The Motor Cycle* was most enthusiastic. Headlining its report, 'Spectacular Racing Before Big Crowds at the Reconstructed King's Oak Speedway, Loughton', it went on to say, 'Thrills! Thrills!! Thrills!!! 17,000 spectators at the King's Oak Speedway, Loughton, had a full quota of them on Monday when the Ilford Club staged a dirt-track meeting on a track which is a marvellous improvement on the one

Programme cover from the second day's racing at High Beech on 9 April 1928.

used at the first event nearly two months ago. There were two meetings on Monday – one in the morning and one in the afternoon – and 7,000 people attended the first and 10,000 the second.

'For the first time in this country real, honest-to-goodness broadsiding was seen, no fewer than three riders demonstrated their ability to proceed round the track in the approved fashion.' The three riders in question were Digger Pugh, an Australian who had become the track adviser and machine examiner, and those two veterans of the first meeting, Colin Watson and Alf Medcalf. Pugh gave several demonstration rides, but Watson and Medcalf actually took part in the day's racing and were the stars of the show. Watson, riding a 246cc New Imperial, won the morning's 250cc event and was second in the 350cc race. In the afternoon he won both the 250cc and the 350cc races. Medcalf, on his 494cc Douglas, won the morning's 500cc event after a wonderful tussle with Gus Kuhn and in the afternoon was well on his way to victory when he fell. He also recorded the fastest time of the day for the 294-yard circuit of 34.92mph. All races were run over five laps.

The next meeting was held on 14 April and saw the debut of Roger Frogley, another English rider destined to become a great star. He had seen the track for the first time only the previous day when he had been given some tuition in the art of broadsiding by Digger Pugh, and yet he was said to have thrilled the crowds time and again and

managed to establish two new track records – 35.28mph for five laps and 38.01mph for a one-lap flying start. Other winners that day included Gus Kuhn and Jack Barnett.

Following this meeting, the riders got together at the King's Oak to discuss the future of dirt-track racing from their point of view, with particular reference to the dangers of signing contracts and the need to keep the sport clean. Jack Hill-Bailey urged them to start an association and it was unanimously agreed to form the Dirt-track Racing Riders' Association with the object of protecting and safeguarding the riders' interests. Lionel Wills was appointed secretary/treasurer and the membership fee was set at 2s 6d (12.5p).

Roger Frogley broke the track record on his first competitive appearance at High Beech. He became the first Star Riders' champion (British Section) in 1929.

The great Australian Vic Huxley smashed the one-lap flying-start track record at High Beech in his first-ever ride on English soil.

High Beech's sixth meeting held on 5 May was a red-letter day as it saw the debut of the legendary Australian Vic Huxley in this country. 12,000 spectators turned out at the King's Oak on that bright sunny day to witness riding the like of which had not been seen before in Great Britain.

Following his meeting with Stanley Glanfield in Australia and his visit to High Beech on 19 February, Mr A.J. Hunting decided to bring over his troupe of top riders to show the British what real broadsiding was all about. Aboard the *SS Oronsay* with Mr Hunting were Frank Arthur, Charlie Spinks, Hilary Buchanan, Ben Unwin, Jack Bishop, Cecil Brown and Victor Nelson Huxley. A few days out of Naples, Huxley and Brown were urgently requested to finish their journey overland so that they could arrive in time for the High Beech meeting. They finally arrived on 4 May, the day before, to find a brand new Isle of Man TT Douglas waiting for Huxley at the premises of Glanfield Lawrence in Tottenham Court Road in the centre of London. Huxley and Brown worked through the night to convert the machine from a road racer to a dirt-track machine. Having not ridden a bike for six weeks and been up all night, Huxley took to the King's Oak circuit on a totally unfamiliar machine. In his first ride he smashed the one-lap flying start record, becoming the first rider to lap in under 20 seconds, recording a time of 19.8, which equated to 40.7mph He later went on to break the five-lap record with a time of 107.6 seconds, which was 1.6 seconds faster than the current record. Huxley took no part in the actual day's racing, but all the talk amongst the crowd afterwards was about the way this incredible Aussie had broadsided round the bends laying his machine over almost parallel to the ground. Up until then speedway had been exciting enough but this man was something else. The *Speedway News* said that 'To watch Vic Huxley ride for the first time is enough to send a shudder down the spine of anybody … To the uninitiated he appears to be the personification of almost suicidal recklessness.'

Forever after nicknamed 'Broadside', Huxley, of course, went on to become one of the greatest speedway riders the world has ever seen. He remained at the top of the tree until 1936, becoming Star Riders' Champion in 1930 and runner-up in 1929, 1931

Dicky Smythe, another top Australian rider of the pioneer days. He felt that High Beech was the best-shaped circuit in Britain.

and 1932. He was also British Individual Champion three times and captain of Wimbledon. Between 1930 and 1936 he rode for Australia in 34 out of a possible 35 Test matches, was captain in 27 of them and scored a total of 286 points. Perhaps his most incredible feat was to hold one or more records on every track he rode on. In 1930 he held no less than 52 separate track records on the 35 tracks he'd competed on.

Following the meeting on 5 May there was a three-week gap in racing at High Beech to allow time for further alterations to be made to the track which was lengthened to 394 yards.

By the time High Beech resumed on 26 May, a number of new speedway venues had opened in London, including Stamford Bridge on 5 May and Crystal Palace and White City on 19 May with Wimbledon and Harringay about to follow on 28 and 29 May respectively. With the Ilford Club unable to offer the same sort of cash inducements as the big London clubs, the top English riders, such as Roger Frogley, Colin Watson and Gus Kuhn began to drift away while the Australians were conspicuous by their complete absence following Huxley's debut. In some respects, High Beech now took on the aspect of a training track, where young, up-and-coming riders tried out before moving on to the big time. Buster Frogley (Roger's brother) and Jack Parker both put in one or two appearances before moving on in this way.

Jack Parker was in fact that very rare thing in speedway, a works rider. He had been sent to High Beech by BSA to see what the possibilities were for marketing a specialised dirt-track machine. On his arrival at the track, he was put into a Handicap Event. Having not ridden speedway before, he was given a sixteen seconds start. By the end of the afternoon, he had graduated to a scratch rider, having won the Handicap Event and finishing second to Roger Frogley in the Scratch Event.

At the end of July, an international match was held which attracted back some of the big names, with Dicky Smythe and Ben Unwin representing Australia and Colin Watson and Jack Barnett representing Great Britain. Smythe and Unwin said that although the track was a little small for their liking they nevertheless felt it was the best-shaped track in the country and one that could be ridden flat out all the way round. Smythe, being true to his word, went flat out and attacked the track records, breaking both the one-lap and the five-lap records.

The Ilford Club used the Australians' recommendation in their future advertising saying, 'We unfortunately cannot offer you the best of transport facilities, but we can offer you real broadsiding all round the track if you come to the King's Oak speedway at High Beech.'

Later in the year, on August Bank Holiday, another top Australian, Frank Pearce, confirmed what Smythe and Unwin had said when he told the crowd that King's Oak was by far the best cinder track he had seen in Britain, and the only one he had ridden with his throttle full out for five laps.

At the beginning of September, the *News of the World* donated a 25 guinea trophy to be competed for by sixteen riders each Saturday afternoon. It was to be awarded to the competitor who either won the event on three consecutive occasions or on four occasions altogether. The competition did not last long as local hero Jack Barnett was awarded the trophy on 6 October having won the event on four out of the six occasions it had been run. The icing on the cake that day for Barnett was that he also broke the one-lap track record, recording a time of 18.4 seconds, a speed of 43.80mph.

High Beech's first season ended on 20 October with meeting number twenty-seven. Since that historic first meeting on 19 February, about thirty other speedway tracks had opened in Great Britain. At the end of a highly successful season, Jack Hill-Bailey noted with some satisfaction the strides both the sport itself and the riders who had started at King's Oak had made. He pointed out that the leading English riders of the day, the Frogley Brothers, Gus Kuhn, Jim Kempster, Colin Watson, Reg Pointer and Alf Medcalf, had all had their first ride at High Beech. Finally, he added, 'The season is over on 'the dirt' and the engines of the machines of the Ilford Club lads will now be fitted with low compression pistons, to wallow through mud and watersplashes, probably to compete in the Exeter Trial on Boxing Day … However, speedway racing in my humble opinion, has provided a means for the motor-cyclist to have his sport with safety to the man in the street and we at King's Oak are proud of the fact that, through the club's efforts, we have produced some of the finest riders.'

Programme cover from the last meeting of High Beech's 1928 season, 20 October.

Over the close season the track was again altered and the new 361-yard King's Oak circuit reopened on Easter Monday 1929 with two meetings, one in the morning and one in the afternoon. The new season was opened by two leading riders, Vic Huxley and Colin Watson. By the end of the morning's racing, to nobody's surprise, the new five-lap track record belonged to Huxley. In the afternoon yet another top Australian, Frank Arthur, took Huxley's place and established the new one-lap flying record.

Jack Barnett, continued to appear at meetings during the early part of 1929 but was surprisingly beaten in a best of three match race series on 6 April by Allen Kilfoyle, who later went on to race for Lea Bridge and West Ham. This meeting was also notable for the first appearance in this country of the Australian champion, Max Grosskreutz.

On Whit Monday, High Beech witnessed what, according to the *Speedway News*, was the finest race yet seen in England, when local hero, Jack Barnett took on the great Australian 'Cyclone' Billy Lamont in a match race. Both riders rode flat out for the five laps but the deciding factor, according to the *Speedway News* reporter, was 'steadiness'. Jack Barnett just held the advantage for the first three laps, but coming out of the last bend onto the home straight to start the fourth lap, Barnett overdid his slide which carried him from his line on the outside right across the track to the inside. Lamont, who was only just behind and, unusually for him, riding the inside line, squeezed through before Barnett came across. Nine riders out of ten would have shut off seeing Barnett careering across the track, but not the reckless, daredevil, 'Cyclone'. The move paid off and Lamont was in the lead. Barnett regained control and chased after Lamont. Coming round the final bend he managed to draw level, but Lamont, who was now in his favourite outside position, just managed to hang on down the finishing straight to win by about a machine's length. The race resulted in a new five-lap track record of 39.87mph.

The reason for the change in status of High Beech and its ability to once again attract riders of the calibre of Huxley, Arthur, Lamont and Watson was due to Bill Cearns. Cearns was now the track's major backer and he used another of his positions, that of a director of International Speedways Ltd, to ensure the appearance of their contracted star riders at the King's Oak. The fact was, that it was now becoming a sort of outpost of International Speedways itself, so much so, that at an extraordinary meeting of the company on 17 May 1929, they agreed to increase their share capital. They offered 1,400,000 additional shares with the express purpose of raising enough money to be able to acquire both the company operating Stamford Bridge Speedway and the High Beech Speedway.

As well as the new influx of top stars, regular riders continued to appear throughout 1929 included Barnett, Dennis Seaman, Fred Law, Norman Humphries, Syd Edmonds, Charlie King and Ed Farley. Mr W.E. Mason, the owner of the King's Oak Hotel, put up a fine trophy which was awarded weekly to the rider who recorded the fastest time of the afternoon. It was very rarely awarded to anyone other than Jack Barnett, though Syd Edmonds managed to wrest it from him one week. By the end of the season, Barnett was in possession of both the one-lap and the five-lap records.

Although High Beech did not enter the Southern League, inaugurated that season, they did form a team to race challenge matches against the London tracks. Their best

Jack Barnett rode in the first meeting at High Beech and later became captain of the King's Oak team in 1930 and 1931.

win was a 26-8 defeat of Lea Bridge. They also managed to beat Wembley, although they lost to league champions, Stamford Bridge.

Reflecting on the 1929 season, Jack Hill-Bailey was concerned that attendances had dropped and they had only managed to keep King's Oak going because of the financial support afforded by Alderman Smith and Bill Cearns. Partly because of the take over by International Speedways and partly because of other commitments, Alderman Smith decided he could no longer support the track. This left Cearns more or less in complete control on behalf of International Speedways. As well as being a director of that company, Cearns was also proprietor of the Hall Green track in Birmingham and a director of Coventry Speedway, so he certainly knew all about speedway management. He was determined to improve attendances at High Beech and to this end made a number of alterations. The track was once again completely relaid, admission charges were reduced to 1s 3d from 1s 6d, the programme charge was reduced from 4d to 3d, pencils were made available for 1d each, covered accommodation was provided and the long-deferred promise of a grandstand was made good. Cearns also realised that it was essential to enter High Beech into the Southern League if they wanted to increase the crowds. This had been the saviour of other London tracks.

High Beech opened its 1930 season on 12 April. Although it was a dull and chilly day, a large crowd turned out to see England's newest league team, nicknamed the Foresters, resplendent in their maroon and light blue colours. The team consisted of Jack Barnett (captain), Syd Edmonds, the brothers Phil and George Bishop, Stan Baines, Stan Taylor and Charlie King.

The following week, Cearns put together a programme of top stars to try to combat the fact that it was Cup Final day. The riders included Vic Huxley, Billy Dallison, Frank Arthur, George Greenwood, Tiger Stevenson and Jack Parker. Cearns' plan worked as the crowd that day was the highest since that very first meeting on 19 February 1928. The new stands were full to capacity and the car park was jammed. Even in this

Left: *Syd Edmonds rode for King's Oak in 1930 and 1931, becoming captain following Barnett's crash in May 1930.* Right: *Stan Baines, a member of the Foresters in 1930 and 1931.*

company, it was no surprise that Vic Huxley was the outstanding rider of the afternoon and won the two main events.

On 1 May, Jack Barnett was injured following a crash involving West Ham's Con Cantwell and was ruled out of the team until 7 June. Syd Edmonds took over as captain. With Barnett out of the team, they were unable to give of their best and they finished the league in eleventh place out of thirteen teams, having lost every single one of their away matches and four (out of twelve) of their home matches. It was a similar story in the *Evening News* London Cup as they beat Wembley at home 52-44 but lost in the second leg by the thumping margin of 71 points to 25.

On 20 July the Riders' Benevolent Fund was inaugurated with a garden party at the King's Oak. Riders from every Southern League track turned out (except for the Leicester team, whose transport broke down en route), as did promoters and ACU officials, to support the venture. Johnnie Hoskins acted as an auctioneer, while his six-year-old son, Ian, gave an exhibition ride on the world's smallest speedway machine. In all £500 was raised.

Although the High Beech team itself was not too successful, it did have one great success at an individual level. During the season, a series of match races took place between London riders and those from the provinces. The winners were brought together in a Grand Final, the winner of which was to receive a special Gold Trophy plus £50 donated by Bill Cearns. The final was held towards the end of August and included High Beech riders, Phil Bishop and Syd Edmonds. Bishop managed to reach the final

Above: *The 1930 High Beech team. From left to right: Jack Hill-Bailey (promoter), Charlie King, Phil Bishop, Geo. Bishop, Jack Barnett (captain on bike), Syd Edmonds, Stan Baines, Stan Taylor.*

Right: *Programme cover from the 1930 London Cup tie, King's Oak v. Wembley. King's Oak won the match 52-44.*

"THE GOODWOOD OF SPEEDWAYS"
(RIGHT OF ADMISSION RESERVED)

3d. PROGRAMME 3d.
Pencils 1d. AT Pencils 1d.

King's Oak
SPEEDWAY
HIGH BEECH

SATURDAY, AUG. 9th, 1930
AT 3.30 P.M.

3rd SEASON MEETING No. 24

To-Days Big Event:

King's Oak *v.* Wembley

"EVENING NEWS"
LONDON SPEEDWAY CUP

PRICES OF ADMISSION (Including Tax):
1/3 Covered Terrace (Juveniles) 6d.
2/- Covered Seats. - 3/- Grand Stand.

Proprietor—W. J. CEARNS.
Racing Manager—R. J. HILL-BAILEY.
All Communications to: 41 HICKLING ROAD, ILFORD
(Telephone - ILFORD 0850)

OFFICIALS:
Clerk of Course—R. J. HILL-BAILEY.
Stewards { A.C.U—D. MALCOLM
(King's Oak)—T. S. WRIGHT.
(Competitors)—R. H. COX and E. SNOW.
Starter—J. HILL.
Machine Inspector—M. ASHMAN. Timekeeper—D. PAGE.
Judge—L. W. BONE. Announcer—E. WILLIAMS.
Medical Officer—DR. R. CONNON ROBERTSON.

MEETING HELD UNDER THE GENERAL COMPETITION RULES OF THE AUTO CYCLE UNION.
A.C.U—PERMIT No. T.A. 260

"EUROPE'S PIONEER DIRT TRACK"

Line-up for the £50 Gold Trophy held at High Beech in 1930. From left to right, back row: Jack Hill-Bailey, Mrs W.J. Cearns, Bill Cearns, unknown mechanic. Front row: Vic Huxley, Phil Bishop, Syd Edmonds.

run-off but was up against the favourite, Vic Huxley. Luckily for Bishop, Huxley suffered engine trouble during the race and was forced to retire leaving High Beech's Phil Bishop the proud owner of the Gold Trophy and the £50 cheque. Due to what had happened in the final, Cearns donated another gold trophy to be raced for by Bishop and Huxley at the High Beech meeting on 6 September. This time there was no mistake for Huxley and he walked off with his consolation prize.

The 1930 season finished at the end of September with a match against West Ham. A special presentation was made to Jack Hill-Bailey to thank him for all the work he had put in over the last three years into making High Beech such a success story. In a speech to the crowd, Bill Cearns paid tribute to the work done by Hill-Bailey, saying that, 'as most trophies in speedway were won by sheer pluck and determination, it was only right that Mr Hill-Bailey, who had displayed these qualities over a considerable period, should be suitably rewarded.' Following this speech, the riders presented Mr Hill-Bailey with a Harley-Davidson machine.

More alterations were made to the track in time for the start of the 1931 season, with a new red ash surface being laid. The Australian Frank Pearce was signed up for the team which now included Jack Barnett, Syd Edmonds, Billy Dallison, Reg Hutchins, Phil and George Bishop and Stain Baines. The first match was on 2 May, when they beat Wembley by 30 points to 24. Inexplicably, Barnett completely lost his form and shortly after the start of the season was transferred to West Ham. His place was taken by a new Australian sensation, the nineteen-year-old Bobby Blake. When Blake arrived in England he made straight for High Beech, where he borrowed a machine, a set of leathers and promptly went out to break the track record in his first ride. Cearns imme-

Phil Bishop receives the Gold Trophy from Mrs W.J. Cearns.

diately signed him up for the team. He built up a big following at King's Oak but at the end of the season he returned to Australia where he had a bad accident practically losing the use of one arm. He never returned to this country.

The Foresters had a much more successful season, winning 16 of their home matches and even winning 3 away, to finish the league in 6th place. Unfortunately, the improvement in the team's performance was not reflected in the crowd numbers as these continued to fall during the season. William J. Cearns was now practically keeping the track open single-handedly and he was no longer prepared to pour money into it. It was estimated that he had spent something like £20,000 of his own money in supporting High Beech since the track opened in 1928. It looked doubtful whether the track would open at all in 1932 but, although they withdrew from the league, they did open for another year of open meetings. It was not a success and when Charringtons, the brewers who owned the King's Oak, massively increased the rent, it was all over. High Beech closed down in August 1932.

There were moves to recommence speedway at the venue in 1933 and a number of people within the sport looked at the possibility of reopening it as a training track. The *Speedway and Sports Gazette* backed this move and called on Jack Hill-Bailey to 'use his influence with Mr Cearns so that a few of our novices can have proper training and plenty of practice.'

A short-lived revival took place in 1935 when New Cross leased the track to open a novices' riding school run by Roger Frogley, but this did not last long.

Another revival took place in 1937 when the North London Motor Club took over the venue following their move from Barnet. Former leading Barnet riders Ron Clarke, Art Sweby and Cyril Anderson became the top riders at their new club as the Foresters reformed and, over the next three seasons, took part in inter-club matches with other local amateur clubs such as Dagenham, Rye House and Smallford. Although the others went on to form a small league, the Sunday Dirt Track League, in 1938, High Beech stayed out though they raced all of them in challenge matches and managed to go through the season unbeaten. Had they entered the league they would probably have won it. The big meeting of the year for 1938 was the High Beech Championship won by Ron Clarke. He received the trophy from none other than the reigning world champion, Jack Milne.

Racing once again came to a halt in 1939 with the outbreak of war. A planned opening after the war in 1947 did not happen but the following winter the track was once again back in action as a training track and the track was then altered for the start of the 1949 season. Although further training sessions were held in 1949 and 1950 they were not successful and the King's Oak finally closed its doors. The track that had given Great Britain speedway quickly became overgrown and forgotten.

However, on 19 February 1961, exactly thirty-three years after that first meeting, the Veteran Dirt-Track Riders' Association met at the King's Oak to unveil a plaque which read: 'King's Oak Speedway, High Beech, Epping Forest. On a track behind this hotel on Sunday, 19 February 1928, was held the first motorcycle "Dirt-Track" meeting in Europe. This commemorative plaque was placed here by members of the Veteran Dirt-Track Riders' Association and unveiled on Sunday, 19 February 1961 by Mrs K.M. Hill-Bailey and Johnnie S. Hoskins.' Unfortunately the plaque went missing some years later, but has now been replaced with one in the Forestry Conservation Centre which stands on the old centre green. It says, 'This plaque, donated by the Veteran Speedway Riders Association, marks the site of Britain's first Speedway (dirt track) which opened on 19 February 1928'.

But in fact, it wasn't quite all over for racing at the famous old track, as the ex-Wembley and New Cross rider, Jimmy Gooch leased it in 1967 to give private lessons. When these lessons came to an end, that really was it, although there was to be just one more occasion on which speedway bikes would roar round the circuit. This last occasion was on 18 February 1968, when thousands of supporters and former riders turned out to celebrate the fortieth anniversary of the birth of speedway in this country. About twenty-five veterans enjoyed a nostalgic spin around the track riding machines of the 1928-30 era including a BSA, two Rudges, a Norton, a Martin-JAP and about half a dozen Duggies. Amongst the veterans who turned out were Roger Frogley, Wal

Opposite: *The start of a race at High Beech in 1938. Note five riders in the race.*

Right: *High Beech in 1960 showing how dilapidated the stadium had become. The start markings, however, are still clearly visible.*

Phillips, Syd Edmonds and the former darling of King's Oak, Jack Barnett. During the afternoon, an elderly supporter produced an album of cigarette cards including one of Barnett. He asked Jack to autograph it for him. As he did so, the supporter told him he had waited nearly forty years to get his autograph!

All hope of reviving speedway on the site was lost on 23 June 1971 when the Forestry Conservation Centre was opened on the spot.

Speedway supporters from all over the country and further afield still flock to the King's Oak in February every year to commemorate the birth of British speedway at anniversary events organised by Peter Lipscombe and John Chaplin of the *Vintage Speedway* magazine.

2
EASTBOURNE

Although there are reports of at least one earlier meeting taking place at Arlington in 1928, the track was officially opened on 5 August 1929, on land formerly owned by the Duke of Devonshire but now belonging to the Eastbourne Motor Sports Club. The main event of the day was the Arlington Scratch Race won by Les Ashdown. The track was described as 'an oval one with two very difficult bends to negotiate.'

The second meeting, attended by approximately 1,000 spectators, was held on 24 August with thrills being provided by local riders, Rod Dutton, Jimmy Horton and Bert Hele. Dutton was the best rider on view, setting a new track record of 87.8 seconds for four laps in heat two of the Arlington Scratch Race. He went on to win the final. In the final of the Hailsham Handicap he seemed to be going even quicker but unfortunately he hit the safety fence on the last lap and Horton was able to avoid him and go on to win the race. Everyone was agreed that Mr Henley and Major Bird, the two promoters on behalf of the Eastbourne Motor Sports Club, had put on two very impressive meetings.

The opening season's third and final meeting was held on 14 September. This meeting attracted some visiting riders including Sparks Burgess and Bert Gerrish, but it was too dry for records to be broken with Horton setting the fastest time of 91.8 seconds in winning the Arlington Scratch Race final. In a special match race, Horton was defeated by Burgess.

Arlington reopened for business on 21 April 1930 with the visit of a local boy made good, Bryan Donkin. Donkin was a local lad who had gone on to better things and was now a member of the Crystal Palace team. His method of taking corners was, according to the *Eastbourne Courier* (the local paper), a 'revelation to the spectators and even to the local riders, who admiringly studied the way that he proved the theory that the faster you take corners the safer you are.' He was, of course, in a completely different class to the sort of rider the crowd was used to seeing. In his first exhibition race he 'literally screamed round the four laps, flattening out at corners with a full throttle, and keeping the spectators on tip-toes at the daring way he dived from each corner down the straight with his engine revving at full peak, cutting out only a fraction of a second before opening out full and lying over to take the next bend.' (*Eastbourne Courier*) When the chequered flag fell, he had lowered the track record by an incredible 9.4 seconds to 78.4.

Once again, Jimmy Horton was amongst the best of the local riders, but this time he was beaten in the Arlington Scratch Race final by Rev Reynolds, though he did win the President's Challenge Cup.

Bryan Donkin reappeared on August Bank Holiday Monday, 4 August. This time he proved to be something of a disappointment and repeatedly fell at the same place on the track. In his first match race against Sparks Burgess, he fell and the race had to be re-run and although Donkin went on to win, it was in the relatively poor time of 98.4 seconds.

Bryan Donkin, a member of the Crystal Palace team in 1929. As a native of Eastbourne he returned to his home town in 1930 to show the juniors how it was done.

The star of the afternoon turned out to be the Australian, Steve Langton, who had a peculiar style of riding which involved standing on his right footrest and putting his left leg out stiffly. His match race with Donkin turned into a bit of a farce as twice Donkin fell and twice Langton stopped to wait for him to get up. When Donkin fell for a third time, he waved Langton on. Langton went on to win both the Arlington Scratch Race final and the Eastbourne Handicap. A new rider whose name appeared for the first time in the programme was a young Tiger Hart. He reached the final of the Arlington Scratch Race, having won both his heat and his semi-final.

Racing continued in this vein for the next few years, with mostly local riders and occasionally a visiting rider from London or elsewhere. These riders were never really top names and were, for the most part, juniors sent by their parent clubs to gain experience including Stan Lemon from Wimbledon and Benny Lee from West Ham. One such hopeful to arrive on the scene in 1934, was a young rider who had been trying to break into the Crystal Palace team, George Newton. The eighteen-year-old Newton had caused a sensation in 1932 when, in his first outing for Crystal Palace as reserve at West Ham, he had equalled Vic Huxley's track record. However, he was not able to live up to this astonishing start and by 1933 was struggling to get into the team. A broken leg at Plymouth put his career even further back and it was felt that the young George would benefit from a few outings on the Arlington circuit.

On his arrival at the start of 1934 he immediately lowered the track record to 73.8 seconds. Newton was one of the most spectacular riders speedway has ever seen. He was a master of balance. He very rarely put his foot down on the track and could change direction off the back wheel. He went on to be a leading light for New Cross, qualifying for three World Championship finals, until illness more or less finished his career in 1939, although he did make a short comeback after the war.

Other leading riders at this time included Harvey Swanson, Rube Wilson, Jack Riddle, George Saunders, Bill Roberts, Charlie Page, Lou Burger and Charlie Dugard. It was in 1934 that Charlie Dugard began the Dugard family's long association with the management of the track, when he and Tiger Hart bought a share in the club. In fact, Dugard's association with the track went back even further than that as he had first ridden there in 1931.

In 1938 a Sunday Dirt Track League was inaugurated. This was comprised of a number of the smaller tracks in the south-east of England, namely Rye House, Smallford, Dagenham (who ran two teams, Dagenham and Romford) and Eastbourne. Eastbourne got off to a good start when, in their first league fixture, away to Dagenham, they ran out victors by 44 points to 39. The first heat resulted in a 4-2 win for Eastbourne, when Tiger Hart got the better of the Daggers' captain, Frank Hodgson. Tiger Hart therefore became the first rider ever to win a race for Eastbourne in an

Below: *George Newton in typically spectacular action. He rode at Arlington in 1934, going on to become one of England's leading riders just before the Second World War.*

Right: *Charlie Dugard first rode at Eastbourne in 1931 and remained connected with the club all his life as rider, manager, promoter, owner and sponsor. His children and grandchildren have continued the Dugard family association to the present day.*

A programme cover from the 1938 season, the year Eastbourne won the Sunday Dirt Track League.

THIS MAY BE THE LUCKY NUMBER ☞ 12147

EASTBOURNE
(ARLINGTON)
DIRT TRACK

A.C.U. PERMIT

"Eastbourne Gazette & Herald" Photo

PROGRAMME

WEATHER PERMITTING

3^{D.}

RIGHT OF ADMISSION RESERVED

official league fixture. There was another first for Eastbourne in the next heat when H. Collins became their first rider to be excluded. His crime was to break the tapes. The Eastbourne team for this match included Tiger Hart (captain), who scored a maximum, H. Collins, Danny Lee, Charlie Dugard and Stan Johns. Other riders to appear during the season were Stan Lemon, Bob Lovell, Charlie Page, Dick Harris, Harry Browne and Jack Kemsley. Eastbourne proved far too strong for the other teams in the league and finished their first season as a league team as champions. The league was discontinued for the 1939 season and Arlington returned to a diet of open meetings and individual races.

On the outbreak of the Second World War, racing ceased at the track which was requisitioned by the army for the purpose of training dispatch riders. By the time they'd finished with it the track had sunk two feet and was little better than a mud bath and the terraces were overgrown with weeds. It was not a promising sight, but it was at this point that Charlie Dugard stepped in and bought the track outright. He filled the track up with clinker and gradually got it back into shape.

After a lot of hard work, Arlington was ready to open for the 1946 season running a series of open meetings. Again it was mainly seen as a nursery track for the London clubs, but in 1947, Eastbourne entered a team into the newly-formed National League Third Division. With a team consisting of Basil Harris, Wally Green, Jock Grierson, Jimmy Coy, Harry Saunders, Ken Tidbury, Ron Clark and Alan Briggs, the team carried on from where it had left off in 1938 and won the league. This time, however the victory was by the narrowest of margins as they won the title on race points from Cradley Heath.

Wally Green, on loan from West Ham, was the top rider with an average of 9.68. His ambition had always been to ride for Wembley so when he was demobbed from the army he wrote to Alec Jackson to ask for a trial, but Wembley already had more juniors than they could handle and Jackson advised the young Wally to apply to West Ham. After a trial at Rye House, he was offered a contract. The West Ham management decided he should get some experience in the Third Division and sent him off to Southampton. He was given a second-half ride but, unfortunately, his front tyre came off while he was leading. After the meeting he approached the Southampton promoter, Jimmy Baxter, and asked him if he wanted to keep him. Baxter consulted his programme and said, 'No, you came last.' As he was leaving, another man approached Green and said, 'My name is Charlie Dugard. Will you ride for me? I am the manager of Eastbourne.' The following week, Green was in the team as reserve. When Eastbourne's best rider, the young Wimbledon loanee Dennis Gray, fell and severely damaged his hand in the Supporters' Cup on 24 May, Green was given his chance in the team and never looked back.

He was ably supported by Basil Harris, average 8.96 and Jock Grierson, 7.39. In the end-of-year Third Division rankings, Green was placed fourth, Harris fifth and Grierson tenth. Green later went on to become runner-up in the 1950 World Championship.

In spite of having a 100 per cent record in league competitions, Dugard had lost £2,000 on the venture and decided not to run Eastbourne in the 1948 Third Division. Instead, he moved the team across to Hastings. His reason for doing this, was that Hastings had much better facilities than Arlington, which was still essentially just a track in an open field in the middle of nowhere, with an old timber garage converted into dressing rooms with no running water. The riders had to use buckets. Hastings, on the

Harry Saunders (right) a leading member of the 1947 Division Three championship side. In Southampton colours, the Australian, Steve Langton (left), who rode at Eastbourne in the early 1930s.

Eastbourne's 1947 Division Three Championship winning team. From left to right: Basil Harris, Ron Clark, Wally Green, Ken Tidbury (on bike), Bob Sivyer, Harry Saunders (kneeling), Jock Grierson, Jimmy Coy.

other hand, had much better facilities including a large grandstand. It was also much nearer to a centre of population, being on the edge of the town. Dugard hoped this would lead to an increase in crowds.

Although no longer in the league, Arlington did continue to run a few meetings in 1948, mostly challenge matches against other non-league teams such as Rye House and High Beech, or open championships. Alec Gray and Dan English rode for the team. One tragedy occurred at the track on 13 June, when Hastings rider, Eric Dunn, fell and was struck on the head as he lay on the track. He died two days later in hospital. Shortly after this the track closed, but it did open again for training sessions throughout the winter.

Charlie Dugard continued to operate Arlington as a training track until 1954 when a new league was formed, the Southern Area League. This consisted of Rye House, Brafield, California, Aldershot, Ringwood and Eastbourne. Eastbourne's proud record of winning every league they'd ever entered was rudely shattered as they finished bottom of the league with just six points.

The intention of this new league was to give junior riders experience. This was a very laudable aim but unfortunately the league did not get off to a happy start. Aldershot was forced to close after ten matches as it was losing money, Ringwood reduced admission prices in an attempt to increase its crowds, while Brafield had an injunction issued against it to prevent Sunday racing.

On loan from Wimbledon, Dennis Gray rode for the 1947 Eastbourne team.

Eastbourne had its leading rider, Norman Street, banned because he was too experienced. Once he'd gone, the Eagles had nothing. Their top scorer, Steve Bole, averaged less than five a match! Their first win came on 15 August and they managed just one more win all season. Eastbourne tried out no less than eighteen riders and not one of them measured up to league status.

It seemed that things could only get better in 1955, but in fact, they got worse. The Eagles managed to use a total of 23 riders in 12 matches and once again finished bottom, this time with just 1 win and 2 points to their credit. Wally Willson was top scorer with 46 points from 8 matches. During the season, Ringwood closed and Dugard spent £300 buying Merv Hannam and Harold Carder from them. In Hannam, Eastbourne at last had a decent rider – he finished third equal in the Southern Area League Individual Championship Final – and it was hoped that a new team could be built around him in time for 1956. Tom Reader also reached the final of the Southern Area Individual Championship, finishing 7th with 8 points.

As it happened Hannam did not stay, but Harold Carder was appointed team manager and he managed to unearth some real talent for the 1956 campaign. His first find was a fast-gating Australian by the name of Ray Cresp. His form in the Eagles' first away match was nothing short of sensational and it helped Eastbourne to their first away win since the league started. Unfortunately, Cresp was too good for the Southern Area League and after only three matches, in which he scored 34 points, he left for bigger things at Wembley. However, two other new riders appeared, Jim Heard, who top-scored with 81 points from 12 matches and Leo McAuliffe, who not only scored 65 points from 9 matches but also went on to win the Southern Area League Riders' Championship with 14 points. Jim Heard was second. It was all a far cry from their first two seasons as the Eagles finished in second place behind Rye House.

At the end of the season, McAuliffe was swapped for Southern Rovers' Colin Gooddy, but this was a bad move on Eastbourne's part as Gooddy was injured after just three matches and took no further part in the season. The experienced Frank Bettis was signed up and, following a battle with the Control Board, was allowed to stay. Not surprisingly, he became the Eagles top rider with 94 points from 10 matches. Jim Heard again rode well scoring 75 points. Maury Conway was the third heat leader. He caused something of a surprise in an exciting Southern Area League Riders' Championship Final. At the end of the 20 heats, he and Leo McAuliffe had tied on 13 points and a run-off was held. The result of the run-off was a tie. Again the two riders went out to decide the issue and this time McAuliffe won a great race by a very narrow margin. Jim Heard came third while Maury Conway's brother, Noel, also an Eastbourne rider, came fifth. A promising young rider who turned out for Eastbourne in 1957 was a New Zealander on loan from his parent club, Wimbledon, by the name of Ivan Mauger. Charlie Dugard's son, John, also made his debut for the Eagles.

Early in 1958 the idea of a new Junior League, or Second Division, that would include the Southern Area League teams plus National League junior teams, was discussed. Seven teams expressed an interest, those being Exeter, Yarmouth, Rye House, Aldershot, Swindon, Norwich and Eastbourne. However, it soon became apparent that the idea was a non-starter. Exeter and Yarmouth wanted ten-heat matches, Swindon and Norwich were only able to offer three home dates, while Rye House, Eastbourne

Left: *Jimmy Coy, another member of the 1947 team.* Right: *Basil Harris, a heat leader with the 1947 Eastbourne team, was ranked as 5th best rider in the Third Division that year.*

and Aldershot decided that the proposed pay rates for the new league were too high and withdrew altogether. They agreed to reform the Southern Area League along with the nomadic Southern Rovers team. However, Aldershot closed in May after two poorly attended meetings, while Rye House was unable to open until August because of extensive rebuilding work. With only Eastbourne and Southern Rovers able to run, the league was abandoned and Eastbourne reverted to a diet of open meetings and challenge matches.

The Southern Area League was revived in 1959 with five teams, Eastbourne, Rye House, Aldershot, Yarmouth and Ipswich. Colin Gooddy returned to take over the captaincy from Frank Bettis and became the Eagles' top scorer. He averaged over 11 points per match and was unbeaten away from home. He was well supported by Dave Still and Gil Goldfinch, until the latter was transferred to Ipswich. Ross Gilbertson turned out several times for the Eagles as did another Dugard son, Bobby. Eastbourne ended the season as champions.

With the introduction of the Provincial League in 1960, the Southern Area League folded. Eastbourne applied to enter the new league but was turned down, on the grounds that its track was not up to standard, so it continued with open meetings and challenge matches. With a team consisting of Colin Gooddy (captain), Jim Heard, Ross Gilbertson, John and Bobby Dugard, Dave Still and Bob Warner, the Eagles took on and generally beat, a number of Provincial League teams, including the champions, Rayleigh, who they beat 42-30. Individually, Ross Gilbertson, who also rode for Poole in the Provincial League, was the top rider and won the Easter Trophy, the Supporters' Trophy and the Southern Area Championship at Arlington.

Veteran Bill Osborne joined the team for 1961, which, his signature apart, stayed much the same as the 1960 line-up. Five challenge matches were held against Rye House (twice), New Cross, Ipswich and Poole, with the home side winning all of them. Once again, Ross Gilbertson enjoyed the most individual success by winning the Sussex Championship and the Silver Helmet.

On 1 July, Bill Osborne opened a training school at the track. This ran on alternate Saturdays and on into the winter months. A machine was available for hire at a cost of £3 for 12 laps, although Osborne was not in favour of novices turning up without their own equipment, 'Any lad who expects to become a speedway rider must own his own bike,' he said. Among his first-year discoveries was Johnny Guilfoyle.

At the end of the 1961 season, there was talk of the Southern Area League being revived yet again with teams from Eastbourne, Rye House, Yarmouth and Weymouth competing, but it failed to materialise.

With the non-appearance of the Southern Area League, Charlie Dugard decided to take the plunge and apply for membership of the Provincial League again. The proposed team was John and Bob Dugard, Frank Bettis, Bill Osborne, Jimmy Gleed, Jim Heard, and Bob Warner. Dugard was also proposing to use Colin Gooddy, as he claimed he was an Eastbourne registered rider, even though he was now riding for Ipswich. On 18 March the Arlington track was inspected by ACU officials who passed it fit for Provincial League racing provided track warning lights were erected and the safety fence was improved.

Programme cover for the Southern Area League Eastbourne v. California match on 17 April 1954.

Just under one month later, the Control Board made a further inspection and felt that neither of the two items referred to by the ACU had been improved sufficiently to allow for Provincial League racing. This meant that although the other promoters were prepared to accept Eastbourne into the league, the Control Board refused them permission. The final announcement came on 19 May.

And so, for the 1962 season, it was back to the usual fare of challenge matches and open meetings. In all, the Eagles raced 12 challenge matches, 9 of them at home, and won 6. The team consisted of Frank Bettis, Bob and John Dugard, Jim Heard, Dave Still and Des Lukehurst. Colin Gooddy put in 4 appearances averaging 11.25, while Pete Jarman put in 3, averaging 11.00. Of the regular riders, Bettis was top scorer, averaging 7.70. Individually, the honours went to Bobby Dugard, who won both the Sussex Championship and the Supporters' Trophy. Ross Gilbertson made a welcome return to the track in April to take the Easter Trophy.

The 1963 season started as normal but, after just two meetings, Eastbourne were told that they could no longer book top Provincial League or National League riders. Charlie Dugard was very unhappy about this decision as he said that without these riders the crowds would decrease and he would lose even more money on each meeting. As it was, it was really only his love of the sport that had kept Arlington going over the last few seasons. In June he put on speedway as part of a composite meeting and was subsequently fined £20 by the Control Board for using National League riders in the event. This was the final straw and Eastbourne closed for the rest of the season. The Speedway Riders' Association were horrified at the closure and made a protest to the Control Board about their new rule. The ruling was eventually reversed but, in spite of that, Eastbourne remained shut for the rest of the season.

Before 1964 began, Charlie Dugard spent about £1,000 on improving the track to try to get it accepted into the Provincial League. He rebanked the track and built a new stand for 1,000 spectators. Instead of the Provincial League however, Eastbourne entered a new league in 1964, the Metropolitan League, which had been set up as a successor to the old Southern Area League. As well as Eastbourne, this league comprised Ipswich, Rayleigh, Newpool (a joint Newport/Poole Junior team), Weymouth and Exeter 'B'. Unfortunately the league was a bit of a shambles as Exeter pulled out after just one match and not one of the teams actually completed their fixtures, Ipswich coming nearest with 6 out of 8; Eastbourne managed 4. Also, the riders seemed to swap teams with alarming regularity, so that, for example, Geoff Penniket, while being Eastbourne's second-best scorer, also rode for Newpool, Malcolm Brown rode for Rayleigh and Weymouth, Wal Morton rode for Ipswich and Weymouth and Vic Ridgeon rode for Eastbourne and Rayleigh. After one outing with Exeter 'B', Des Lukehurst became the Eagles top scorer, finishing up with 26 points. Not surprisingly, Ipswich won the league while Eastbourne took the runner-up spot, losing just one match away to Ipswich.

After this, Charlie Dugard finally became terminally disillusioned with the current state of lower league speedway and decided to call it a day. He therefore closed Arlington to speedway at the end of the season to concentrate on stock car racing. Over the next few years, Charlie Dugard continued to operate stock cars at Arlington, pulling in crowds of up to 8,000 on Sunday afternoons. Every year there were rumours that Eastbourne would return to the speedway fold but it was not until 1969 that it at last became a reality.

Following a four-year gap, the Eagles returned to league racing in the British League Division Two under Arlington Promotions – which was in effect Dave Lanning and Bob Dugard with help from old Eagles favourite Colin Gooddy. Lanning made his intentions clear right from the start when he said, 'It is no good staging speedway at Eastbourne with a mediocre team. We have to win all our home matches – and a good few away ones into the bargain. We are going to be the smartest team in the league and anyone who rides for us must have immaculate equipment … I'm mounting a publicity drive to make sure everyone in Sussex knows about Eastbourne speedway. We'll run every other Sunday afternoon.'

Over the winter, Arlington Promotions poured thousands of pounds into improving the stadium, probably spending more money on the place than had been spent in its entire history up to that point.

The new era dawned on 6 April when the Eagles beat the King's Lynn Starlets by 39 points to 37. The new Eastbourne team was a combination of old and new with the biggest potential find being the sixteen-year-old Dave Jessup, who was making his league debut. He rode in all 30 league matches and in Eastbourne's one and only cup match that season, recording a very respectable 6.62 average. Channel Islander Hugh Saunders was another making his debut in British League racing. He did even better than Jessup, averaging 7.00. At the other end of the scale, Lanning brought two old-timers, Reg Trott and Alby Golden, out of retirement. This too, however, was a master-stroke, as both of them took on the mantle of heat leader. Ex-Wimbledon and Norwich star, Reg Trott, was appointed captain and scored 309 points in 30 matches for an average of 8.70. Former Southampton favourite, Golden, was not far behind, averaging 7.88. The Eagles' top rider, however, was Barry Crowson, who was wrested away from Canterbury after a bitter close season struggle. He knocked up a string of high scores

Bob Andrews and Tommy Sweetman cross the finishing line at Arlington in 1st and 2nd places to give California a 5-1 in the 1954 Southern Area League match.

but about halfway through the season was whisked back to his parent club, West Ham. His average at the time of his departure was 9.93. The other regular members of the team were Derek Cook, Laurie Sims and Tony Hall.

The loss of Crowson and an unfortunate injury to Saunders, which kept him out for several matches, badly affected Eastbourne's chances of carrying out Lanning's wishes of winning all their home matches and 'a good few away ones'. Nevertheless, they performed well enough for their first season back in league racing, finishing mid-table having won 14 and drawn 2 of their 30 matches. One little oddment from that season was that the first-ever dead heat in Division Two of the British League occurred in a race at Eastbourne on 25 May when Crowson tied for first place with Crayford's Archie Wilkinson.

Eastbourne's reasonable first year back in league racing brought clear hopes of better things to come and the crowds returned to support the Eagles. So many attended the first meeting of the following season (1970) that hundreds were actually turned away! Lanning's policy of unearthing potentially great sixteen-year-old youngsters continued when he drafted a young Gordon Kennett into the side. Kennett was given his first run out on a speedway track on 29 March and by 12 April found himself in the team. At the end of his first season he had ridden in 29 matches for the Eagles and scored at an average of 6.79 points, better even that Jessup's debut year. However, there is no doubt that this was Dave Jessup's year. This remarkable seventeen year old went from junior to top rider, finishing the season with an average of 9.66 and winning the British League Division Two Riders' Championship Final. To cap it all, he almost, but not quite, led the team to their first British League Division Two title, as they finished in second place behind Canterbury. Jessup's advance was so rapid that he made a number of Division One teams sit up and take notice. In the end, he was signed by Wembley for the 1971 season.

Eastbourne's 1971 British League Division Two championship winning team. From left to right, back row: Laurie Sims, Malcolm Ballard, Dave Knight, Roger Johns, Mac Woolford. Front row: Reg Trott, Gordon Kennett.

Behind Jessup, the rest of the team all scored like heat leaders. Derek Cook was second with an average of 8.44, the wily old captain, Reg Trott, scored at 7.52, while Alby Golden, Phil Pratt (signed from Reading in mid-season) and Mac Woolford all scored at over 6 points per match. Laurie Sims recorded the lowest average and that was only fractionally below 6 at 5.98.

With Jessup and Kennett both future World Championship runners-up, it seemed that Dave Lanning had a real talent for spotting the stars of the future. And it didn't finish with those two, as two other youngsters, Roger Johns and Gordon Kennett's brother, David, put in brief appearances during the year and also showed great potential. One of the reasons Eastbourne was able to unearth such precocious talent was its training school which ran regularly through the winter months. This cost £2 plus £4 10s for the hire of a bike for 20 laps.

With their ever-improving youngsters, it looked as though next year the Eagles would go one better and become champions. However, the season started off badly when Jessup moved permanently to Wembley, Alby Golden decide to call it a day, Phil Pratt refused to ride for them and Derek Cook was whisked back to his parent track, Poole, after four matches in which he'd scored at an average of 10.25. However, none of this seemed to faze the Eagles youngsters, as after twelve matches, they were unbeaten and top of the league. The Kennett brothers, as expected, had improved on their 1970 performances and were now heat leaders. Roger Johns came into the team as a more than useful second string, but it was yet another youngster, Malcolm Ballard, who proved to be this year's sensation. In his first four matches in league speedway, he scored paid 9, paid 10, paid 11 and paid 14. Just 50 days after making his debut, he became an international when he rode for Young England against Young Sweden at Ipswich on 17 June. Three days later he turned out for Young England again, this time on his own track. He was top scorer with 14 paid 16. He finished the season with an average of 8.74 and was Eastbourne's top scorer. Lanning had done it again!

The previous year, when finishing second, Eastbourne had had seven riders who scored at over 6 points per match. This year, not counting Derek Cook, they had eight with the lowest being Mac Woolford at 6.67. This would have been enough to make the Eagles' 8th best rider a heat leader in the Sunderland team! Of course, all this meant that Eastbourne did indeed go one better than 1970 and finish the season as champions having lost just 7 matches out of a total of 32 ridden. The other members of that amazing title-winning outfit were Laurie Sims, Reg Trott and Bobby McNeil.

The Eastbourne team was rewarded with a civic reception at which Eastbourne's mayor, Councillor John Robinson, congratulated the Eagles on their achievement. Dave Lanning commented that this was 'an unprecedented gesture in speedway history.'

Following their success, Eastbourne felt that they should be automatically promoted to Division One but this was refused, so they applied in the normal manner for membership, which was also refused because they were not prepared to pay the £3,500 licence fee. Bob Dugard said he felt Eastbourne were 'entitled to promotion as the new Division Two champions, but if we do well again in 1972 we will go for the top grade even if it means buying a place.'

There were a number of enforced changes to the line-up for 1972 with still more teenagers. These included Trevor Geer and sixteen-year-old Paul Gachet (who was a

product of the Eastbourne winter training school and came in for Dave Kennett, who had been snapped up by Hackney), Laurie Sims and Mac Woolford. Confidence was high as the Eagles started the season but they were soon hit by injuries as first Malcolm Ballard tore ligaments in both his leg and hand and then Derek Cook fell at Berwick injuring his head and arm. Both of them came back after missing just a few meetings, but Cook's comeback was marred by another injury and he missed a few more matches. Once back in the saddle, Ballard continued his meteoric

Bob Dugard, son of Charlie Dugard, shown here as a young rider in Wimbledon colours. Like his father, Bob has been involved with Eastbourne in one capacity or another all his adult life and remains so now.

rise to the top, averaging 9.94 for the season, while Gordon Kennett also showed great improvement in style if not in actual points. Gone was a lot of the wildness, which had earned him the nickname 'Cowboy' and in came a more polished style. The biggest improvement of all, however, came from Bobby McNeil, who rose from reserve to heat leader during the course of the season.

As all the youngsters were doing so well, Reg Trott decided it was time to retire which left Malcolm Ballard, at the ripe old age of twenty-two, as the oldest member of the team. Trott's retirement allowed Gachet the opportunity to show what he was made of and as the latest in the long line of teenage whizz kids he achieved an average of 5.14 in his first year of competitive racing. Another newcomer to the team, although he only rode in three matches was yet another Dugard, Charlie's son and Bob's brother, Eric. Although Eastbourne did well enough, they were not quite able to make up for the loss of David Kennett and Laurie Sims from the team or for Reg Trott and Derek Cook for part of the season. In the end they had to relinquish their hold on the Division Two title, finishing in fifth place.

With the loss of the top two, Malcolm Ballard and Gordon Kennett to Oxford and Derek Cook to Canterbury, things did not look promising for Eastbourne as 1973 dawned. When they lost their first match 54-24 away to Barrow and their second 51-27 away to Boston, Lanning and Dugard knew that something had to be done. The first thing they did was to

Left: *Neil Middleditch joined Eastbourne as a sixteen year old in 1973. He is now the Team GB manager.*
Right: *Trevor Geer first rode for Eastbourne in 1971 as a teenager. By 1974 he had become a heat leader. He returned later as manager and co-promoter.*

sign up Mike Vernam. Good scoring from Vernam at their next two away matches saw the Eagles draw with Sunderland and then record their first away win at Berwick. Meanwhile, Eastbourne youngsters, Bobby McNeil, Roger Johns and Paul Gachet were all continuing to improve and by May things started looking a lot better. When Vernam left for Hull later in the season his place was taken by yet another sixteen-year-old talent in Neil Middleditch, son of the former Hastings and Poole star, Ken.

It was an event surrounding Neil Middleditch, which was to cause a great controversy later in the season. In the ninth heat of the match against Long Eaton, Middleditch broke the tapes and was excluded. Eastbourne argued that Long Eaton rider, Norman Strachan, had rolled forward and it was this that had caused Middleditch to start and that therefore the start should have been ruled unsatisfactory and all four riders put back in. The referee, Mr E.W. Roe, refused to change his decision and Eastbourne refused to continue with the match, handing Long Eaton five 5-0s.

Eric Dugard scored steadily but got laid up during the season. His place was taken by the veteran and former Eastbourne favourite, Ross Gilbertson. In his short time with the Eagles he proved he was still a top man and finished the season as the second highest scorer behind Bobby McNeil. McNeil's average was 9.34, Gilbertson's was 8.88. Roger Johns became the third heat leader, turning in 8.59. All of this meant that, far from having the poor season it looked as though they might have, the Eagles climbed two places in the table to finish in third place.

By now, the Eagles had become easily the youngest team in the league. When they beat Boston on 18 August, the oldest rider in the team was 20 years and 55 days. The age of many of the Eastbourne team created an unexpected problem as Dave Lanning pointed out that they had difficulties in transporting their riders to meetings as 'half of the team aren't old enough to drive.' Lanning's help in getting them to the track each week didn't stop them throwing him into the Arlington well, which was situated in the middle of the centre green, at the end of each season!

As well as being top scorer, it was a highly successful year for Bobby McNeil on an individual level, as he took the Silver Helmet from Workington's Lou Sansom in July. He also came second in the Division Two Riders' Championship after losing out to Boston's Arthur Price in a run-off for first place.

There were more changes to the team for 1974, as Dave Lanning was determined to get back to the top of the league so that he could apply for that Division One place. Ross Gilbertson retired and Roger Johns left to try his luck with First Division Wimbledon. In their places came Mike Sampson from Barrow, veteran Pete Jarman from Cradley and, unbelievably, yet another outstanding sixteen-year-old prospect from the winter training school by the name of Steve Weatherley.

Sampson and Jarman propped up the middle order, while, once again the youngsters continued to improve. McNeil remained top man and Trevor Geer and Paul Gachet joined him as the other two heat leaders with averages of 8.46 and 8.30 respectively. Neil Middleditch and Steve Weatherley both recorded six plus averages. It was, however, to be a frustrating season for Eastbourne as they finished runners-up to Birmingham by just four points, having drawn three away matches and lost no less than five by the tantalising score of 40-38. Just 14 more race points would have netted the

Above: *Steve Weatherley, yet another precocious teenage talent to join Eastbourne in the early 1970s. His career was cut short by a tragic accident at Hackney in 1979.*
Right: *Eric Dugard, another of Charlie's sons, rode for Eastbourne from 1972 to 1981.*

Eagles 15 match points and a victory in the league by the runaway margin of 11 points.

Since joining the Second Division in 1969, Eastbourne's record now looked like this: eighth, second, first, fifth, third, second. Perhaps the most impressive thing about this run of success was that it was nearly all down to the never-ending stream of teenage discoveries coming out of its own training school. This incredible run continued into 1975, as Gachet, Middleditch and Weatherley became the three heat leaders following the departure of McNeil and Geer. Gachet and Middleditch both upped their averages to over 9, 9.87 for Gachet and 9.62 for Middleditch, while the seventeen-year-old Weatherley, in only his second season, turned in an incredible 8.06. On 3 August Weatherley became the first rider to get round the Arlington circuit in under 60 seconds when he set up a new track record of 59.8. Of course it goes without saying that they were joined by yet another teenage prospect. This time it was Colin Richardson. Still at school, Richardson joined the team and like his predecessors, immediately showed what he was made of, finishing the season with a 5.24 average. Although Eastbourne suffered a slight fall in the league to fourth place, they did manage to win the New National League (as the British League Division Two had now been renamed) Knock Out Cup for the first time. They beat Workington 83-72 on aggregate in the final, having knocked out the league champions, Birmingham, in the second round.

Once again, Eastbourne lost its top two riders to Division One as Gachet left for White City and Middleditch went to his father's old club, Poole. This year, however, there weren't two riders ready to take their places. Steve Weatherley did what was asked of him and became a National League (yes, the name had been changed yet again!) superstar but there was a big gap between him and the second heat leader, who turned out to be Eric Dugard. Pete Jarman's 6.75 average, which made him the third heat leader, was evidence of how much the Eagles had fallen. True, they unearthed their usual teenage training school prospect in Steve Naylor, but unfortunately he broke his ankle in a road accident after 13 matches and his season was over. Colin Richardson improved a little on his 1975 season and still showed exceptional promise, but the Eagles needed more than promise as they slumped to eighth place in the league. Weatherley's average was the best yet recorded by an Eastbourne rider since its return to league racing in 1969 as he turned in a very useful 10.35. He also came second in the Junior Championship of Great Britain where it was his misfortune to come up against another young teenager just starting out in speedway by the name of Michael Lee.

In spite of its poor season, the Eastbourne management, now back in the sole hands of the Dugard Family (Charlie, Bob and John) had ambitious plans for the stadium and launched a development fund aimed at improving facilities so that they could bring First Division speedway to Arlington. The plans included a new covered grandstand with a restaurant, bar and glass enclosure overlooking the track.

Then suddenly, in 1977, it all came good again as Richardson's promise turned into the real thing. As usual, Eastbourne's number one from the previous season left for the First Division. Steve Weatherley was off to White City. In his place, Eastbourne welcomed back Dave Kennett. With that one change in the line-up, Eastbourne's poor showing in 1976 turned into a total triumph in 1977 as they annexed both the League and Cup with some considerable ease. Richardson averaged 10.63, the highest average yet by an Eastbourne rider; Kennett averaged 8.37 and Dugard, 8.25. But the real revelation was Mike Sampson. Sampson had plodded along with the Eagles since 1974 averaging 6 or 7 points per season. This year his average shot up to 10.09. Pete Jarman also began the season well, scoring at 7.5 per match, but after 19 matches he decided to call it a day to allow yet another in the long line of Eastbourne youngsters to win a permanent place in the side. This year it was the turn of Paul Woods, who finished the season with an average of 6.85.

The team steamrollered its way through the opposition. In one two-month period, from 12 June to 12 August, they won 14 straight league matches as well as performing a

An Eastbourne programme cover from speedway's 50th anniversary year, 1978.

Mike Sampson first rode as a second string for Eastbourne in 1974. In 1977 he blossomed into a top heat leader.

Knock Out Cup double over reigning league champions and cup holders, Newcastle. At the end of the season, they had won 29 out of their 36 league matches to finish seven points clear of their nearest challengers, Rye House. On top of this they had won the Cup Final by the convincing margin of 41 points, 98 to 57, having annihilated Berwick in the home leg by 61 points to 16.

Individually, Richardson had a tremendous season. He scored 20 maximums from 35 matches and won the National League Riders' Championship at Wimbledon in spite of having the 'flu. He also took the Silver Helmet from Brian Clark on 31 May and defended it successfully against Tom Owen, Ted Hubbard and Steve Koppe, before losing it to Martin Yeates on 3 October.

During the season, Eastbourne held a special challenge match against Ipswich, the Division One champions. The Eastbourne team was not formed of the usual suspects but was a team made up of their discoveries who had since moved on. The Eastbourne line-up was: Gordon Kennett, Steve Weatherley, Trevor Geer, Bobby McNeil, Dave Jessup, Roger Johns and Neil Middleditch. They defeated the British League champions by 42 points to 36. It was a very proud moment for all those involved with Eastbourne's winter training school.

With the inevitable happening and Colin Richardson moving off to Wimbledon, Bob Dugard took the decision not to replace him as they were concerned that the 1977 team had been too strong! In his piece in the programme for the opening meeting of the 1978 season, Bob Dugard said, 'We got caught up on the success treadmill last year. Never was a more successful NL team tracked than the 1977 Eagles, but it had dreadful drawbacks. No NL team reached the 30-point scoreline. Here and there were very few cases of genuine effort on the track to provide value-for-money entertainment, but in the main the majority failed miserably in their responsibility, which caused us to make a policy decision that goes completely against the grain. We have purposely weakened our team in the hope that you the fans may once again see some competitive racing.' He went on to explain that there had been a dramatic fall in attendances last season, 'purely due to the fact that our overall strength made it impossible for any team to provide reasonable entertainment, and a lot of fans justifiably stayed away.'

With its weakened team, Eastbourne still managed to finish fourth in the league and retain the Knock Out Cup. This completed ten seasons in the Second Division, during which time they had won two championships, two Knock Out Cups, finished runners-up in the league twice and third once. They were easily the most successful Second

Division team of its first ten years and 1978 summed up the reasons for their success, as six of the seven regular team members were products of the Arlington training school. David Kennett and Eric Dugard averaged over 8 points per match, Roger Abel and Steve Naylor over 7 and Paul Woods 6.64. This year's new find was John Barker, who came in as reserve, scoring 5.79. The only non-Eastbourne trained member of the team was Mike Sampson.

During the season, several Friday meetings were tried out to see if the crowd numbers would hold up should the Eagles decide to apply for Division One status. Although the crowds were never really outstanding, they were healthy enough to convince the Dugard family that it was now time to take the plunge and move up to the top echelon. With Bob Dugard's other promotion at White City in obvious difficulties, he applied to have the licence transferred and so, for the first time in its history, Eastbourne entered speedway's first division and became a member of the British League. The man that had been involved with Eastbourne speedway since the early 1930s, Charlie Dugard, became promoter.

After a decade of success in the Second Division, Eastbourne did not find life so easy amongst the big boys. There were, of course, a number of changes to the team, with most of those brought in to bolster the team being former Eastbourne riders such as Gordon Kennett, Steve Weatherley and Trevor Geer while Roger Abel, David Kennett, Eric Dugard, Steve Naylor and Paul Woods all stayed on. The only non-Eastbourne product to start the season was the Finn Kai Niemi. The Eagles' hopes were pinned on Gordon Kennett, Kai Niemi and Steve Weatherley to lead the team. Kennett and Niemi lived up to expectations and started the season well. Weatherley started well at home but was finding it difficult away from home and just as there were signs that he would

The 1977 Double-winning Eastbourne team. From left to right, back row: Eric Dugard, Pete Jarman, Colin Richardson, Mike Sampson. Front row: Steve Naylor, Roger Abel, David Kennett.

at last come good, disaster struck on 8 June when he was paralysed in the crash at Hackney which took Vic Harding's life. This tragedy knocked the stuffing out of the team. 'All we wanted to do was get the season over. It affected some members of the team very badly,' was Bob Dugard's comment. Trevor Geer in particular was very badly affected by the accident although he managed to soldier on to the end of the season. The accident overshadowed the whole season at Arlington and the fact that they finished 16th out of 18 teams was largely irrelevant.

For the start of the 1980 season, serious consideration was given to the race day. For many years, Eastbourne had been a Sunday track. With their elevation to the First Division, they had changed to Friday evening but, in spite of the presence of top stars, attendances did not rise. On just a few occasions during the season they had reverted to Sunday afternoon. On those occasions the gate showed a significant increase. In 1980 therefore, it was decided to run more Sunday meetings, with 21 of the 31 fixtures being run on that day. The long awaited grandstand-restaurant complex was also opened in time for the 1980 season.

The American Steve Columbo had been signed up to join Gordon Kennett and Kai Niemi as the third heat leader. He arrived in this country and then promptly flew out again before riding in one league match leaving the Eagles with just two heat leaders. Eastbourne's first match was away to Hull. In the second half, Niemi was involved in a bad crash which resulted in a serious arm injury, keeping him out for several weeks. A number of other foreign riders were tried. The Swede Borje Klingberg lasted three matches before becoming homesick and wanting to go home, the Pole, Jozef Kafel, raced in five matches averaging 0.92, while another Pole, Jan Puk, managed to do even worse than that by riding in two matches and failing to pick up a single point.

Eastbourne turned to one of its own and recalled Paul Woods from Crayford where he was on loan. He fitted into the third heat leader spot but at an average of just 6.28. Fortunately Niemi returned, but then Kennett was taken into hospital suffering from diabetes and was forced to rest. At the time of his enforced absence he was averaging 9.71. It was another season to forget for the Eagles as they managed just 8 wins out of 16 at home and finished 16th out of 17 teams. The only bright spot was the signing of Finn Veijo Tuorieniemi in July. He finished the season with a 6.12 average and showed promise of better things to come. On an individual level, Kai Niemi made the World Championship Final where he scored eight points.

Over the close season, Bob Dugard took over the promotion of the club from his father, bringing in his old colleague from Oxford and White City days, Danny Dunton, as his co-promoter. Both of them realised that much needed to be done to bring Eastbourne up to strength and there was a great deal of activity in the transfer market over the winter. Both Gordon Kennett and Niemi went on to the transfer list. A swap between Niemi and Birmingham's American star, Kelly Moran, was arranged but Dugard refused to allow Niemi to leave the club until the American had actually arrived in Britain and signed the agreement. With no sign of Moran arriving, Niemi lined up for the Eagles in their first match of the season at Hackney in the League Cup. Having been assured that Moran would be available for the following Sunday's meeting at home to King's Lynn, Dugard let Niemi go. As the tapes went up for the first heat, Moran was still

David Kennett rode for Eastbourne from 1970 to 1971 and from 1977 to 1983.

en route following his transatlantic flight. He arrived halfway through the match. Not surprisingly, he came last in his first two rides. However, those first two rides were to be the only time all season that Moran disappointed the Eastbourne management and fans. His combination of showmanship and sheer class brought him instant popularity and was one of the major reasons why Eastbourne were one of the few tracks in the British League that year to report increased attendances. Meanwhile, Gordon Kennett had dropped his transfer request following discussions with Charlie Dugard who had offered him a generous sponsorship deal from his own machine tools business.

Other new signings in 1981 included the Pole, Robert Slabon, and yet another Finn, Olli Tryvainen. Unfortunately, Slabon was injured halfway through the season and was forced to return to Poland, his place being taken by Eric Dugard. With Kennett and Moran as numbers one and two, the third heat leader spot continued to remain in the capable hands of Arlington discovery Paul Woods.

Once again it was not a great year for Eastbourne as they finished 13th out of 16, but the slow process of team building had begun and the Eagles were looking forward to a better 1982 as Bob Dugard announced in December a £25,000 team-rebuilding project. He also announced that there would be a return to the old policy of unearthing their own discoveries. Dugard felt that since joining the British League not enough attention had been paid to this aspect of the club. Foreigners were costing a lot of money and their commitments did not always coincide with Eastbourne's needs. A new 135-yard training track was prepared in the corner of the car park. On this Dugard hoped to train youngsters between the ages of six and fourteen. Alan Johns was put in charge of the project and two of the first junior hopes he discovered proved to be yet another generation of the Dugard family, Paul and Martin. Bob Dugard spent part of his £25,000 on buying another American, Ron Preston, from Poole. With Kennett, Moran and Woods all staying on, Eastbourne started the year with four recognised heat leaders. Unfortunately they had no one to support them and while the four scored well enough, Kennett, Moran and Preston all scoring over 9 a match, the next highest was new signing from Sweden, Lillebror Johansson with an average of just 3.55. The result was a marginal improvement in Eastbourne's league position as they climbed just one place to 12th.

Below: *The Finn Kai Niemi was signed up as a heat leader when Eastbourne joined the British League in 1979.*

Right: *Borje Klingberg did not have a happy time at Arlington. He rode in just three matches for the Eagles in 1980.*

Eastbourne had a difficult year with its charismatic American star, Moran. In June he was fined £1,000 for failing to arrive for a match with Ipswich. He was in trouble again in August when the track doctor ruled him unfit to ride in the match at Belle Vue. This match was 24 hours after Moran had qualified for his second World Championship final. The Eastbourne management were not impressed with the doctor's ruling. They issued a statement which said, 'the rider had been celebrating reaching the World Final the previous night in Sweden, and had not slept for more than 24 hours and was obviously in no fit condition to ride.' Moran was fined £10 by the referee and reported to the Control Board. Moran said that the whole thing had been a mix-up and although he agreed he had been celebrating and was a little hung-over, which he felt was only natural, he said the real reason why he had not slept was because, 'there was a lot of confusion about the homecoming arrangements' and that he seemed to be driving around Sweden for half the night. Moran's World Final appearance resulted in his scoring 11 points and finishing in fourth place.

There was a shock for Gordon Kennett at the end-of-season Supporters' Club meeting when he heard that he had been transfer-listed by Bob Dugard. 'I was surprised. I thought I would be the last one to go. I am one of the only two English riders at the club and I have been with Bob for twelve years – my entire speedway career,' he said afterwards. Dugard put Kennett's fee at £15,000 and said he needed the money to go towards covering a £20,000 plus operating loss for the 1982 season. If he was unable to raise £15,000 for Kennett, Dugard said that Eastbourne was in danger of closing. Fortunately, King's Lynn agreed to the fee and it looked as though speedway at Arlington was saved.

However, there came another bombshell as Kelly Moran said he would not return to England for the 1983 season. With no money to replace him, Dugard asked the BSPA to put Eastbourne's racing licence on ice for a year while he built up the club's finances. The BSPA refused to agree and instead promised to help the Eagles assemble a competitive side. Three names were put forward to replace Kennett and Moran: John Cook, an American and the Poles Edward Jancarz and Roman Jankowski. In the end, Eastbourne had to settle for John Eskildsen and Mike Lanham, two good solid team men but neither of them could be called top-class replacements.

Just as the season was about to start, Dugard's troubles got even worse as Eastbourne's one remaining heat leader, Ron Preston, announced he would not be returning to Arlington until May. Management assistant and programme editor, Tony Millard, said he was prepared to fly to America to try and convince Moran and Preston to change their minds and return to Eastbourne.

The final decision on whether to operate at all for the 1983 season was taken at a meeting of Eastbourne supporters at the end of March. Dugard told them that, 'the initial reaction was to pack it all in. We could wind up the club quite easily. But our second thought was if the supporters want us to carry on, we will do so. Quite frankly, we will have a terrible team. You supporters are going to be humiliated by some of the results.' A show of hands amongst the supporters showed that there was overwhelming support for the club to continue and that they agreed to do all they could to help raise funds. Jim Langford, already one of the club's major individual sponsors, was put in charge of co-ordinating fund-raising efforts. Another positive outcome of the meeting was the reactivation of the dormant Supporters' Club as well as the setting up of a new branch in Brighton to join the highly successful Hastings Supporters' Club.

One last attempt by Dugard to persuade Moran to return failed. Moran intimated in a telephone call that he was prepared to come to Britain for the

The charismatic Kelly Moran became immensely popular with the Eastbourne supporters in his two years with the club, 1981 to 1982.

England-USA Test series and that he might stay on for two weeks to take part in a few Eastbourne matches. Dugard was not impressed. 'This proposal is completely useless,' he fumed, 'it would do more damage than good to Eastbourne Speedway and make us look ridiculous.' Moran was immediately transfer-listed for £20,000. Dugard also called for the American star to be banned from international and World Championship racing in Britain. As far as Preston was concerned, it became obvious by April that he had no intention of returning to Arlington in May. He had gone to Mexico and, in spite of Dugard leaving a couple of dozen messages with friends and relatives, he had not contacted the Eastbourne management to let them know what he was doing.

Eastbourne prepared for the new season with a team consisting of Paul Woods, Lillebror Johansson, Peter Schroek, Barney Kennett, John Eskildsen, Trevor Geer and Mike Lanham. Before a wheel was turned, Johansson broke a foot while guesting for a Dutch team at Canterbury. Then in heat one of the first match of the season, Schroek collided with the safety fence and broke his collarbone. Barney Kennett lasted just under one lap of Eastbourne's second match on Easter Sunday, falling and splitting open his forehead. Three races later, Eskildsen fell in front of Geer with both riders receiving collarbone injuries putting them out for two months. When Geer returned he broke his toe and chose to retire. Already the weakest team in the league, it had, by the end of its second match lost five of its riders, leaving just captain Paul Woods and Mike Lanham. The Easter Sunday fixture attracted a crowd of 1,500. Four years previously the corresponding fixture had attracted 8,000 paying customers. Could things get any worse?

The answer to that was 'yes', as straight after their one and only away win of the season, when Eastbourne should at last have been able to celebrate something, their new signing, Zimbabwean Denzil Kent, was arrested and served with a deportation order for overstaying his permitted time in Britain. In the end he escaped deportation, but had to pay a £250 fine. Eastbourne's last home match finished off the season as it had begun, with a 16-point defeat at the hands of Reading. In spite of this, the Eagles seven were applauded by the fans who reserved the biggest cheer of the night for skipper, Paul Woods, who through it all had managed to improve his average to 8.94. He told the crowd that he wanted to remain an Eagle and hoped for better things from the 1984 season. Incredibly, after this complete nightmare of a season, the Eagles did not finish bottom of the league, ending up 14th out of 15. What bottom team Swindon's season must have been like can only be imagined!

It was touch and go, but Eastbourne managed to sign up yet another top American in time for the 1984 season. Having given up all hope of persuading either Kelly Moran or Ron Preston to return, Dugard turned his attention to Reading's Bobby Schwartz. A mystery sponsor agreed to come up with the £25,000 asking price and Eastbourne just beat Exeter to his signature. He started as he meant to go on, scoring a 12-point maximum in Eastbourne's first match against King's Lynn. Like Moran before him, this charismatic showman and great rider won over the Arlington crowd and he became a great asset to the club. He finished the year with a 9.42 average.

Paul Woods started off well, but a crash that left him with fractured ribs put him out for a while. On his return, he seemed to be suffering some reaction from having to shoulder all the burden of keeping the team going in 1983. At one time he even retired

The 1982 Eastbourne team. From left to right, back row: David Kennett, Ron Preston, Lars Hammarberg, Paul Woods. Front row: Kelly Moran, Gordon Kennett (on bike), Börge Ring.

saying, 'I am sick and tired of speedway. It is ruining me mentally.' But he was back within a month completely revitalised, scoring paid 12 in his first match. Eskildsen was much improved on his 1983 performance, nearly 2 points improved in fact, as he recorded an 8.07 average for the season. The three heat leaders had good backing from the new signings, former Eagle Olli Tyrvainen, the Czech Antonin Kasper, and former master of the Arlington track Colin Richardson, who was making a comeback for the club where he had started his speedway life.

It wasn't a great season – the team finished 11th in the league – but it was a world away from the year before. Eastbourne's financial troubles however, were far from over. In November, Bob Dugard announced that the club's losses for the season had been in the region of £40,000, £10,000 worse than the 1983 figure. A fractional increase in support, up 3.5 per cent on the previous year to an average attendance of 1,260, had been heavily outweighed by substantially higher running costs. Having unsuccessfully put forward plans to the British Speedway Promoters' Association (BSPA) for a new pay policy and equally unsuccessfully tried to obtain a new sponsorship deal, the Dugards decided there was no alternative but to drop back into the National League. In some ways, the decision came as a relief to both the Eastbourne management and its supporters. As a Second Division team it had been the most successful in the country, while as a First Division team it had done nothing but struggle. In addition, as a Second Division team, there had been the satisfaction of being able to develop its own raw talent, whereas as a First Division team it had to get out the cheque book to sign up foreign riders in an attempt to keep pace with the rest of the league.

1985 was just like old times down at Arlington in more ways than one. Gordon Kennett returned to captain the side, a new sixteen-year-old training school product by the name of Martin Dugard came straight into the team with a five plus average and the Eagles won a trophy, the Knock Out Cup. Kennett's average for the year was 10.47. He was given strong heat-leader support by Colin Richardson, who decided against staying in the British League in favour of staying with Eastbourne and new signing from Scunthorpe, Andy Buck. The ever-present Keith Pritchard, Paul Clarke and Chris Mulverhill made up the rest of the team. Towards the end of 1985, Russell Lanning, son of Dave Lanning, having been signed up as general manager two seasons before, signed

another two-year contract with the club. The switch to National League racing had made a big difference to the club, he said, 'There is so much keenness around the place. People are looking forward to next season in a way they haven't done for years.'

The resurrection of Eastbourne Eagles was complete in 1986 as once again they took the League and Cup double in style. They won the league by 6 points and they did not lose one match in the Cup, home or away. It was certainly a return to the good old days, as Martin Dugard progressed to become second highest scorer behind Gordon Kennett, both scoring 11 maximums during the course of the season. Yet another training school protege, Dean Standing, broke into the team with a 7.06 average, while still one more sixteen year old, Dean Barker, had several outings at reserve

The American, Ron Preston, only had one season with Eastbourne, 1982.

and showed great potential. Colin Richardson, Keith Pritchard, Andy Buck and Chris Mulverhill were still there giving solid support.

Individually too, Martin Dugard had a successful year, as he won the Silver Helmet from Les Collins on 28 September and made five successful defences, the most of any rider during the season. He lost it to Nigel Flatman on 17 October on what turned out to be the final challenge of the season. Colin Richardson and Gordon Kennett also won the Silver Helmet during the season.

To pull off the league and cup double in 1986 was a great achievement, but it had been done before in the Second Division/National League by Belle Vue Colts, Crewe, Boston, Birmingham and Eastbourne themselves. What had not been done before was to follow up that feat by doing it again the following season. The writing was on the wall for the other teams as soon as the season started. The Eagles' first eight home National League matches resulted in scores of 52-26 (Peterborough), 57-21 (Boston), 55-23 (Rye House), 56-22 (Exeter), 54-23 (Long Eaton), 53-25 (Berwick), 53-25 (Middlesborough) and 57-21 (Canterbury). This was followed by a crushing 62-33 defeat of Poole in the second round of the Knock Out Cup. In all, Eastbourne won every single one of its home matches as well as seven away, including at Mildenhall, the team that finished runner-up.

Paul Woods stayed with Eastbourne throughout their first British League campaign, 1979 to 1984.

The Zimbabwean, Denzil Kent, was nearly deported in 1983 for overstaying his permit.

A programme cover from Eastbourne's 1984 season, their last for a while in the British League.

Eastbourne's cup performance was even more amazing when they won it in 1987, as it meant that, not only had they won the cup three times in succession, but that they had not lost a National League cup tie since 1976. In recognition of this outstanding accomplishment, the trophy was awarded to them outright. Much of the success was due once again to the famous Arlington teenage production line as 1987 saw Martin Dugard, Dean Standing and Dean Barker all progress further. Dugard moved to the top of the score chart with a stunning 10.40 average, the second best in the whole league, while Dean Standing became an outstanding second string on 7.33. Gordon Kennett continued to score prolifically while the Supporters' Rider of the Year, Andy Buck, improved his average by over 1.5 points to become the third heat leader. All the riders in that history-making team gave of their best, the others being Keith Pritchard, Darren Standing and Steve Chambers.

In its first period in the old Second Division/National League, Eastbourne was the most consistent and best team, but in the three years since returning, the team had done even better than that and had totally dominated the league. In 13 years of Second Division/National League racing, Eastbourne had lost just 8 home matches and had 71 away wins. No other team came anywhere close to equalling, let alone beating, a record like that.

With Eastbourne now on top of the world the news came as a bombshell when, in January of the following year, Bob Dugard announced that Eastbourne would be closing down for at least a year. This was in protest to the National League Promoters insisting that the Eagles must abide by the 42-point limit. With Dean Standing requesting a transfer, the Eagles average had come down to fractionally above the limit at 42.08, but the management committee was still pressing for Eastbourne to lose another rider. Dugard was incensed that they should stick so rigidly to the letter of the law. He said, 'I'm not prepared to con the public by putting out a below-quality side simply to satisfy this particular rule. We are having to increase admission prices, but I am being asked to reduce the quality of the product for the supporters. I know they will not stand for it. It would be financial lunacy to run under the circumstances. We have had a wonderful three years and are quite rightly expected by our public to maintain certain standards. I have not got the heart to continue. If we can't keep our three heat leaders, we will not open this season.' Dugard went on to say that he believed the loss of one of his star riders would trigger a 20 per cent fall in attendance. He said he intended to loan out all his riders for the next season with a view to a possible relaunch in 1989. Russell Lanning, who had left Eastbourne to join Wimbledon, contacted Dugard immediately offering him his support and said he would work hard to find a solution to the problem.

Fortunately, a solution to the impasse was reached before the start of the season when Channel Four television presenter Gareth Rogers agreed to take over the running of the club for the next twelve months. Under the terms of the deal, Rogers agreed to rent Eastbourne speedway from the Dugard family's Oxspeed Company, with Dugard handling all contractual matters involving riders and acting in an advisory capacity while Rogers would take over as promoter. It was agreed that the Eagles would retain Gordon Kennett, Andy Buck, Keith Pritchard and Dean Barker but that Martin Dugard would move up to First Division Oxford. All this close season wrangling left its mark on the team and by mid-season the Eagles were in the unaccustomed position of being in the bottom half of the table. Gradually, however, the old Eastbourne spirit began to reassert itself and a fine finish to the season saw them climb the table to end the year in third place. Once again it was Gordon Kennett who guided the team through a difficult first half into the sunnier climes of its final position, with a 9.97 average. Andy Buck gave

The 1985 Cup-winning Eastbourne team. From left to right, back row: Keith Pritchard, Chris Mulverhill, Russell Lanning (team manager), Andy Buck, Colin Richardson. Front row: Derek Harrison, Gordon Kennett (on bike), Paul Clarke.

strong support while Dean Standing, who had stayed on after all, moved up to become the third heat leader. Dean Barker and Keith Pritchard, whose testimonial year this was, and Darren Standing all gave solid support. This year's junior find was David Norris. His first match, at home to Stoke, came just 24 hours after his sixteenth birthday. He scored eight paid ten from four rides. Rogers commented that the sight of this youngster in full hair-raising flight around the track was 'a real golden moment which will live in my memory as long as I'm in speedway.'

As the 1989 season began, Gareth Rogers found a much-needed co-promoter to share the work, in the shape of former Canterbury boss, Chris Galvin. The only major change to the team line-up was the departure of Dean Standing, but the improvement of Dean Barker more than made up for his loss. In fact, Barker's early season form was so good that Rogers put his name forward to be considered for the forthcoming Test series against Australia. This was a move Rogers was soon to regret as Barker was chosen for the Second Test at Edinburgh but instead chose to ride in an open meeting at Oxford, for which he claimed he had a prior booking. The National League management committee slapped a £500 fine on Rogers for giving Barker permission to ride at Oxford rather than in the Test and Barker himself was warned that he could face disciplinary action. To complicate matters still further Bob Dugard, who was still harbouring resentment over the 42-point limit affair from the previous year, launched a bitter attack on the National League chairman, Mervyn Stewkesbury. Barker was eventually cleared of wrongdoing but Rogers agreed to pay his fine. Rogers' action infuriated Dugard still further as he felt it completely undermined the principled stand the club had made on the issue. There were further difficulties both on and off the track, during which both riders and supporters openly expressed their views to the press giving their opinion on what they thought of the way the club was being managed. Following all this, the whole situation came to a head on 28 October at the annual end-of-season dinner and dance, when an unseemly fracas took place and fists flew. David Norris collected minor injuries during the scuffle and immediately put in a transfer request.

In spite of all its troubles, the team plugged away and did its best. Gordon Kennett, as ever, was the perfect ambassador for the club, recording a 9.60 average. Behind him the ever-improving Dean Barker also recorded a 9 plus average, while David Norris's average went up to 7.04. Unfortunately for the Eagles, Barker's season was cut short when he received multiple injuries following a horrific pile-up at Hackney on 8 September. Following in the Arlington tradition two more youngsters with great potential were discovered in Ben Howe and David Mason. The club arranged for them to make exchange visits to widen their experience with Howe going to Australia and Mason to Denmark.

After a traumatic season the Eagles finished up in seventh place in the league, their worst position since their return, while in the Cup they reached the third round before being knocked out by Poole 113-79. Rogers summed up his second year in charge with the following words, 'The continued development of junior talent is one of the most positive points I can look back on. In honesty, though, 1989 will not go down as one of Gareth Rogers' – or Eastbourne's – favourite years. My motivation is very low. Bob Dugard has said don't throw the towel in. But a certain faction have demoralised me. You don't mind if people aren't going to row the boat with you, but you don't need the abuse.'

The Czech, Antonin Kasper, rode for Eastbourne in 1984.

Despite everything, end-of-season attendance figures revealed that there had been an 11.79 per cent increase giving a total of 26,820 cash customers, with the average attendance rising from 992 to 1,090. In spite of his hint that he may quit, Gareth Rogers agreed to stay on. As he told the supporters in the first programme of the new season, 'The past problems have to be put to the back of our minds.' David Norris had left for Ipswich for a fee of £12,000 and Dean Barker had left for Oxford. In their places came Austrailian Tony Primmer and former Arlington favourite Paul Woods. Gordon Kennett missed the first few matches of the season following an injury to his left shoulder in a pre-season practice session. His place as captain was temporarily taken by Keith Pritchard.

Without Kennett, Eastbourne's National League season did not get off to the best of starts as they lost 74-22 to Peterborough, 66-29 to Wimbledon and 62-33 to Hackney. It wasn't until their first home match of the campaign, against Long Eaton, that they managed to chalk up a win, but even that was only by the narrow margin of 49-47. Kennett's return brought some stability to the side, but it still wasn't the sort of season that the Eastbourne patrons had been used to over the years.

The problem was that there was no real heat leader support for Kennett. Andy Buck struggled against a viral infection that finally forced him to retire altogether in September. Although Tony Primmer and Paul Woods did their best, they still finished up with averages of only just over the 6-point mark. The one bright spot was the form of new Aussie, Brian Nixon, brought into the team midway through the season making everyone wonder why he hadn't been brought in before. The outcome was 11th place in the league and an early exit from the cup, 120-72 to Hackney, in the second round.

As the 1990 season ended, Gareth Rogers again expressed doubts about whether the track could continue, but it appeared as though Bob Dugard had come to the rescue as he obtained financial backing to take the team back into the Sunbrite British League. Dugard named his new team and the application went in confident that it would be accepted. No sooner had he done so than Mervyn Stewkesbury came up with a plan for evening up the leagues (there were currently nine in the Sunbrite British League and seventeen in the National League) and for automatic promotion and relegation to take

The 1986 double-winning Eastbourne team. From left to right: Martin Dugard, Chris Mulverbill, Andy Buck, Keith Pritchard, Gordon Kennett, Dean Standing, Dean Barker.

place. This plan received the backing of the National League promoters on 6 December who further agreed that the teams to be promoted in the first instance to even up the leagues would be Poole, Ipswich, Berwick and Wimbledon, with Eastbourne on 'stand-by'. Dugard insisted that for him it was 'First Division or bust', to which Rogers added, 'The message is clear from my own bankers. I can't afford another season in the Second Division.' Following further discussions between the Eastbourne management and the National League, Dugard announced on 21 December that the track would close as they had not been given any assurances about automatic promotion. Although he agreed to defer a final decision, there was to be no change of heart and Dugard and Rogers carried out their threat to close down Eastbourne.

Fortunately for the Arlington faithful, if not for the Plough Lane fans, the close down only lasted a few months. On 5 June 1991, Wimbledon director, Don Scarf announced in his club's final programme that 'during the winter as amalgamation got underway it became obvious to me that we had to go First Division or close, so we decided to give it a go. Despite all our efforts, we failed to find a team sponsor and although our attendances have been slightly higher than last year, we have been losing over £2,000 per meeting, a situation that obviously could not continue. In order to honour our commitments we are moving our operation to Arlington…' This was a tragedy for Wimbledon but a reprieve for Eastbourne as Don Scarf and Peter Brown moved their British League Division One team to the Sussex Coast with the first match taking place on 30 June. The team kept its nickname and therefore became known as Eastbourne Dons. Of course there was a complete change of personnel from the 1990 Eastbourne team except for

Gordon Kennett who came back to ride for the new team. The rest of the Dons were Neville Tatum, Bobby Ott, Deon Prinsloo, Nathan Simpson, Jesper Olsen, John Davis, Andy Graham and Armando Castagna with former Eagle, Trevor Geer, acting as team manager.

Wimbledon had already had a poor start to the season and things did not get much better in their new home as they finished the season in 12th place, one from bottom. Andy Graham was the star performer with an average of 9.44. The following season, 1992, Eastbourne reverted to being the Eagles and Trevor Geer joined Peter Brown as co-promoter. There were wholesale changes to the team, as firstly, after seven years continuously and ten altogether, Gordon Kennett left Arlington. Kennet had been a great servant to the club having made a total of 477 appearances and scoring 5,339 points. Others to leave included Bobby Ott, Armando Castagna, Jesper Olsen and Deon Prinsloo, for whom Eastbourne was unable to obtain a work permit. In fact, the only two Dons to remain as Eagles were skipper Andy Graham and Nathan Simpson. Andrew Silver, former Eagle, Olli Tyrvainen, and Glenn Doyle were signed up as replacements. Neville Tatum returned from his loan to Ipswich later in the season.

The new team started off well with a 14-point victory over Arena Essex in the Gold Cup and it looked as though they were in for better things. But this was a false dawn as

Left: *Darren Standing rode for Eastbourne from 1986 to 1990.*

Above: *David Norris first rode for Eastbourne in 1988 and has had several spells with the club.*

the Eagles then lost their next nine matches. Attendances dropped alarmingly and a crisis meeting was held at the club. A new pay structure was put in place which related riders' earnings to crowd levels at home matches. Team changes were urgently needed and the Swede Stefan Danno was signed up. A paid 10 on his debut was a promising start, but shortly afterwards, Andy Graham, captain and top scorer, asked for a move to Cradley Heath. His place was taken for one meeting by Bobby Schwartz and then permanently by Peter Nahlin. In September yet another old favourite returned to Arlington when Paul Woods made a brief comeback for the team.

None of these changes did much to improve Eastbourne's lot as they lost every single away league match as well as five of their home matches. The team hovered in the bottom three all season and with automatic promotion and relegation now the order of the day, Eastbourne found itself in the position where it had to win its last home match against Arena Essex on 25 October to stay in the First Division. Reserve, Tyrvainen gave one of his best performances of the season to score 10 paid 12 points. In spite of this, it looked all over for Eastbourne as, at one point, they trailed the Hammers by 7 points. With one heat to go however, the Eagles had pegged back the deficit and were leading by 3 points, 43-40. In the last race, Arena Essex's Brian Karger shot away from the gate, but in a nail-biting effort Andrew Silver and Peter Nahlin managed to grab a share of the points and save the match and First Division status for the Eagles. This victory consigned Swindon to bottom place in the league. It was a final irony that both Andrew Silver and Peter Nahlin had been signed from Swindon. At the end of the season, Nahlin proved to have been Eastbourne's top rider turning in an average of 8.63 with Andy Graham on 7.18 and Andrew Silver on 6.58.

Not only did a member of the Silver family help to save Eastbourne's First Division place on 25 October, but it was also the day that another member of the Silver family, Andrew's father, Len, saved the club from closing down. The poor attendances had once again raised doubts over whether Eastbourne could continue in 1993, but Len Silver agreed to take over as promoter of the club along with Jon Cook and promised that Arlington would stay open. Silver, had of course, had many years experience promoting at Hackney, Rayleigh and Rye House, though he had been absent from speedway for seven years looking after his skiing business. He looked forward to this new challenge with relish. 'We have to be much more positive in our publicity and get away from abusing our own sport at every opportunity,' he said, 'It's a great sport and we have to start selling it to the public at large as that. If anybody wants to kick up a fuss from the centre green phone they should be allowed to do so – the crowd love that sort of thing – but if someone tries it as things stand at the moment they get fined, which can't be right.' 'Leaping Len' was back!

At a Supporters' Club meeting at the end of the season a positive vote was taken on moving the Eagles' race night to Saturday. Silver agreed and Eastbourne's regular race night was changed, although there were still eight Sunday dates pencilled in. The Dugard family agreed to invest in excess of £25,000 on upgrading the floodlights. One of Len Silver's new ideas for publicity resulted in the appointment of a Community Relations Officer, whose job it was to approach local councils with a view to arranging school visits in order to raise the club's profile. He was also to be responsible for inves-

Neville Tatum rode for the short-lived Eastbourne Dons team in 1991.

tigating the possibility of obtaining grants. The man appointed for this role, was local policeman Peter Brown (no relation to the former promoter). With the return of two former Eastbourne stars, Martin Dugard and Dean Barker, to join Peter Nahlin and Andrew Silver, the team took on a much more solid appearance. And when yet another former Eagles' favourite, David Norris, joined later in the season, it looked rather more like the sort of Eagles team the patrons were used to. A bid by Len Silver to buy Savalas Clouting from Ipswich for £15,000 was turned down.

The league itself turned into something of a three-horse race with Eastbourne vying with Belle Vue and Wolverhampton for top honours. In the end, Eastbourne just missed out and had to be content with 3rd place on 61 points just 2 behind both champions Belle Vue and runners-up Wolverhampton. The fourth placed team, Arena Essex, were a further 8 points adrift. Dugard's return saw him as top scorer for the team with an average of 8.98, just in front of Nahlin on 8.02. David Norris took the third heat leader spot.

Although 1993 was a much better year for the Eagles, it was tinged with sadness, as Charlie Dugard died on 8 April. Charlie had been involved with speedway racing at Arlington almost since the beginning and, was, of course, the father of John, Bob and Eric and grandfather of Martin and Paul, all of whom had ridden for Eastbourne. Since Charlie's first involvement with the track back in 1931, the Dugard family had been synonymous with Eastbourne and Bob, of course, was still involved in its operation. The Dugard family had stepped in many times over the years to rescue Eastbourne financially and to pour money in from their own pockets to keep the track going when it would otherwise have closed. Charlie had, right from the beginning, held the view that Eastbourne should bring on its own youngsters and through the training school, which he set up and masterminded, it had done just that. Names like his own grandson, Martin, Dave Jessup, Gordon Kennett, Steve Weatherley, Colin Richardson and David Norris were all products of his training.

There is no doubt therefore that Charlie would have been proud of the announcement made at the end of the season that Eastbourne had managed to land a £40,000 sponsorship deal to help youth development at Arlington. Although sponsorship was nothing new in speedway, this deal was unique as it represented the first major investment by the Government through the Business Sponsorship Incentive Scheme for

Sport. The idea was that the fund would match pound for pound the investment put in by two major companies, Len Silver's Silverski Holidays and Dugard's own Machine Tools Ltd.

Having made a giant stride forward in 1993, Eastbourne returned to its winning ways in 1994 by lifting the Speedway Star Cup and finishing runner-up in the league. As usual, success in 1993 meant that Eastbourne had to part with one of their riders to keep under the points limit. Reluctantly they allowed Peter Nahlin to go, leaving them with Martin Dugard, Andrew Silver, Dean Barker and David Norris as well as Paul Dugard, Stefan Danno and the sixteen year old, Darren Shand. Although there was no team place for him, Eastbourne also signed up the Swede, Stefan Andersson, with a view to using him in the 1995 season. As it turned out it proved to be a shrewd move, as after just one match, Andrew Silver decided he'd had enough of speedway and gave it up. Andersson was immediately drafted into the team, scoring seven paid ten on his debut.

With a more or less settled side, the Eagles had their best season since their old Second Division days. Averages of 9-plus from Dugard and Norris and 8.98 from Barker saw them finish as runners-up in the league to runaway champions, Poole. But even better was to come in the Cup as they carved their way through the opposition to reach the final, where they were up against Cradley Heath. The first leg was a total triumph for the Eagles as they trounced the Heathens by 59 points to 37. The second leg was a foregone conclusion especially after the first heat when Martin Dugard roared away

from the gate, defeating home skipper Greg Hancock with Stefan Andersson passing Scott Smith to make it a 4-2 for Eastbourne. Heat two, the reserves heat, was even better for the Eagles as Paul Dugard and Scott Swain, riding in only his fourth match for Eastbourne, took a 5-1. Although Cradley did make a comeback later in the meeting and, in fact, eventually went on to win it by 49 points to 47, they were never in with any real chance as Eastbourne ran out winners by 106 points to 86. It was also a triumph for the joint team managers, former Eagles' favourites, Steve Weatherley and Trevor Geer. There were also a couple of individual successes for the team as Stefan Danno qualified for the World Final, scoring two points, and Martin Dugard finished in third place in the Division One Riders' Championship.

John Eskildsen rode for Eastbourne in 1983 and 1984.

During the 1994 season, Len Silver decided it was time to hand over the reins and Bob Dugard came back as co-promoter with Jon Cook.

Before the 1995 season started, Eastbourne were able to announce the biggest sponsorship in the history of the sport as they clinched a £30,000 deal with the multi-billion dollar Korean based conglomerate, Hyundai. The deal was secured because of the good relationship existing between C. Dugard (Machine Tools) and the Hyundai Corporation.

A major reorganisation took place over the close season as Divisions One and Two were amalgamated to make one league of 21 teams to be known as the Premier League. Some equalisation of team strengths took place and Eastbourne lost David Norris to Reading, but, generally, Eastbourne did not come off too badly and were able to hang on to Martin Dugard, Barker, Danno, Andersson, Shand and Swain. Stefan Ekberg and Paul Whittaker were brought in to the team and everything was ready to capitalise on their success of 1994. And capitalise they did. With Dugard once again having a tremendous season and scoring at over ten points a match, with Barker still improving to 9.35 per match and with Danno at over 8.7, Eastbourne carried all before them romping home in the League by 8 clear points to take the title of league champions for the 8th time. The difference being that this time, for the first time in their history, they were champions of the country's top league.

Eastbourne's chances of retaining its title in 1996 were badly affected by the loss of Dean Barker who missed the whole season due to a broken leg, an injury he had sustained on the day Eastbourne had clinched the 1995 title against Exeter. Barker had been in the best form of his life and his loss was a bitter blow to Eastbourne. Neville Tatum joined Dugard, Danno and Andersson and David Norris returned. Tatum left after just three matches to be replaced by Alan Mogridge in a swap deal with the London Lions.

Dugard remained the undisputed number one at Arlington, turning in yet another 10 plus average, while Andersson emerged as a real star, scoring 9.11 for the season. Norris came good towards the end of the year but he had also suffered a broken leg towards the end of the 1995 season which he had sustained in the Overseas Final. Dean Standing was tempted out of his four-year retirement in June to try and make up for the injuries, but at the beginning of September he too broke his leg. In all it was a good effort by the Eagles, but there were too many injuries and they finished the season in third place. Eastbourne also entered a team, the Eaglets, into the Conference League. They were not a success, winning just one match and losing 13 to finish in 12th place out of 13 teams.

At the end of the 1996 season there was yet another reorganisation of the league as some of the leading teams felt the Premier League was too big and that a smaller, more elite league should be created. Eastbourne opted to join this new league of just ten teams. The Eagles prospects in the new Elite League looked good as they managed to keep all their riders from 1996 with the addition of Dean Barker, who was now ready to return. An early season away victory over Ipswich, the Eagles first since 1979, gave them cause to think that there could be another league championship on the way. This, however, was followed by a controversial 73-17 drubbing at Poole, with accusations from the Eastbourne team about Poole's abuse of the rules regarding tyres. After this

Left: *Stefan Danno rode for Eastbourne from 1992 to 1999. He twice finished 12th in the Grand Prix standings.*
Right: *Darren Shand joined Eastbourne as a sixteen-year-old in 1994.*

aberrant result, the season went well for the Eagles and they came very close to pulling off the double, finishing second in the league and once again winning the cup. Although their averages were slightly down on the previous year, Dugard, Andersson, Barker, Danno, Norris and Mogridge proved themselves to be a formidable outfit and, as the season went on, they got better and better. The Cup Final against Poole was proof of this as they outgunned Poole in both legs. A win at Wimborne Road by 6 points set the Eagles up for a convincing victory and when they stormed into a 16-point lead after just 6 races, it was all over. Dugard and Danno both scored maximums while Andersson dropped just 1 point. There were ten 5-1s to Eastbourne as the Eagles raced to a 50-point aggregate victory.

For 1998, Eastbourne retained Martin Dugard, Stefan Andersson, Stefan Danno and David Norris and brought in the 1992 World Champion, Gary Havelock and Scott Robson. Dean Barker again missed the season, this time due to a badly broken arm. Dugard continued to dominate proceedings at Arlington with a league average of 8.86, but Andersson was down on scoring power to a mere 6.29. Danno also could only manage 6.89. In the end, Norris proved to be second to Dugard with 7.20. The signing of Havelock proved to be something of a failure and he was eventually transferred to Poole, his place being taken by a succession of riders, including an old Eastbourne friend, Peter Nahlin, but none of them came good either. Eastbourne's real problem was its away form. They managed to win just 2 out of 21 official fixtures, strangely enough both wins came within a four-day period in June. Their home form was a lot better as they lost just 5 matches, 4 of them to the league and cup champions, Ipswich. In all, this performance resulted in a mid-table place as they came 5th out of nine teams. Stefan Danno had the most success individually as he finished in 12th place in the World Championship Grand Prix series and was also ranked 12th in the first ever FIM Official World Rankings.

Over the close season, a major change was made to the track by radically widening the exit on turn two. Following a visit there at the beginning of April, Ipswich complained that the track was now the wrong shape as it was no longer formed with two straights joined by smooth curves. Ipswich promoter, John Louis, said, 'You could say it was cone, or even pear-shaped.' Jon Cook, on behalf of Eastbourne, said that Arlington was the shape of the future. He said the Speedway Control Board had inspected the track and were most complimentary about it. He added that his supporters liked the new shape and that they were voting with their feet. 'Our crowd on Saturday night [for the Ipswich match] was massive, the place was heaving. We are at the forefront of change for speedway.' He felt the new shape gave more room for 'riders who want to race.'

Yet more changes were made to the league as teams were increased from six to seven riders. Dugard and Norris returned, as did Barker making yet another comeback from serious injury. In a move which took everyone by surprise, Eastbourne then signed up the first Russian to race in British league speedway, when they signed up Roman Povazhny. American Josh Larsen was also signed up while the two reserve spots went to Brent Collyer and Seemond Stephens, who was attempting to jump straight from the Conference League to the Elite League. It didn't work and after six matches he left for the Premier League, his place being taken by Mark Lemon. Lemon proved to be something of a disappointment and he too left after 14 matches to be replaced firstly by Stefan Danno on a temporary basis and then permanently by Peter Nahlin.

Once again Dugard led the way for the Eagles but his average was well

Stefan Andersson first joined Eastbourne in 1994 and has been in and out of the team ever since.

down on what had come to be expected as he managed just 7.81. He was also involved in the most talked-about incident of the year as he physically attacked former team-mate Stefan Andersson in full view of the Sky cameras following a bad crash between the two. With Dugard's scoring being down he only just managed to retain the top spot with Nahlin, Norris and Barker all recording 7 plus averages as well. In many ways Dean Barker was probably the success story of the year as he had had to come back from a bad arm injury wearing a special glove to be able to race. It was not a good year for Eastbourne and they finished the year one from bottom of the table. In the Craven Shield they also finished 9th out of 10, while in the Speedway Star Cup they were knocked out in the first round.

During the season, a 70th anniversary meeting was held with former riders Andrew Silver, Dean Standing, Malcolm Ballard, Paul Woods, Keith Pritchard, Eric Dugard, David Kennett, Barney Kennett and Trevor Geer all taking part in the special parade. The meeting was started by Jimmy Gleed, a member of the 1950s Southern Area League team.

After making several changes to the team for the 2000 season, Jon Cook announced 'We are in for a season to remember.' And he was right. Into the team came England international and Grand Prix rider, Joe Screen as well as Paul Hurry and Petri Kokko. Out went Peter Nahlin, Roman Povazhny and Josh Larsen. Martin Dugard, David Norris, Dean Barker and Brent Collyer stayed. It looked a good line-up, but the season started badly as both of Eastbourne's opening league matches ended in defeat. Then it happened and the team clicked into gear as they reeled off 10 matches without defeat – including 4 away. Even so, King's Lynn were still favourites to take the league as they had also had a tremendous start to the season and at one point were 12 points clear of the Eagles. Bit by bit however, Eastbourne pulled back the deficit. In July, Collyer was dropped from the team and his place taken firstly by Per Wester and then by Stefan Danno. As fate would have it, the last match of the season was against King's Lynn and it came down to whoever won it would be champions. Danno was out injured but even worse, Dugard was also injured and unable to race. Cook brought in two guests, Savalas Clouting and Scott Nicholls.

The atmosphere at Arlington on 30 September was absolutely electric. It was estimated that a crowd of 6,500 turned up, including many from King's Lynn. Eastbourne took the lead in heat two thanks to their reserves, Kokko and Clouting, taking a well-deserved 5-1. To add to the tension however there was a dispute over whether the result should stand as the flag marshal had shown the yellow flag instead of the chequered flag at the end of four laps. Much to team manager Olli Tyrvainen's relief, the referee said the result would stand. Gradually, thanks to some excellent riding, particularly by Norris and Screen, the Eagles pulled ahead. At the end of heat twelve, the scores stood at Eastbourne 42 King's Lynn 32.

The Knights had one last trick up their sleeve as they gambled on sending in Jason Crump as a golden double tactical substitute. From the start it was Boyce for King's Lynn who took the lead in front of Clouting, Norris and Crump. Norris and Crump both moved past Clouting and then Norris went after Boyce, taking him on the last lap. Boyce slowed up to allow Crump to take the four points for coming second. It was a 5-3 for

A third generation Dugard, Charlie's grandson, Martin, rode for Eastbourne in two separate periods between 1985 and 2001. In 2000, he became the first British rider to win the British Grand Prix.

King's Lynn, but it was not what they wanted. They now needed two 5-1s and a 4-2 to take the title. Heat thirteen saw Screen and Nicholls up against King's Lynn's Crump and Leigh Adams, who was so far unbeaten. As the race got underway, Nicholls went down on the third bend and was excluded. Screen was left to face the two Australians alone. He just managed to get to the first bend in front of Crump, but it was Adams who chased him all the way. It was a photo finish, but Screen held on by a whisker to give the Eagles the match and the Elite League title. It had been an all-round team effort for Eastbourne, something that was indicative of the season as a whole.

After his comparatively poor form in 1999, Dugard had returned to the top of the pile, recording a 9.67 average, with Joe Screen on 8.82. David Norris, Paul Hurry and Dean Barker all scored at more than 7 points per match. Individually, Stefan Danno once again finished 12th in the Grand Prix, while Joe Screen came 16th. But perhaps the best performance of all came from Martin Dugard, who appeared at the British Grand Prix as a wild-card entry. Not only did he win it, but in doing so, became the first British rider to win his own country's Grand Prix.

With Dugard, Screen, Barker and Norris all lining up for the 2001 Eagles, there were high hopes that Eastbourne could become the first team to retain the Elite League title, but a dreadful injury to Joe Screen at King's Lynn on 25 April, when he broke his thigh, put a real damper on the season. As Jon Cook put it, 'It takes a lot for everyone in the club to pick themselves up from that. To lose Joe was a blow that we were just not to recover from.'

The club received another blow when Dean Barker was also injured and missed 10 matches in the middle of the season. Two former Eagles, Stefan Andersson and Roman Povazhny came back during the season to help out but after 25 April there was really no chance of Eastbourne retaining its title. In the end the team finished the table in 7th place. Dugard was once again top man with 8.16, but Dean Barker as second-heat leader could only manage 6.8 and David Norris recorded 6.7. Two newcomers to the team, Brent Warner and Joonas Kylmakorpi covered the reserve spots well enough, though at times, owing to Eastbourne's injury list they were forced into the team. On one memorable occasion at Coventry on 14 April, Brent Werner rode in 7 races scoring 19 paid 20.

There was another memorable occasion, again in April, on the 28th of the month, when Eastbourne recorded the highest score ever in the Elite League, beating King's Lynn 75-0. The Knights' management had withdrawn its team in protest following a dispute over the eligibility of Danny Bird to ride at no. 7 in place of the injured Lee Redmond. Eastbourne still had to ride every race to earn the points. The fastest time

An Eastbourne programme from its highly successful 2002 season.

of the night was 58.4 seconds (track record 55.3). Bob Dugard called King's Lynn's decision 'unbelievable' and said, 'I can see no possible way they [the King's Lynn promoters] can keep their licences.'

Eastbourne Eaglets ran again in 2001, entering the Southern Junior League with a team that included Daniel Giffard, Barrie Geer, Jason King, Chris Geer, Matt Fern and a name very familiar to long standing Arlington patrons, Edward Kennett. This time the Eaglets had a far more successful time than their big brothers as they won the league, winning 6 out of their 8 matches.

With Martin Dugard deciding to retire, Eastbourne needed to find a top-class star to replace him in time for the 2002 season. At first they thought they'd found him, when they signed up Poland's Grand Prix star, Krzystof Cegielski, but then Cegielski had his licence withdrawn by the Polish authorities. With just days to go before the start of the season, Eastbourne was left with just one top-class rider in Joe Screen, who was raring to go after his long lay off. Fortunately for Eastbourne, the Elite League promoters had brought in a new rule for 2002 banning Elite League teams from having more than one Grand Prix rider unless they'd had three the year before in which case they could have two. This left a number of Grand Prix riders without British clubs for 2002. One of those was England's last world champion, Mark Loram. Within 24 hours of Cegielski's enforced exit, Loram was in the team. With two top English riders, both noted for their dare devil all-action style, Eastbourne could once again look forward to the season and hopefully put the dismal 2001 season behind them. Along with Loram and Screen, the Eagles retained Dean Barker, Stefan Andersson, David Norris and Toni Svab, who had joined towards the end of the previous season. The other new signing was Savalas Clouting, who joined the club nine years after Len Silver had first offered £15,000 for him.

At the beginning of 2002 there was a change in the management set-up at Eastbourne as BSPA President, Terry Russell joined Jon Cook as co-promoter. Bob Dugard, as stadium owner, continued to concentrate on stadium matters while Dugard Machine Tools continued as club sponsors.

2002 proved to be yet another outstanding year for the Eagles. No fewer than 6 riders recorded averages of over 6.8, the only exception being Clouting on 4.23. Loram took over the number one spot from Dugard with 9.51, while Screen proved to be the perfect number two. For the second time in three years, Eastbourne topped the Elite League. However, yet another rule change this year meant that this was not enough for them to be crowned Elite League champions. Instead, a play-off system was introduced, with Eastbourne having to meet the winners of the run-off between the second, third, fourth and fifth placed teams for the right to be called champion. This final race-off, a two-legged affair, between Eastbourne and Wolverhampton took place on 25 September and 2 October and resulted in a win for Wolverhampton. Eastbourne fans were able to take some consolation in the fact that yet again their team won the Cup, beating Peterborough in the final, 94-86 on aggregate. In any other year, Eastbourne would once again have been proclaimed winners of the double.

And so, as 2002 came to an end, Eastbourne found itself top of the league for the 10th time in its history. It has also won the cup relevant to its league 9 times. Other

Gordon Kennett first rode for Eastbourne as a sixteen-year-old youngster in 1970. His last season with the club was over twenty years later in 1991. In all he rode 477 times for the club, scoring 5,339 points.

honours include winning the Premiership in 1995 and 1996. Strangely enough, Eastbourne have never won the fours in any of the leagues they have been in. In some ways this is a reflection of the fact that the Eagles have always gone for strength in depth. Although they have had their share of star riders, the team behind them, right down to the reserves, has always given full support.

Eastbourne has now been going since 1929, with, apart from the war years, just one short break for four years in the 1960s. In all, the public has been able to watch speedway at Arlington for 64 years. There is no other track in the country which can match this record. For at least 61 of those years the Dugard family has been involved in one capacity or another. On many occasions they have saved the track from extinction by digging deep into their own pockets. Eastbourne's contribution to British speedway is incalculable – not only because of its longevity, not only because of its impressive league and cup record but also because of its commitment to training youngsters, which has continued from pre-war days up to the present.

3

RYE HOUSE

Rye House opened for speedway in 1935. It is said that the speedway was opened on land which had once been a watercress field but was now the site of a track built privately in 1928 by a Mr Frogley for his two sons, Roger and Buster, to practice on. To begin with in 1935 it catered mainly for amateur riders and was a breeding ground for new, young talent. The speedway itself was part of a general Sunday afternoon's entertainment as spectators watched the racing and took part in horse riding or a row on the River Lea. It was a very relaxed atmosphere, far removed from the business side of the sport that was being carried on in nearby London.

Right from the very beginning, all the London clubs took an interest in what was going on at Rye House and representatives used to visit frequently with a view to

spotting possible talent. Hackney's Australian star, Dicky Case, set up a training school at the track under the aegis of the Hackney Motor Club. The cost was 19s for the first lesson and 15s thereafter. Tom Bradbury-Pratt, the promoter at Harringay, put up a special cup for novices. In 1936, this was won by Reg Allen. Some of the other riders who appeared at these early meetings included Percy Brine, Bert Spencer, Keith Harvey, Bill Mathieson, Archie Windmill, Ron Clarke and Fred Cutt. The operation continued in this way until 1938, in which year Rye House joined with Eastbourne, Smallford and Dagenham in the Sunday Dirt Track League.

Rye House opened its first league season on Easter Sunday with a special Easter Championship, a silver cup going to the winner. Among those

Hackney's Australian star, Dicky Case, founded the training school at Rye House.

taking part were Malcolm Craven, Fred Curtis, Les Bowden, Roy Duke, Steve Langton, Ken John and Jock Hamilton. For half-time entertainment a motor ball match was laid on between North Hants and Hackney Wick. Colin Watson also made a guest appearance, setting up a new track record of 88.8 seconds.

Before the league season started, the Rye House Cubs staged a challenge match against The Rest. That first Rye House team consisted of Les Trim (captain), Jock Hamilton, Ken John, Johnny Myson, Jack Milross, Dellow, D'Alessandro and Morris. The Cubs' captain, Les Trim, won the next big event at the track when he took the Rye House Amateur Championship. The cup was due to be presented by none other than the 1936 World Champion, Lionel Van Praag, but owing to injuries sustained in the Test match at Belle Vue he was unable to appear and Trim received the cup from Mrs Case instead.

Given recent developments in the sport with regard to play-offs it is interesting to note that the Championship was run over the usual 20-heat format, but that the title was decided by a run-off between the four highest scorers. Trim led from start to finish, although he was strongly challenged by Jack Hyland on the last bend. According to *Speedway News*, Trim received 'a great ovation from those "Toughs" who had braved the elements to witness some excellent racing throughout the afternoon.'

Rye House continued with its diet of inter-club matches and open events throughout the season. On 3 July and again on 17 and 31 July, the American stunt rider Putt Mossman visited the track. Stunts performed included crashing through a flaming board wall. He returned yet again on 28 August with his troupe of stunt riders, this time to perform a stunt especially invented for Rye House when he took off from an inclined ramp and jumped 60 feet over two cabin cruisers moored in the River Lea.

Although the Sunday Dirt Track League did not operate in 1939, Dicky Case continued to develop the track and his training school. For the first time he organised the hire of machines and leathers for novices. Before the season started, he decided to give up riding so that he could concentrate on the school. Les Trim continued as captain, although he was now also riding for Crystal Palace in the Second Division, and Rye House imported a couple of Hackney juniors, Stan Dell and Nobby Stock to the team. Their opening match of the season saw them defeat High Beech by 49 points to 35, Dell top scoring with 10 points.

Although the Second World War put a stop to most speedway racing in this country, Rye House managed to continue to put on a number of meetings. In 1940, Dick Case's Speedway ran 6 meetings. In 1941 Case managed to organise 14 meetings and in 1942, a further 6. 4 more were run in 1943 under the auspices of the Harringay Speedway Motor Club and Light Car Club (Harringay MC and LCC). These wartime events brought in new support from people who had never seen the sport before, for example, Mr A.B. Kennell of Holland-on-Sea. Mr Kennell had never been to a speedway meeting in his life before, as Holland-on-Sea was miles away from the nearest track. However, during the war he came to find himself in Hoddesdon and went across to the speedway. He wrote in his diary afterwards, 'In the afternoon I saw my first motorbike dirt-track meeting.'

As soon as the war finished, Case, who also happened to own the pub next door to the Rye House track, was back in overall charge of the training school, which recommenced in 1945. Rye House now became recognised as the premier training track in

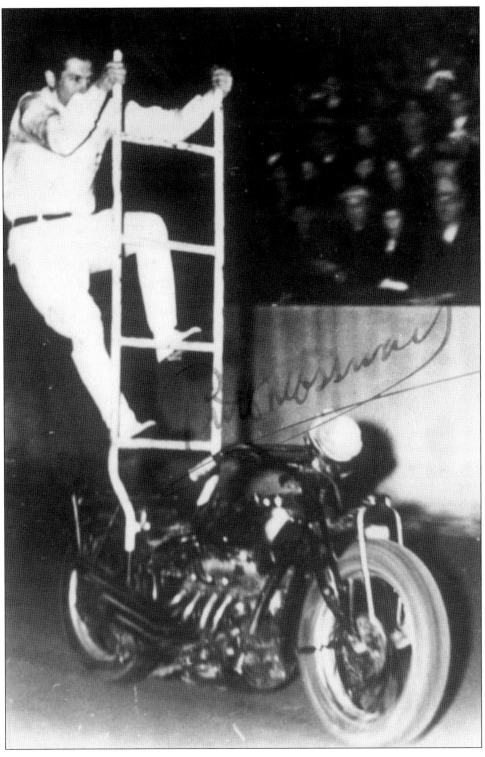

Putt Mossman, the American stunt star, appeared at Rye House several times in the 1930s.

A wartime programme cover dating from 1940.

Official Programme **3ᵈ**

Second Meeting SUNDAY, JUNE 2nd at 3.45 p.m.

Rye House
Speedway

HODDESDON HERTS.   Phone: HODDESDON 2857.

HARRINGAY SPEEDWAY M.C. & L.C. Club.
Affiliated A.C.U. South Mid. Centre

Steward	E. B. HOWLETT
Clerk of the Course	... G. KAY
Timekeeper	J. M. PHILLIPS
Chief Pit Marshal	J. BROOKER

Hon. Secretary of the Meeting:
G. KAY, 337a Green Lanes, Palmers Green, N.13.
Telephone: Palmers Green 1233
St. John Ambulance Brigade, Hoddesdon Section,
in attendance

RYE HOUSE
v
HACKNEY WICK
COMMENCING AT 3.45 P.M.

the country and was used by the North London tracks, West Ham, Harringay and Wembley, to find and train novices and juniors. Harringay's training sessions were overseen by Nobby Stock and Joe Bowkis. Each had their own day allocated to them. Wembley's day, for example, was Wednesday. Its manager, Alec Jackson, used his day to excellent effect. At the start of the 1946 season, it was felt that the fairest way to allocate riders to league teams was to allow each team to retain two of their pre-war riders and then to pool the rest. The clubs then drew from this pool. After drawing Bill Kitchen and Bob Wells, Wembley pulled out, saying it would fill the rest of its team places with juniors trained by Jackson at Rye House. The four were Bill Gilbert, Roy Craighead, Alf Bottoms and Bronco Wilson. Wilson was tragically killed in a crash at Harringay in 1947, but Gilbert, Craighead and Bottoms all went on to play a major part in what was arguably the greatest team ever to race in league speedway. Later in 1946, Alec Jackson pulled off an even bigger 'coup' when he signed up Split Waterman following a try-out at Rye House.

Being so near the river did cause its share of problems as in the spring of 1947, not only the track, but also Dicky Case's pub, were flooded. The *Speedway Gazette* suggested the tune, 'There are ferries at the bottom of my garden', would be an appropriate theme song for Rye House! In 1948, the Harringay MC and LCC ran 17 meetings at the track, while Case continued as chief instructor. The outstanding discovery of the year was a fifteen-year-old schoolboy by the name of Reg Fearman.

For the next few years, George Kay, on behalf of the Harringay MC and LCC, continued to serve up a fortnightly diet of open meetings and challenge matches on Sundays. At the end of each meeting the riders would line up outside the pay box, while George Kay paid them their earnings in two shilling pieces and half crowns from the day's takings. Behind the scenes, training continued throughout the year under the direction of at first, Dicky Case and later on Pete Sampson and Bill Mathieson. The track at this time was 440 yards round and was laid outside the dog track with a corrugated iron safety fence between the riders and the public. Discoveries in 1949 included Jack Hughes, Alf Viccary and George Mugford, while in 1950 the best-known name to emerge from the training school was Ron How, later to ride with great distinction for Harringay, Wimbledon and England. He qualified for 9 World Championship finals, coming 5th in 1964. 1951 saw the arrival of Cyril Maidment, Ronnie Genz and Bobby Croombs. In 1952 it was Stan Bedford's turn. He won the Rye House Championship. Alf Hagon was another discovery that year, while the 1953 Novice of the Year was Gerald Hussey who had had just three weeks experience comprising 14 practice sessions before winning the Rye House Championship Final. Hussey later went on to ride for West Ham, Norwich and Leicester and to qualify for the 1958 World Championship Final. Tragically, he died following a crash while driving in a midget car race in 1960. Other discoveries that year included Len Silver, Gil Goldfinch and Jim Tebby.

Rye House's return to league racing came with the inauguration of the Southern Area League in 1954. Nicknamed the Roosters, Rye House's team was led by Stan Bedford and included top scorer Vic Ridgeon, Dave Slater, Jim Heard, Derek Clark, Al Sparrey and Dave Still. The league was a close-run affair, with three teams tying on 18 points for second place, but just in front, with 20 points, came Rye House. The final of the Southern Area League Riders' Championship was held at Rye House, but it was not won by a home rider as Alby Golden of Ringwood took the trophy.

Rye House won the League more convincingly in 1955, losing just 2 matches out of the 12 raced. Vic Ridgeon, Al Sparrey, Dave Slater and Jim Heard continued to ride well for the team, but it was the return from National Service of twenty-one-year-old Mike Broadbanks that made all the difference. In what was, in effect, his first full year in speedway, Broadbanks was not only top scorer in the league but he also won the Southern Area Riders' Championship. This latter victory was in front of a 6,000 crowd at his home track with a faultless maximum in spite of starting off the day ill in bed with a temperature well into the 100s. Vic Ridgeon came second, while Dave Slater took fifth place. After meetings, Broadbanks used to take a dip in the River Lea to cool

One of Rye House's best post-war discoveries, Ron How. He went on to ride for Harringay and Wimbledon.

Left: *The programme cover from the 1954 Southern Area League Riders' championship final.*

Below: *The 1955 Rye House Roosters team. From left to right, back row: George Kay (promoter), Vernon Brown, Vic Ridgeon, Bill Simpson, Stan Bedford, Mike Broadbanks. Front row: Dave Slater, Al Sparrey (on bike), Jim Heard.*

down, jumping in from the bridge next to the track. On one occasion, he unfortunately went straight through the deck of a cabin cruiser that was passing underneath which he hadn't noticed.

1956 saw Rye House do the hat-trick as they took the title for the third year running. Mike Broadbanks had moved on to better things with Wembley, leaving Vic Ridgeon as top scorer with 113 points in 11 matches. Strong backing once again came from Dave Slater, who was known as 'Slater the Gater' on account of his fast gating, and Al Sparrey who were ably supported by Gerry King, Bobby Croombs and new training school discovery, Brian Brett.

Dave Slater's third place was Rye House's best in the Southern Area League Riders' Championship for 1956. Vic Ridgeon, who was most people's favourite to take the title, had a nightmare of a meeting. In his first race an oiled-up plug prevented him from starting. He won his second and third races but in his fourth a faulty clutch put him out at the start. For his final ride he borrowed Bobby Croombes' machine and promptly blew it up. Eastbourne's Leo McAuliffe won the Championship. His only defeat of the day came from Rye House's Gerry King in the most exciting race of the afternoon. McAuliffe got away from the tapes but was chased hard by King, who just managed to squeeze past McAuliffe literally as they crossed the finishing line.

It was not to be four in a row in 1957. In fact, the Roosters had to suffer the ignominy of coming bottom of the league, winning just 5 out of 12 matches. This fall from grace was partly explained by the fact that Ridgeon decided to retire mid-way through the season, leaving Gerry King and Bobby Croombs to carry the team. Dave Slater was the third heat leader but he had a poor season in comparison with his first three. Croombs was the highest-placed Rooster in the Riders Championship, but he could only manage 8 points to come 9th.

As detailed earlier in the chapter on Eastbourne, the Southern Area League did not run in 1958. In any case, Rye House did not open until late in the season because of extensive building works being carried out at the stadium, which resulted in a brand new track being built on an adjoining site which had formerly been the stock car circuit. The referee's box was on the infield next to the starting line. This meant the referee had to turn round and round to watch the race. If the four riders were racing it out in two pairs half a lap apart, the referee was in the position of having to choose which pair he watched because when he had one pair in sight the other would be going past the back of his head!

As Rye House raced on a Sunday, they received a number of objections from the Lord's Day Observance Society. To try and overcome these objections, the local vicar gave a short sermon in the interval. Rye House's opening meeting on its new track took place on 3 August when Brian Meredith won the August Trophy. Just six meetings took place in 1958.

Rye House returned to Southern Area League racing in 1959 under the managership of Fred Peachey with, apart from Bobby Croombs, a completely new line-up. Tommy Sweetman was the top man, scoring 68 points from 8 matches. Support came from Ronnie Rolfe, Ernie Baker, Clive Hitch and, discovery of the year, Stan Stevens. However, it was not a good year for the Roosters and they finished the table in 4th

World Champion, Ronnie Moore, at Rye House on the day the new track was opened in 1960. In the background are Terry Keats and Bob Warner.

place, equal on match points with bottom team Ipswich, but with a slightly better race points average.

The track was rebuilt yet again at the end of 1959, this time by Mike Broadbanks and his father, Alf, or 'Pop', as he was affectionately known. Mike Broadbanks was now in charge of the speedway and training at Rye House. The 325-yard track was moved back to its original position, only this time with the greyhound track round the outside. The old speedway track became a go-kart track. The new track was opened in 1960 with a special best-of-three match race series between Broadbanks and Ronnie Moore, the World Champion, which Moore won 2-1. This was followed by the All Star Trophy donated by Moore, which was won by Tommy Sweetman from Stan Stevens and Clive Hitch.

Rye House, now under the name the Red Devils and managed by Freddie Millward, continued to run a series of challenge matches with Tommy Sweetman as captain. Others in the team included Clive Hitch, Stan Stevens, Colin Pratt, Pete Sampson, Jim Gleed, Bill Wainwright and Sandy McGillivray. Vic Ridgeon decided to make a come back in 1961 and was signed up by Wolverhampton in the Provincial League. However, he also found time to turn out for his old club, Rye House, joining Tommy Sweetman, Geoff Mudge, Roy Trigg, Ken Vale, Clive Hitch, Pete Sampson, Sandy McGillivray, Colin Pratt and Terry Keats to form the basis of that year's Red Devils. Trigg proved to be top scorer, with Pratt and Sweetman close behind. A Rye House novice who began to command attention during the season was a young man who rode under the name of Tyburn Gallows. He rode once for the Red Devils, scoring one point and also won the Junior Plaque at the end of the season. He took his unusual name because he said he was Great Britain's assistant hangman.

In spite of not being in a league, Rye House still managed to draw in large crowds for its meetings. Part of this was due to Millward, who always knew how to combine the necessary showmanship with essential organisational skills and part to the exciting racing which was served up Sunday after Sunday. The 1961/62 winter season training

The new Rye House track just after it had been rebuilt in 1960. Vic Ridgeon is the rider in the lead.

school threw up an unusual novice in sixteen-year-old Ray Cousins, who decided to revert to leg trailing. He said he had decided to model his style on 'Cyclone' Billy Lamont as he felt that leg trailing was a much more spectacular style. Rye House continued its diet of open meetings and challenge matches under the promotion of Gerry Bailey and Jack Carter, with Mike Broadbanks as club steward and chief instructor. But before they could get on with the 1962 season, the Control Board announced that Tyburn Gallows was no longer to race under that name and was to revert to his real name, Raymond Humphries. He was also banned from wearing his C.N.D. race jacket. Later, Humphries changed his name by deed poll to Tyburn Gallows so the Control Board couldn't stop him using it.

A new name was unearthed at the start of 1962 as Norman Hunter made a sensational debut. In Rye House's opening meeting, he scored 11 points from just 4 rides to finish 3rd. In his last ride he even had the temerity to pass Rye House's captain, Tommy Sweetman on the final turn. He had only been practising for four months.

After a successful season, Rye House was thrown into a crisis at the beginning of 1963 by the Control Board ruling that only reserves and the lowest scoring second strings in the Provincial League were allowed to race at Rye House in future. This was on the grounds that it was a training track and by using top

Because Rye House ran on a Sunday in the 1950s and 1960s, entry was for members only, so every time you went you had to join the Supporters Club! This is a membership ticket from 1964.

RYE HOUSE
SPEEDWAY

"The home of the Red Devils"

Nº 2679

**'SUNDAY MIRROR'
WORLD CHAMPIONSHIP TROPHY**

1964 SEASON
SIXTH MEETING

SPEEDWAY CHAMPIONSHIP
OF THE WORLD
(ROUND ONE)

SUNDAY, JUNE 21st AT 4 P.M.

**OFFICIAL
SOUVENIR PROGRAMME ONE SHILLING**

Tommy Sweetman, captain of the Rye House Red Devils, in the early 1960s.

The programme cover from Rye House's first ever World Championship qualifying round, 21 June 1964.

Provincial and National League stars they were denying juniors the chance to get experience. Mike Broadbanks said it could mean the end for Rye House. He agreed that the theory sounded good, but what it didn't take into account was the fans. Rye House needed enough customers each week to make Rye House a paying proposition. If fans were served up a regular diet of just trainees they would stop coming and then the track would have to close leaving no places for trainees at all. Broadbanks cited the examples of former Rye House trainees, such as Geoff Mudge, Norman Hunter and Colin Pratt who had now made it to the top. The supporters wanted to see them and wanted to see how the new juniors got on against them. Broadbanks tried one meeting under the new rules but complained afterwards that, 'The fans just didn't stay through the whole meeting.' He also made the point that the new juniors needed the experience of racing against more established riders if they were to learn. Fortunately common sense eventually prevailed and the ruling was rescinded.

When the big split between the National and Provincial Leagues came in 1964, Rye House threw in its lot with the Nationals, which meant that Provincial League riders were banned from using the track. This led to some top names appearing at Rye House during the year, including former Rye House discovery, Norman Hunter, now a heat leader with West Ham, Martin Ashby, Jimmy Gooch, Reg Luckhurst and Wimbledon's Bob Andrews, who won both the Gerry Hussey Memorial Trophy and the Ronnie Moore Trophy. Also, for the first time in its history, it was chosen to stage a World Championship round. Coventry's Les Owen won this meeting from Norwich's Tich Read. A former world number three, Jack Biggs, took part in the meeting, coming fourth.

There were rumours at the end of the season that Rye House was to close its doors to speedway and concentrate on stock cars instead. However, a new consortium consisting of John Bailey, Bill Wainwright and Tommy Sweetman took over the running of the track. Ernie Hancock was installed as team manager and season 1965 continued in much the same vein as previous seasons except that the new consortium promised to have at least 10 changes of rider from meeting to meeting so that many new faces would be introduced. Clive Hitch captained the team in a series of challenge matches and was supported by Malcolm Simmons, Pete Sampson, Geoff Penniket, Eddie Reeves, Roy Trigg and Tyburn Gallows. Rye House was used for a different form of training on 21 March as ITV sent its camera team down to the Hertfordshire track prior to its televising the 'real thing' at West Ham and Sheffield later in the season.

The 1966 season proved to be a very poor season with many matches being affected by bad weather resulting in very low crowd attendances. At the end of the season, the

Bob Andrews receiving the 1964 Gerry Hussey Memorial Trophy from Mr and Mrs Hussey.

The 1961 Rye House Red Devils team. From left to right, back row: Colin Pratt, Peter Sampson, Bill Wainwright, Ronnie Rolfe, Stan Stevens, Freddie Millward (manager), Jim Gleed. Front row: Clive Hitch, Tommy Sweetman (on bike), Sandy McGillivray.

consortium decided they'd had enough and closed Rye House to public meetings. The training school continued but it was to be another three years before the track re-opened to the public under former promoters John Bailey and Jack Carter, trading as Carter & Bailey Ltd. Ernie Hancock remained as speedway and team manager.

In previous years, the Rye House team had been made up of loanees from the regular league teams, but this year the promoters decided to put together their own team so that supporters were not faced with seeing a rider in Red Devils' colours one week and then in opposition colours the next. The 1969 team was Tyburn Gallows, Ron Edwards, Tiny White, Nigel Rackett, Fred Sweet and Barrie Smith. In all it raced 4 matches, winning 2 and losing 2. Amongst those successful at individual meetings this year were Dave Jessup and Ted Spittles.

The early 1970s saw Rye House continue as a training track with a series of public open meetings. The promoters were now Johnny Guilfoyle and Bill Mathieson, though the proprietors were still Carter and Bailey. A new safety fence was erected in 1971. Among the trophy winners during these years were Brian Foote, who won the Gerry Hussey Memorial Trophy in 1970 and 1971, Dave Jessup, who won the Skol Lager Trophy in 1970, Stan Stevens, who won the Ace of Herts Trophy in 1972 and Barney Kennett, who won the Lea Valley Park Trophy in 1973.

Then came 1974 and, with it, the biggest change to Rye House's status since speedway had begun there in the mid-1930s. At the end of the 1973 season, Rayleigh was forced to close down as the site was to be redeveloped. Len Silver, on behalf of the promoters, Allied Promotions, immediately began to look round for another track so that the Rockets could continue. At first he thought he had found it at Crayford, a track which had closed in 1970. However, there were planning problems at Crayford and Silver continued his search for a new home. It occurred to him that Rye House would be the ideal spot as there was already a track in existence. It was also used to running at weekends, which was Silver's preferred option – Crayford would have had to run mid-week. Silver therefore approached Bill Mathieson who still held the rights to run speedway at the venue and Mathieson agreed to pass them over to Allied Presentations for nothing. Peter Thorogood was installed as manager and a few alterations were made to the track by putting in some banking and making it shorter. After some new additions to the stadium itself had also been made, with terracing for the back straight, an office, a brand new Tannoy system, new dressing rooms and moving the pits to the other side of the track, Rye House was ready to embark on its new career as a British League (Division Two) track. At the beginning of April, the team was announced as Bob Young (captain), Brian Foote, Red Ott, Pete Wigley, Trevor Barnwell, John Gibbons, Steve Clarke, Peter Cairns with Peter Moore and Allen Emmett hopefully to rejoin the Rockets after injury. There were further alterations to the track at the end of June as it was widened.

The season started well with wins at home and away over Elllesmere Port and Sunderland, but, after that, things started to go badly wrong. First Red Ott broke his collarbone after just four matches and then Steve Clarke fractured his skull and both were out for the season. Peter Moore returned from injury but he was just a shadow of the rider who had once been the World number 4. Bob Young couldn't get to grips with the track and for all Pete Wigley's efforts, the scores just would not come. Attempts to improve the team led to new riders coming into the team. Bob Cooper was signed from Leicester and former Rye House favourite, Clive Hitch, was talked out of retirement. When Hitch proved to be a great success, Peter Thorogood turned to more Rye House veterans in Stan Stevens and George Barclay. Stevens' long lay-off proved too much, but Barclay, who had been riding for Canterbury, did well

Hugh Saunders rode for Rye House Rockets from 1975 until 1979. He then became team manager.

Bob Cooper rode for Rye House from 1974 to 1979.

enough. Through it all, Brian Foote proved himself to be the number one at Rye House, but his average was only 7.93 and that wasn't really good enough for a number one. In the end, Rye House finished 16th out of 19 in its first season.

There were wholesale changes to the team before the 1975 season started. Out went Clive Hitch, Trevor Barnwell, George Barclay, Peter Moore, Pete Wigley and Stan Stevens. Even the manager, Peter Thorogood, left to cross the Thames to open up Crayford. In his place as manager at Rye House came former Red Devil, Colin Pratt. Of the 1974 Rockets, Bob Young stayed, but gave up the captaincy to another survivor, Brian Foote. Bob Cooper stayed and Steve Clarke attempted a comeback following his fractured skull. John Gibbons also stayed. Unfortunately neither Clarke nor Gibbons were able to reproduce the promise they had shown the previous year and after ten appearances each, both left the side.

The Rye House management had high hopes of the newcomers to the side, Tiger Beech, Dingle Brown, Hugh Saunders and Kelvin Mullarkey, signed after a tremendous fight with Boston. Unfortunately the injury jinx struck again as first Brown injured his foot and was out for over a month and then Mullarkey broke a collarbone. Barry Duke was signed from Swindon as cover but, after just two meetings, he too received a head injury and was out for some time. Pratt then drafted in a Rye House junior, Karl Fiala, and although he showed a lot of promise in his first season he was not the answer to Rye House's problems. Brian Foote improved on his 1974 scoring, upping his average to 8.39, to remain the Rockets' number one with Hugh Saunders performing reasonably well as the number two on 7.46. But it was once again a season to forget, as Rye House finished the league in 14th place.

There were further changes to the management over the close season as Colin Pratt joined Len Silver as director. Pratt's first moves were persuading Hackney's Ted Hubbard to join the Rockets on loan and signing up one of the most promising of the winter trainees, the sixteen-year-old Bob Garrad. Rye House entered its third season with what seemed on paper its best team so far, consisting as it did of Ted Hubbard, Bob Cooper, Kelvin Mullarkey, Hugh Saunders, Brian Foote, Karl Fiala, Bob Garrad and Tiger Beech. Unfortunately, Beech decided to retire after the first match and Cooper, third heat leader the year before, started very badly. So badly in fact that Ashley Pullen was drafted into the team in his place. Cooper later returned when Foote collected a foot injury.

In spite of these setbacks however, it was a much better year for the Rockets. Hubbard proved to be a real star man as he turned in an average of 9.17. Mullarkey, Saunders and Foote all scored at over 7 points per match and Garrad had a great first season recording 6.09. Fiala also continued to improve and finished with 6.73. For the first time since their elevation to the big time, the Rockets were able to mix it with the top teams in the league as they finished 5th out of 18.

With an ever-improving and settled team, Rye House did even better in 1977 as they finished runners-up in both the league and cup to runaway league winners, Eastbourne. Mullarkey and Garrad improved out of all recognition, Mullarkey to

The ever popular Ashley Pullen rode for Rye House from 1976 to 1980. In three of those years he was ever-present.

Karl Fiala joined Rye House as a teenager in 1975. By 1979 he had become the Rockets' leading rider.

become the undoubted star of the team with a 9.14 average while Garrad, in only his second season, became the Rockets' third heat leader on 8.07. Hubbard continued his winning ways and he too finished with a 9 plus average. Unfortunately he missed ten matches through injury, as did Karl Fiala, otherwise they might even have challenged the mighty Eagles for that top spot. The other two members of the team, Ashley Pullen and Bob Cooper, rode in all but one of the team's official fixtures between them and provided the basic stability at reserve level that enabled the top boys to challenge for the title.

Rye House's most glorious moment, though perhaps its most frustrating as well, came when it met First Division Hackney in the Inter-League Knock Out Cup and went down by just one point, losing 39-38. In all, it was a season to be proud of and, with a basically young team, brought promise of good things to come.

However, 1978 was to be another year of nearly, but not quite. Free of injury, Hubbard moved back to the top of the score chart just ahead of Mullarkey. Fiala's improvement continued and he managed to snatch the third heat leader spot with a 7.84 average to Saunders' 7.56 and Garrad's 7.46. Pullen also moved up the score chart with 6.78. The emergence of two more youngsters saw Cooper lose his team place after just four matches as first Peter Tarrant and later Kevin Smith came into the team, both finishing fractionally under 5 points per match. Rye House's strength in depth was such

Left: *Ted Hubbard, averaged over 8 points per match for Rye House every year between 1976 and 1979.*

Right: *Kevin Smith rode for the Rockets from 1978 to 1980.*

The 1977 Rye House National League runners-up. From left to right, back row: Ashley Pullen, Bob Cooper, Bob Garrad, Karl Fiala, Ted Hubbard, Kelvin Mullarkey. Front row: Garry Monk, Hugh Saunders (on bike), Kevin Bowen.

that the top six all managed to score at least 2 maximums and even Smith scored 9 paid 11 against Newcastle. The Rockets were undefeated at home and won 8 matches away. It wasn't quite enough and they finished in 3rd place behind Canterbury and Newcastle, both of whom won 12 matches away, although, ironically, Rye House was one of the only two teams to beat Newcastle at Brough Park. There was slightly better news in the Knock Out Cup as they reached the final, finishing runners-up to cup specialists Eastbourne 83-73 on aggregate.

With Fiala, Garrad and Smith all coming good in 1979, the league title should have been the Rockets' for the taking. For the third year running, Rye House was able to track a settled team. To give some idea of the team's strength, Hubbard was number five with an average of 8.16 and, although Smith's average improved to a massive 8.20, even that wasn't enough to give him a heat-leader spot. Karl Fiala shot to the top of the Rockets' score chart with 9.20, closely followed by Garrad on 9.11. Mullarkey managed to hang on to the third heat leader spot with 8.71. Pullen and Saunders took the reserve positions with averages of 7.34 and 6.57 respectively. When the number eight, Peter Tarrant, was called upon during the season he also acquitted himself well, averaging 5.23, enough to win him a place in practically every other team in the league.

The Rockets kept their unbeaten home record and also managed to win 11 matches away as well as drawing 1. At one stage in the season they put together an unbroken string of 19 successive league wins. But they were involved in a neck-and-neck fight with Mildenhall for the league title. The two were well in front of the rest of the teams in the league and the destination of the title really came down to Rye House's last

A full-throttle action shot of Kelvin Mullarkey and Kevin Smith.

match of the season, away at Mildenhall. Unfortunately for the Rockets, both Kevin Smith and Hugh Saunders were injured and unable to take part in this vital, winner-take-all, match. Peter Tarrant was brought in and rider replacement used, but they were unable to match the firepower of Mildenhall and so finished the season as runners-up.

There was however, a consolation prize as Rye House took the Cup for the first time, beating Berwick in the final by 92-64 after a thumping victory in the first leg by 54 points to 24. Ironically, the Rockets had defeated Mildenhall in the semi-final, winning both legs.

Rye House, having come second in the league in 1977, third in 1978, second in 1979, cup runners-up in 1978 and cup winners in 1979, were becoming the new power in the National League. All of this had also been done with basically the same team, which had now been together for three years. And they had become a real team, riding for each other. Kelvin Mullarkey's massive total of 70 bonus points in the league plus another 14 in the cup gives some indication of just what a team they had now become.

At the end of the year, Colin Pratt left the club and Len Silver appointed Hugh Saunders, who had decided to retire, the new team manager. Instead of looking for an experienced replacement for Saunders, Silver stuck to his policy of encouraging juniors from his training schools at Rye House and Hackney and the place went to Simon Aindow, who unfortunately broke his wrist. Silver then experimented with some other youngsters, Andy Fines, Barry King and Carl Squirrell, before settling on Fines. Ted Hubbard also left the team, to be replaced by Peter Tarrant. The rest of the 'team of all talents', Bob Garrad, Karl Fiala, Kelvin Mullarkey, Kevin Smith and Ashley Pullen rode in every single one of Rye House's official fixtures. It was this stability of the ever-improving top five that at last gave Rye House its first league championship as the Rockets held off Newcastle's challenge to take the title by a single point.

Rye House wrapped up the title at Middlesborough on 9 October. It was a match the Rockets needed to win, otherwise the title could go to either Newcastle or the home side, Middlesborough. With just 4 races left, Rye House were 6 points behind. Fiala was brought in as a tactical substitute and he and Garrad recorded a 5-1. Fiala was out again in the next race, this time with Smith. Again it was a 5-1 to the Rockets. Rye House were now 2 points in front. In the penultimate heat, Middlesborough scored a 4-2 to make the scores all level going in to the final heat. It was real nail-biting stuff as Fiala came out for his 3rd ride in 4 heats. A 4-2 to the Rockets gave Rye House a 40-38 win on the night and they took the league title. Garrad, Fiala and Mullarkey all recorded 9 plus averages for the season, while Smith scored at 8.43 and Pullen at 6.84. All 5 recorded at least 2 maximums each and Tarrant also contributed 1. Mullarkey once again contributed a massive number of bonus points in league matches, just 2 short of the previous year with 68.

Rye House had at last achieved its ambition and with such a young team looked set to dominate the National League for the next few years as long as the team could be kept together. As it turned out this was not to happen. Both Smith and Garrad decided it was time they moved on to the British League, Pullen was recalled to his parent track, Reading, while Fiala stunned both management and fans by announcing his retirement at the age of just twenty-five. It left Rye House looking desperately for replacements to maintain the high standards the supporters had now come to expect. Of the successful

1980 team, only Kelvin Mullarkey, Peter Tarrant and Andy Fines remained with Barry King and Carl Squirrell ready to step into the two reserve spots.

Silver's first signing was Steve Naylor, Crayford's top rider in 1980. Naylor was followed by Kevin Bowen and then Rye House had a team of sorts. But before the league campaign had even got underway, Andy Fines was involved in a crash at Mildenhall and the resulting broken leg kept him out all season. After just four matches, Carl Squirrell broke his ankle. With both Naylor and Bowen struggling to maintain their form, things looked serious for the

Marvyn Cox came to Rye House as a teenager in 1981. By 1982 he was a heat leader and by 1983 he was the Rockets' top rider.

91

Left: *The typical all-action style of Steve Naylor in the early 1980s.*

Opposite left: *Chris Chaplin rode for Rye House from 1983 to 1986.*
Opposite right: *Alastair Stevens, a heat leader for the Rockets in 1985 and 1986.*

Rockets. Only Mullarkey was firing on all cylinders, this year scoring less of the bonus points but more of the real thing. Another junior, Marvyn Cox, was brought into the team and turned out to be a success – as a junior, but Silver was desperate to obtain another top-class rider. His prayers were answered when Bob Garrad asked for a move back to his old team. His spell at Hackney had not been a success due to a string of mechanical problems. Garrad's return, plus the signing of Peter Johns from Wimbledon, at last brought a change of luck to the beleaguered Rockets and they ended a run of 13 consecutive league defeats.

The season finished on a reasonable note, but the improvement came too late to do much about their league position as they fell from number 1 to number 16. Garrad finished the season as top man with an 8.85 average with Mullarkey close behind on 8.39. During the season, Len Silver made some improvements to the spectator accommodation adding 800 seats to increase the seating capacity to 2,000. Apart from Andy Fines returning at the beginning of 1982 to replace Peter Johns, the team stayed the same as the one that had finished the 1981 season. After just seven matches, Kevin Bowen broke a bone in his spine and Johns was back. With a more settled side, the Rockets were able to put the previous season behind them and, although, they were never really in with a chance of the League, their performances were much improved. Two riders in particular shone for the Rockets, Bob Garrad, who improved his average to a massive 9.85 and Marvyn Cox, who became number two man, having chased Garrad for that top spot all season, eventually finishing with an average of 8.87.

In the end the team finished 6th in the league and reached the semi-final of the cup – it was a satisfactory conclusion to a season that saw them getting back to something like the Rockets of old. Just as the 1983 season started, Kelvin Mullarkey decided he was going to retire as he couldn't find a sponsor, though in the end he actually went on loan

to Canterbury. The Rockets line-up for 1983 would look very strange without Mullarkey. He was going to be a hard man to replace. Without Mullarkey, Rye House had to rely on Cox, Garrad and Naylor to lead it home. Cox continued from where he'd left off in 1982, better in fact, finishing the season with an average of 9.83 and coming 3rd in the European Under-21 Championship on the way. He also came 4th in the National League Riders' Championship and won the Silver Helmet from Keith Millard, successfully defending it twice.

In a reversal of the 1982 positions, it was Garrad who was chasing Cox all season, finishing with 9.28. Naylor, as third heat leader, managed an 8.00 average. Unfortunately there wasn't much to back these three up. Peter Johns had a good start to the season, scoring 36 paid points in his first three matches, but an injured thumb put him out for a while. He came back for two matches and then was out again with a back injury. A number of other riders were tried during the year, including Len Silver's son, Andrew, Steve Bryenton, Kevin Bowen, Chris Chaplin, Terry Broadbank and John Barclay, but none of them were able to make that all-important breakthrough which would have propelled the Rockets up the table. In the end they finished in 11th place and were knocked out of the cup in the second round.

With Marvyn Cox vanishing into the British League, things did not look good for Rye House as 1984 started. With Peter Johns missing too and Steve Naylor not available due to a fractured wrist they looked even worse. There was only one thing for it and Len Silver did it. Kelvin Mullarkey was recalled from his loan to Canterbury. Canterbury were far from happy and even slapped an injunction on Mullarkey in an attempt to stop him riding for Rye House. But return he did, though it was not be to his accustomed position of heat leader as Rye House uncovered a new star in Andrew Silver. Silver had had a few outings the year before, but in the first match of 1984, against Milton Keynes, he scored paid 11. In his first four matches, he posted 38 points. Just as it looked as though he would be the sensation of the season he was injured in a crash that affected his ankle and shoulder. He returned later in the season and after a hesitant start, returned to his winning ways. He finished his first full year with an average of 7.79, second behind Garrad. Naylor came back from his injury to finish the season as third heat leader. Once again though, it was a middling year for Rye House as they finished the season in 8th place with an average match score of 39-39.

For 1985, Rye House signed up Neil Cotton and Alastair Stevens. Unfortunately, Cotton just couldn't get to grips with the tight turns of the Rye House track and he was dropped at the end of May. Steve Naylor was injured after just two matches and was out for the rest of the season. Both Garrad's and Mullarkey's scoring was well down on previous years. The only bright spots in an otherwise poor season for the Rockets was the continued improvement of Andrew Silver, who stamped his authority on the team to become undisputed number one, and the form of Alastair Stevens who slotted in at number two to Silver. Rob Woffinden, signed up during the season, became the Rockets third heat leader with an average of 6.84. For a great part of the season, the Rockets were battling to stay off the bottom. In the end they managed to climb to 13th place.

Midway through the season, Len Silver decided to call it a day and sold out to Ronnie Russell. He appointed Naylor as team manager and announced that it was his intention to bring glamour back into speedway. He wanted to make stars of the riders like the old days, he said, 'I'm talking about the Briggos and men like Colin Pratt and Banger. They were the stars at Hackney when we were kids.'

1985 was also Mullarkey's testimonial year. Unfortunately rain led to the postponement of his meeting in August, but it was eventually staged on 27 October, the last

Rye House's Neil Cotton tries to pass inside Mark Chessell of Reading in 1985.

meeting of the year. After the meeting, Mullarkey announced his retirement.

It could be said that the winner in 1986 was the rain. The first three scheduled meetings were all wrecked by rain and there were three further rain-offs during the season. The bad weather did little to help attendances at Rye House but, as Russell said, 'I thought we could have attracted more. Even allowing for rain, I think a winning team will do the trick.' Unfortunately, he never found that winning team. It wasn't for the want of trying though. With Mullarkey retiring and Silver moving to Arena Essex he set about rebuilding the team around Alastair Stevens and Bob Garrad. His first move was to bring in former-England international, Paul Woods, for a fee of £12,000. Paul's arrival was followed by that of ex-Hackney star, Paul Bosley, and Birmingham second string, Linden Warner.

Once again injuries badly damaged Russell's hopes for a league title in his

Rye House Speedway, Sunday 5th October 1986 at 4pm
PRESENTS
A TESTIMONIAL MEETING IN AID OF BOB GARRAD
Official Match Souvenir Programme £1 if sold

The programme cover from Bob Garrad's testimonial meeting on 5 October 1986.

Bob Garrad rode for Rye House from 1976 to 1986. He was the Rockets' number one in 1980, 1981, 1982 and 1984.

An action shot from 1981 showing, from left to right, Kevin Bowen, Steve Naylor and Kevin Teager (Scunthorpe).

first year in charge. Julian Parr, who had joined Rye House at the tail-end of the previous season, broke his collarbone. Next, it was the turn of Warner, who also broke his collarbone. Parr came back and then broke his other collarbone while Bosley aggravated an old back injury. Woods was next to go following a crash at Peterborough which left him concussed. Alan Mogridge arrived at the beginning of August and injected some much needed life into the team, scoring 145 points in 18 matches before being called back to parent club, Hackney. Only Bob Garrad, fittingly enough in his testimonial year, and Alastair Stevens rode in every official fixture for Rye House. Woods ended the season as the new Rye House number one with an average of 8.97. In his short spell in August and September, Mogridge was the number two. Over the season as a whole, Stevens retained his number two position with a slightly increased average and Bosley was number three.

In spite of its run of bad luck, both with the weather and with injuries, the team managed to finish the season in 11th place.

Garrad's testimonial meeting on 5 October proved to be a big occasion, with the World Champion, Hans Nielsen, taking part along with some old familiar names – Marvyn Cox, Andrew Silver and Kevin Smith. Garrad had ridden for Rye House for eleven years since his first appearance as a sixteen year old in 1976. During that time he had been the Rockets number one on four occasions including in 1980, the year of the league championship. Following the meeting, at the grand old age of twenty-six, Bob Garrad called it a day and hung up his leathers.

If 1985 and 1986 were bad, then 1987 was a disaster. Along with the retirement of Garrad, Russell lost Paul Bosley and Alastair Stevens. Their places were taken by Gary

Rolls, Barry Thomas, now in the veteran stage of his career, and Kevin Teager, tempted out of retirement. It was never a great team but the Rye House faithful were hopeful that it could at least hold its own. The Rockets opened with a win over Milton Keynes. Teager was top scorer. As this was the first match of the season in the whole of the National League it meant Rye House were top. It was the only time they were to see that end of the table all season. The Rockets lost their next two home matches as well as their first away match at Wimbledon by 56 points to 22. Julian Parr had a poor start to the season and retired after a spectacular crash against Newcastle on 31 March. Former Rocket, Steve Bryenton, took his place. Linden Warner retired soon after and Jamie Luckhurst came in from Ipswich. But his form was so poor that he also retired. The season just got worse and worse for Rye House and in August and September they suffered a run of five successive home defeats. Paul Woods, average 8.11, and Barry Thomas, average 6.93, tried their best, but with the third heat leader, Kevin Brice, managing just 5.10, they never had a chance. Brice's average wouldn't even have got him into the Eastbourne team! Sure enough, the Rye House Rockets finished bottom of the table for the first time in their National League history.

With the club suffering, the crowds stayed away and the club found itself in financial difficulties. In October the club's bank gave it fourteen days to come up with concrete proposals to save the club otherwise they would have to close it down. Russell immediately launched a £20,000 appeal fund, asking for 200 supporters to pledge £100 each. As if this wasn't bad enough, Rye House was ordered to pay former Rocket, Andrew

The 1986 Rye House team. From left to right, back row: Linden Warner, Julian Parr, Ronnie Russell (promoter), Paul Woods, Kevin Brice. Front row: Alastair Stevens, Bob Garrad (on bike), Paul Bosley.

Silver, £1,350 as his share of the £9,000 transfer deal which took him to Arena Essex. 'This could be the final nail in our coffin', said Russell after the Control Board hearing which found in favour of Silver. 'I've got a meeting with our bank this week ... the fact that we've now got to find even more money is a terrible blow.' He added that 'The Appeal Fund has been going well but there is still a long way to go ... I have been encouraged by the response and we even had a donation from former rider Kelvin Mullarkey.' After a winter of uncertainty over the future of the club, Russell was able to announce in February that the funds were now in place to enable it to run in 1988.

Having saved the track, Russell found himself embroiled in the biggest controversy in the history of the National League when he signed up Denmark's Jens Rasmussen and Germany's Peter Schroek. It had always been the rule that, apart from Australians and New Zealanders, foreigners were banned from the National League. Russell argued that there were no riders of sufficient quality to replace the riders that were leaving, who included Barry Thomas, Gary Rolls and Steve Bryenton. After much argument, the National League promoters agreed that Rye House could sign up Rasmussen as he had been an English resident for five years with an English wife and child. Russell agreed not to bring in Schroek straight away. When he did bring him in he was so disappointing that he was dropped.

The form of Rasmussen however, was the complete opposite as he shot to the top of the Rockets scorechart and remained there all season. He finished with an average of 9.28, which made him the first Rye House rider to finish with a 9 plus average since Marvyn Cox and Bob Garrad, five years previously. His best support came from skipper Paul Woods, while the third heat leader spot was taken by another newcomer to the side, Steve Wilcox. Once again, however, the top riders suffered from lack of support and the team made very little headway in the league, finishing 14th out of 16.

As the season came to an end, Ronnie Russell decided he'd had enough. A dispute over the cost of the stadium rental for 1989 did not help. His farewell speech to the supporters who turned up to the last meeting gave little hope that Rye House would run the following season. Following a meeting between Russell and the Stadium-owners in November however, a more optimistic Russell announced that there was hope for the Rockets after all. A new rent had been agreed as well as a formula for deciding future rent increases. In fact, agreement had been reached on everything except who should pay the £10,500 cost of demolition for the small home-straight stand, which had been pulled down at the beginning of September. After months of discussions, Russell was able to announce in February that Rye House would be running in 1989 after all and that he had taken on the former Mildenhall promoter, Barry Klatt, as co-promoter.

Rye House brought in Mel Taylor to replace Steve Wilcox as the third heat leader and Glen Baxter to give strong second-string backing. With a strong top four in Rasmussen, Woods, Taylor and Baxter, Russell and Klatt were expecting much better things from the Rockets this year. Once again, luck proved not to be with the Rockets as Paul Woods received a bad eye injury after only six matches and missed the rest of the season. Baxter responded to the challenge magnificently and took his place as heat leader. In fact, he did so well that he became the number two man behind Rasmussen, who was

Left: *Jens Rasmussen was the first European to ride in the National League when he signed for the Rockets in 1988.*
Right: *Mel Taylor rode for Rye House from 1989 to 1991.*

having another tremendous season. Taylor also rode well, but, as in previous years, there was no support until the thirty-eight-year-old Kelvin Mullarkey made a surprise comeback for the team on 20 August. In his first outing he scored paid 9 and in his second he did even better with paid 11. He slotted back in the team as top second-string, averaging 5.63 in his 11 matches, and gave the Rye House faithful something to cheer about at last. Far from 1989 being the start of better things, the Rockets finished the season in exactly the same place as the previous year – 14th. At the end of the season Mullarkey retired again.

As the 1990 season approached, major alterations were made to the stadium itself. The old pits area was demolished and new much bigger pits built. Russell explained that, in the old days, most riders just had one bike, now they had two or even more and the old pits weren't big enough to cater for all the extra machines. Hardcore was put down on the car park to prevent puddles and work was also in hand to build a new grandstand on the home straight. As for the team, Russell and Klatt were able to keep the 1989 top three together and add a few new signings in Roger Johns, Scott Humphries, and Nigel Sparshott. Russell had had a turbulent time at Rye House since taking over the promotion from Len Silver, but this season was to prove even worse than anything that had gone before as all three heat leaders were badly injured in the opening weeks of the campaign. Firstly, Taylor broke his arm before the National League campaign even got underway, then Rasmussen injured his leg and wrist and

The most popular rider ever to wear the Rockets colours, Kelvin Mullarkey, rode for Rye House on and off for fifteen years. Between 1975 and 1983 he was ever-present, riding in 295 consecutive matches for the Rockets.

finally Baxter broke his hand. The Rockets lost their first six matches and then Roger Johns broke his wrist. In an attempt to shore up the team, Wayne Baxter, the brother of Glen, and Wayne Bridgeford were drafted into the team and the co-promoters talked three former Rye House riders, Linden Warner, Kevin Teager and that man Kelvin Mullarkey back into the team again. With the return of Rasmussen and then Taylor in August there was a small revival in the team's fortunes, but the damage had been done and the Rockets once again finished bottom of the league with even fewer points than they had scored in 1987, winning just 8 matches out of 32. For the third year running, Rasmussen recorded a 9 plus average and Taylor, when he was there rode well for his 8.86, but the injuries were too much for Rye House.

On 16 September 1990, in a match against Glasgow, Kelvin Mullarkey fell and never again returned to the track. It was a sad end for the Rockets' most loyal servant. Nevertheless his fifteen-year career as a Rye House rider had been a wonderful example to other riders. His exuberant never-say-die attitude had been an outstanding feature of the team for ten years. He had been a heat leader for seven years, captain of the team that had won the cup in 1979 and the league in 1980 and was responsible for holding the team together in the potentially disastrous 1981 season. His commitment to the team was second to none as his massive tally of bonus points in 1979 and 1980 showed. From September 1975 until he left for Canterbury at the start of the 1983 season, he did not miss one match for the Rockets, racking up a total of 295 consecutive league appearances. In 1989, at the age of thirty-eight, he made himself available to answer the call of the club when they were in desperate trouble and did the same again in 1990. There is no doubt that Mullarkey had written himself into the Rye House record books as the most popular rider ever to don the colours of the Rockets.

With the amalgamation of the leagues in 1991, Rye House found itself in Division Two of the British League. The change in status, however, did little to improve its dismal record of the last few years. Rasmussen broke his collarbone in the very first home meeting and, although he returned later in the season, he was not the rider he had been in the previous three seasons. As if that wasn't bad enough, he then managed to

In 1993, Martin Goodwin became the first Rye House rider in history to reach the World Championship British Final.

finish off both his and Rye House's season by breaking his leg. Taylor broke his wrist and suffered concussion following a bad crash in a home match against Glasgow, which the Rockets lost by the mammoth score of 29-60. Rye House's 1991 season was summed up by what happened to Martin Goodwin, who had been signed on loan from Arena Essex. He started the season in tremendous form by scoring 17 in his first two home matches, against Exeter and Hackney, followed by 14 against Peterborough and paid 13 against Ipswich. Then, in July, he managed to get himself suspended for the season by a Control Board tribunal following an incident at Hackney in May when he smashed the window of the referee's box at Hackney with his crash helmet. In between the time of the incident and the tribunal finding he continued with his high scoring, helping Rye House to a first-round cup victory over Stoke, when his winning ride in the last race of the second leg gave the Rockets a 90-89 aggregate score. His loss was a bitter blow to the team and without him, as well as Taylor and Rasmussen, the team struggled through yet another season, finishing in 9th place out of 12.

For the start of the 1992 season, Rye House assembled its strongest looking team for years. Martin Goodwin was back, the Courtney Brothers, Sean and Mark, had been signed from Berwick and Glasgow respectively and Jan Pedersen moved in from Arena Essex. Rasmussen was still injured, but it was hoped that he would return before the season was too old. Under the managership of Norman Kingsbury, it looked as though Rye House might at last escape from its accustomed lowly position. Although the team looked good on paper, it took some time to gel and did not get off to a good start, the low point coming with an 18-point home defeat at the hands of Mildenhall on 20 April. But in some ways this proved to be a blessing in disguise as it shocked the team into putting more effort into their riding.

Russell, however, had a more important worry and that was that the crowds were not flocking back to see the new team. Following a home win against Sheffield, Russell took the microphone to tell the supporters that speedway would not continue at Rye House for many more weeks if attendances did not improve. Mildenhall and Milton Keynes had already closed and he warned that Rye House would soon follow them. In a statement afterwards he said, 'We are in a serious position. We were given a lifeline earlier this season by Terry Russell and Ivan Henry at Arena Essex for which we were very grateful, but we also believed that a successful side would be able to turn Rye House round. That's all I wanted to do. It's not got to be a profit-making situation, just breakeven. But I've exhausted my business money and that of my partner, Barry Klatt, just to prop Rye House up.' The agreement with Arena Essex he referred to was one in which Terry Russell and Ivan Henry had basically agreed to make up any financial shortfall on the understanding it would be paid back later.

With Rasmussen's return in May, things began to improve for the team and, following a further inspired signing in the Swede, Mikael Teurnberg, to replace Trevor O'Brien, who broke his thigh at Exeter, Rye House stormed through the second half of the season enabling the Rockets to finish in 5th place, their highest position since winning the league in 1980. Goodwin had a tremendous season, finishing with an average of 9.67, the third best in the whole league, while Rasmussen and Pedersen both scored at over 7 points per match. The reserves did even better in the Division Two Reserves League as they finished runners-up. Chris Young was the outstanding rider with an average of 10.40, followed by Robert Ledwith on 9.14 and Martin Cobbin on 8.24. In his three matches for the team, Wayne Baxter was unbeaten with 2 full, and 1 paid, maximums.

The relative success of the team did lead to crowds picking up just enough for Rye House to struggle through to the end of the season, but there was no doubt that the club still had serious financial problems to overcome. However, with the erection of

Sean Courtney in action for Rye House in 1992.

 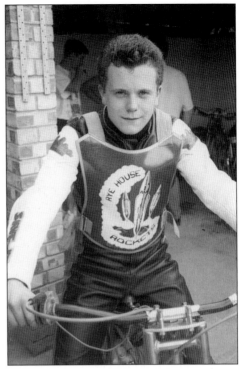

Wayne Baxter rode for Rye House as a reserve from 1990 to 1992.

Martin Cobbin, a leading rider for the Rye House reserve team in 1992.

floodlighting at the track, Russell was hoping that he could run some evening meetings which would bring in the crowds. At the supporters' annual dinner in November he announced that Rye House would definitely run in 1993. In December he revealed that he had completed negotiations with businessmen, Peter Redfern and Roger Shout, and that they would now become co-promoters along with himself. Russell declared that, following the arrival of Redfern and Shout, 'Rye House is on a much firmer footing than it has been for some years. Our intention now is to field the strongest team we can and the end product of that will hopefully be a place in the First Division.'

The new promoters wasted little time in naming their squad for 1993 which, apart from the Courtney brothers, remained much the same as the successful 1992 outfit and included Goodwin, Rasmussen, Pedersen, O'Brien, Teurnberg, Young, Cobbin and Paul Whittaker. Early results proved reasonably encouraging as they won their home matches with a fair amount of ease although they were finding things more difficult away from their own strip. However, the first real blow of the season came, ironically, as a direct result of the success of their captain, Martin Goodwin. Goodwin won the World Championship British quarter-final at Swindon and then scored 8 points in the semi-final at Ipswich. This was enough to take him through to the British Final at Coventry, the first Rye House rider ever to reach this stage of the competition. Undeterred by the First Division opposition, Goodwin went even further and qualified for the Commonwealth Final at King's Lynn. Unfortunately, this event took place on the

same day as the Rockets' home match against Long Eaton. Forced to use rider replacement, Rye House went down to a 61-46 defeat. Although the Rockets were to lose only one more home match all season, these losses, combined with their poor away form meant that they had no chance of taking the title, or even finishing in the top three. Once again crowds began to dwindle. In an attempt to bring back the supporters, Russell moved the start time from 6 p.m., which had been introduced for summer matches, back to the traditional 4 p.m. start time.

In the end the Rockets finished in 8th place, a great disappointment, considering the team they had got together. Goodwin's scoring for the team was down to 8.23, while Rasmussen's was slightly up on 8.04. Both Pedersen and Lawrence Hare, who had been signed up mid-season on loan from Ipswich, scored at over 7. Darren Spicer, another mid-season signing, finished with a very respectable average of 6.93.

At the end of the season, in spite of falling crowds yet again, Russell was optimistic that the team would run in 1994. 'After all my years at Rye House, you would think it would have turned me into a pessimist,' he said, 'but in fact I'm even more of an optimist than ever. Peter Redfern says another 200 people a week and a bit more sponsorship would make all the difference. But just where do we get another 200 from? Crowds are down about 40 per cent on what I was getting in my first year here.'

Unfortunately, Ronnie Russell's optimism was to prove misplaced. At the beginning of December Peter Redfern and Roger Shute announced that they were no longer able to continue in the position of co-promoters at Rye House. Russell desperately tried to put together another consortium. Although the deadline for declarations of intent to run in the Second Division was 31 December, the BSPA agreed to allow Rye House an extension to see if they could keep the track open. But it was not to be and Russell was forced to admit defeat. On 21 January 1994 he contacted the BSPA and informed them that, after 20 years of league speedway at Rye House, the Rockets would not be running in 1994. He asked for the licence to be put on ice for one season and that all Rye House contracted riders be available for loan. Russell said, 'It's a sad day for everybody connected with the club, from riders through to supporters. I'm absolutely gutted that all the efforts to keep the club going this year have come to nothing.' Club captain, Martin Goodwin, added, 'Sundays at Rye House were unique, it really was a family day.'

Jamie Barton was the first rider signed up by Rye House on their return.

In spite of Russell's hopes, Rye House did not return in 1995 and it was to be another four years before attempts were made to revive the old Hoddesdon circuit.

During the winter of 1998/99, two former Rye House supporters, John Stoneman and Steve Ribbons, called a meeting to discuss the possibility of running a team in the Conference League. The meeting responded enthusiastically and Stoneman was elected Rye House Speedway Club chairman and Ribbons treasurer. It was agreed to ask fans to put £50 into a kitty so that they could get together a team which would race under the name of Rye House Rockets. At the present time, a return to Rye House itself was out of the question (as the track had been tarmacked over for use as a stock car circuit) so the club looked around for a track which would agree to allow the team use of it to race its home fixtures on. As a former promoter, Len Silver was approached to see if he would like to become a club member in return for the £50 support fee. Len said he would do better than that and he agreed to sponsor the team. He also arranged with his old friend Dingle Brown, now promoter at Mildenhall, for use of the West Row track as the Rockets' surrogate home track.

Next the club had the task of putting together a team. Jamie Barton was the first to sign up, followed by Simon Wolstenholme, who was made club captain. Gradually the team took shape and the new Rockets were ready for their first match.

Finally, the great day itself came, when, on 9 May 1999, the Rockets reappeared as a league team, taking on King's Lynn Braves at Eastbourne (Mildenhall was unavailable that day). It proved to be a nail-biting return for the Rockets as they fell well behind in the first few heats, only to claw their way back to make the last heat the decider. When Braves' second placed Freddie Stephenson was excluded for crossing the inside line, the faithful Rockets fans who had fought so hard for this day went mad with joy as they saw their team run out victors by 44 points to 43. Wolstenholme had played a true captain's part, scoring paid 15, while Ian Clarke and Jamie Barton had both given him excellent backing scoring paid 8 and 6 respectively. Wolstenholme remained the team's best rider, recording a final average of 8.43. He was given strong support by two later signings, Simon Moon and Peter Collyer. The other regular team members, Jamie Barton, Dean Chapman and Ian Clarke also rode well. Towards the end of the season, Len Silver managed to persuade David Mason out of retirement and in his five matches he recorded an incredible average of 10.67. In their first season back in league racing, the Rockets finished fourth.

Towards the end of 1999, Len Silver stunned the speedway world by announcing that he had reached agreement with Eddie Leslie, the owner of Rye House stadium, to bring speedway back to the track. One of the conditions of the agreement was that the Rockets lay a shale surface before every speedway meeting and then pick it up again at the conclusion, returning it to tarmac in time for the stock cars to run. Silver also came to an agreement with the speedway club that he would take over all the financial responsibilities of the club. Silver said that finances would not be a problem but to be able to lay and lift the track each week he would need a massive force of volunteers.

On 15 May, speedway returned to Rye House for the first time since 1993 and resulted in a victory for the Rockets over Southampton in a challenge match by 48 points to 42.

It was hard work but each week the track was laid before and then lifted after every meeting; although it was physically possible, it was not a desirable state of affairs. Also, it inevitably meant that conflicts of interest arose between the needs of the stadium owners, the greyhound track, the stock car, ministox and mini motorbikes organisers and the speedway club. Silver decided the only way to resolve all this was to buy the stadium. And so, on 14 July 2000, following negotiations with the stadium owners, Len Silver became the owner of Rye House Stadium. 'It has always been my dream to own my stadium, as, in all my previous speedway ventures, I have always had a landlord, so you could say this is my dream come true,' he said afterwards. Greyhounds continued

at the stadium but everyone else, apart from the speedway club, was given notice to quit at the end of the season. Now that he was in charge of the stadium, Silver also felt it made sense for him to take over the running of the speedway. He was already responsible for its finances and therefore promoter in all but name. After discussions with the Rye House Speedway Club, they readily agreed to the new arrangement and Len Silver became stadium owner and speedway promoter.

Meanwhile, there was a team for the team manager, John Sampford, to run. David Mason, Simon Wolstenholme and Simon Moon all stayed on, while Garry Sweet and Nathan Morton joined the team. Following the opening challenge

Garry Sweet rode in the Rye House Conference League team in 2000 and 2001.

match, the Rye House season became one of home wins and away losses. To try and end the run of poor away form, Silver signed up well-known grass tracker, Phil Ambrose. His effect was almost immediate as the Rockets won their first away match at Somerset. Mason carried on from where he had left off the previous season, finishing up with a 10.34 average. Wolstenholme gave strong support with 8.5. Ambrose proved to be the third heat leader with a score of 7.24. Moon, Sweet and Morton all gave good support with 6 plus averages. Mason had a brilliant season individually, taking the Bronze Helmet from Buxton's Paul Burnett and successfully defending it 11 times. Although the team only managed to finish 6th in the league, it did reach the final of the Knock Out Cup. Unfortunately, the Rockets had too much to do after the away leg, which they lost 37-53, and although they put on an outstanding performance at home to win 50-38, with Mason and Sweet scoring paid 14 and 16 points respectively, overall victory was just out of their reach and they went down narrowly on aggregate by 91 points to 87.

One final accolade was awarded to the track this year as one of the Young England *v.* Young Australia Test matches was raced at Rye House. Mason was called up and responded magnificently with two race wins over the Elite League's Travis McGowan.

With the stock cars finally out of the way, Len Silver spent the winter working on the new permanent track which now boasted sweeping shale bends, a new chain-link safety fence and a permanent inside line. The track was now one of the best in the Conference League and was awarded the prestigious Conference League Riders' Championship Final.

The team that started the 2001 season was, for the most part, the same as the one that finished the 2000 season. But the rider who caught the eye in the opening meeting was youngster, Daniel Giffard, who scored 17 paid 19 in 7 rides from the reserve spot. The other eye-catching riders were Phil Ambrose and Garry Sweet who unfortunately, were both injured forcing them to miss some matches. This gave another youngster, Darren Andrews, his chance and he made the most of it. Once again Mason and Wolstenholme were the best two riders, but an injury to Wolstenholme in June meant that he missed his first official fixture for the Rockets since the team's reformation in May 1999. Silver moved quickly and signed up Chris Courage. At the end of the season, Mason turned in a 9.91 average while both Wolstenholme and Courage recorded 8 plus. Morton and Giffard were the top second strings with 6.44 and 6.34 respectively. Once again the team was almost unbeatable at home but could not win away, which meant a middle of the table finish for them, 4th out of 8. Once again the Rockets reached the final of the Knock Out Cup and once again they lost. This time, however, they lost both legs to a rampant Somerset side and were never really in with a chance. At least in David Mason, Rye House had the rider of the season as he took the Conference League Riders' Championship with 13 points. Simon Wolstenholme finished 3rd on 12 points after losing a run-off to Scott Pegler. Rye House also entered a team in the Southern Junior League, but it failed to make much impression and finished in last place, winning just one match. James Cockle proved to be the best rider.

Never one to avoid a challenge, Len Silver sprang his next surprise on the speedway world when he announced that Rye House would run two teams in 2002, one in the

David Mason joined the Conference League team in 1999 and stepped up to the Premier League with Rye House in 2002.

Premier League and one in the Conference League. Two of the 2001 Conference League team, David Mason and Chris Courage, stepped up to the Premier League while Silver set about building the rest of the team from scratch. In came Australian Nigel Sadler, American Brent Werner and English riders, Scott Robson, Mark Courtney and Scott Swain. Werner and Sadler proved to be good buys as they both recorded 8 plus averages. Mason also showed that he could hold his own in the higher league, recording an average of 5.61. It was not, however, too successful a first year in the Premier League and the team finished in 13th place out of 17 teams. Werner had a good season individually, reaching the final of the Premier League Riders' Championship and coming fourth.

Simon Wolstenholme continued to lead the Conference team but received another injury, this time a broken hand, putting him out for some time. James Cockle was promoted from the junior team, but he too suffered an injury, a broken leg, forcing him out of the team. New signings Scott Courtney and Barrie Evans were also injured during the season. In spite of the injuries, however, the team was at last able to put together some away wins and, with its unbeaten home record continuing, spent the season fighting out the lead with Peterborough, Mildenhall and Sheffield. In the end, the Raiders had to settle for 4th place. Also, for the third year running, they reached the final of the Knock Out Cup, although a 58-32 defeat at the hands of Buxton in the first leg gave them very little chance in the return.

4

HASTINGS

Speedway was tried at Hastings in the early 1930s. Organised by the Hastings Motor Cycle Club, the track was situated in Marley Lane, Battle. Local riders such as Vic Pierce and Don Patterson took part along with riders from other clubs in the south of England and London, including Jack Williams, Joe Linn and Vic Harrington. A contingent from the more established Eastbourne track at Arlington, such as Stan Lemon, Tiny Lewis and Doug Buss also took part. The meetings were run along the normal individual events lines and included sidecar racing. The track lasted a couple of years but was not successful and it closed down in 1934.

Speedway returned to Hastings in 1948 when Charlie Dugard moved his Division Three championship-winning side, Eastbourne, to Pilot Field Stadium in Elphinstone Road. Pilot Field Stadium had originally opened in 1923 for Hastings Football Club. Dugard decided the facilities there were much better for a speedway league team than those at Arlington so he moved in lock, stock, and barrel. The 388-yard track was built tightly round the football field and, in consequence, was a strange shape. It was almost rectangular with two very long straights and two very sharp corners which made for two further short straights. Originally, there was also a kink in the track opposite the pits that made a fifth bend, but Dugard straightened this out after complaints from the riders. Nevertheless the track was still a strange shape and described by a number of riders

A programme cover from a pre-war Hastings meeting at Marley Lane, Battle, on 14 May 1933.

as 'dangerous'. The new track opened on 21 April 1948. Wally Green, Eastbourne's top rider from the year before, got off to a flying start, winning all six of his races, earning himself £22 10s in the process. The team was quickly nicknamed the Saxons and Dugard had the rakers led out each week by a Saxon warrior dressed in flowing robes with a King Harold-style bob haircut under a winged helmet.

In the move to Hastings, the old Eastbourne team lost their three Wimbledon loanees, Jimmy Coy, Basil Harris and Harry Saunders. Wally Green, Jock Grierson, Ken Tidbury and Ron Clark remained. Shortly after the season started, Bill Osborne arrived on loan from Bradford and then Dugard signed up the South African, Buddy Fuller, and it looked as though Hastings was all set to retain the title won by Eastbourne. However, injuries put paid to its chances as first Green broke his collarbone and then Fuller also received an injury which finished his season. Green returned, only to break the other collarbone. When Osborne was recalled by his parent club it finally ended any lingering hope that the Saxons might retain Eastbourne's title. The only good aspect about the loss of so many top riders, was that it gave their juniors a chance to race and in Ken Middleditch, Dugard found that he had a real discovery on his hands.

The team finished 6th in the league out of 12 teams, having won 18 home matches and losing 4 and doing the complete reverse away by winning 4 and losing 18. Green managed to appear in just half of the club's fixtures recording an average of 10.61, which shows just what a loss he was. Grierson recorded 9.57 and Osborne 7.89. Frank

Bettis, who appeared in only 12 matches, was the best of the second strings, recording 5.58. Middleditch turned in an average, in his first year of league racing, of 4.37. Green and Grierson were ranked at numbers three and four respectively in the Division Three rankings as a whole. Green also took the Division Three Match Race title from Exeter's Bert Roger, but was unable to defend it because of his injury.

When Hastings opened in 1949 it was without Wally Green, who had been recalled to his parent club, West Ham. Aub Lawson, the Hammers captain, had paid a visit to Hastings during the 1948 season and, on seeing Green ride, had said to him, 'Walter, it's time you came back to West Ham.' And so he did. Grierson, Fuller and Clark all returned, as did Ken Middleditch who, along with Grierson, had been

West Ham junior, Wally Green, was Hastings' top rider in 1948.

Hastings' Ken Middleditch went from novice in 1948 to beat leader in 1949.

wintering out in South Africa with Buddy Fuller. Middleditch's sojourn out in South Africa had done him the world of good and his first few meetings at the Pilot Field showed that he had improved out of all recognition. For the rest of the season he and Grierson were vying for the top spot and at the end of it there was very little to choose between them, Grierson averaging 8.66 and Middleditch 8.36. Fuller proved to be the third heat leader until he fractured his skull in a mid-season crash. Without Green however, the team had no real pretensions of becoming a title-chasing team and it finished the season in 8th place. In spite of his lower average, Middleditch finished the season above Grierson in the Division Three rankings, Middleditch being ranked 5th and Grierson, 8th. The end of the season also revealed Middleditch as the track record holder with a time of 70.40.

As it happened, this record was to stand for all time as Hastings did not reappear for the 1950 season, or ever again. Rumblings of discontent amongst the local community had been heard as far back as June 1948, when thirteen local ratepayers, under the chairmanship of Mr Arthur Parsons, formed an organisation called 'Kill Hastings Speedway', and complained to the council about the noise, threatening at the same time to stop paying their rates. After meetings between the organisation, the council and Charlie Dugard, the residents decided to take their case to court. The case was viewed with great trepidation by speedway clubs all over the country as it was seen as something of a test case. The residents indicted Dugard on eleven charges and employed Sir Hartley Shawcross to present their case. Ten of the charges were thrown out and the residents ordered to pay ten elevenths of the costs. However, the one remaining charge was upheld and this meant the end for speedway in Hastings. In his summing up, the judge, Mr Justice Humphries, said, 'I will add that no attack has been made in the case upon speedway racing. It is completely untrue to say that this is a test case. My decision is not intended to be a decision that speedway racing should be stopped. What I hold is that it is proved to my satisfaction that speedway racing in this particular residential neighbourhood must stop, unless it can be carried on without that noise, without which, according to evidence, it cannot be carried on'. [Quoted in *Homes of British Speedway*] In other words, the Saxons had lost the battle of Hastings. Dugard appealed against the decision but the appeal was dismissed and an application for leave to appeal to the House of Lords was refused. Dugard hoped that speedway could still run in Hastings if other promoters agreed to fit silencers to the bikes, but

The South African, Buddy Fuller, had two seasons with Hastings, 1948 and 1949.

unfortunately he could not obtain the necessary agreement. The last meeting to take place at the Pilot Field track was on 5 October 1949 when Hastings lost to Tamworth 44.5 to 39.5. One of Dugard's reasons for moving his Eastbourne operation to Hastings was to be nearer to a centre of population. It was to prove a costly mistake.

With the track and safety fence still in position, a group of speedway supporters got together in 1975, to organise a petition throughout the borough in support of speedway returning to the Pilot Field. The organisers of the petition, Mr Ray Marchant and Mr Dave Ormerod, said the intention was to hand the petition to the Hastings District Council. They felt that with the new regulations with regard to silencers being made compulsory, they had a good chance of resurrecting speedway at the venue. It was not to be however, and speedway has never returned to Hastings.

5

CANTERBURY

In 1968, at the youthful age of seventy-five, the founder of modern speedway, Johnnie S. Hoskins, decided it was about time to meet a new challenge, so he looked around for a site where speedway had not been held before and came up with Kingsmead Stadium in Canterbury, home of Canterbury City Football Club. Hoskins constructed a track round the outside of the football pitch on Canterbury Athletics Club's former running track and entered a team into the newly-formed British League Second Division.

Hoskins was warned that the venture would not be a success as Canterbury was not the right venue for a speedway, what with being a cathedral town and all. But Hoskins, as usual, was to prove his critics wrong. At least 7,000 people turned up on 18 May, the opening night. 7,000 was the number who paid to get in, many more were thought to have got in for nothing by climbing the walls surrounding the stadium. The gate was something like double that of the record gate recorded by the football club. Johnnie Hoskins, who had done his homework before opening Canterbury Speedway and had talked to all the 'right' people to get the necessary backing for his venture, had invited the Mayor of Canterbury, Cllr B.A. Porter, to be his official guest at the opening.

The match itself was a real thriller as, after twelve heats, the two sides were level at 36 all. It looked all over for the Crusaders, as the team were nicknamed, in the final race when Tyburn Gallows had to pull on to the centre green with a cracked frame, but when Belle Vue's Dave Brockbank fell, it opened up the possibility of a home win. However, the Colts' John Woodcock was just too good for Canterbury's Ken Vale and he held on for the vital win that gave Belle Vue Colts the victory by 39 points to 38.

This was, in fact, Canterbury's second fixture as they had already raced one away match, which, as befitting Hoskins' status, made history as the first match ever raced in the British League Second Division. That was also against Belle Vue Colts with the Crusaders going down by 23 points to 55. The team that night was Lex Milloy, Tyburn Gallows, Chris Raines, Nev Slee, Barry Lee, Barry Crowson and Martyn Piddock. The first riders ever to race in Canterbury colours were Lex Milloy and Tyburn Gallows, who lined up in heat one. It was not a propitious start however, as the Colts took a 5-1, Taffy Owen winning the first-ever British League Second Division race from his partner, Ken Eyre.

As well as being criticised for the venue, Hoskins was also criticised for the team he had put together. There was only one experienced rider, Ken Vale (who was acting as rider-coach) although to some extent Tyburn Gallows was also experienced. The rest were all juniors – Barry Crowson, on loan from West Ham, Martyn Piddock, Chris

Raines, Barry Lee and Nev Slee. Once again, Hoskins was to prove his critics wrong, as, after that first home defeat, the Crusaders did not lose at Kingsmead again all season. Their away form was not too good however and they finished 7th out of 10 in the league.

Hoskins was to enjoy an even bigger triumph over his critics when his youngsters went on to win the Knock Out Cup, thumping Reading 112-80 in the final winning both legs in the process. Crowson turned out to be the best of the juniors and finished the season with an average of 8.44. Top rider however was Peter Murray who came into the team midway through the season. He finished with the remarkable average of 10.05. Vale was the third heat leader but only just as the young Martyn Piddock made big strides through the season to finish on 7.96, just 0.04 behind Vale. Unfortunately, Tyburn Gallows was injured after only six matches, breaking both legs and arms. A number of different combinations were tried at the lower end of the scoring order with Lee and Slee leaving and John Hibben, Pat Flanagan and Frank Wendon joining Raines to swap around the second string and reserve spots. Another young rider to make four appearances in that first season was Graham Miles, who brought a dash of colour to the team by riding in red leathers at a time when all riders wore black ones.

With the recall of Crowson to his parent club in 1969, Hoskins looked round for a replacement and thought he'd found one in the Australian, Jim Crowhurst, but he was not a success and was soon on his way back to Australia. This left a team place open for a seventeen-year-old junior by the name of Barry Thomas who came straight in to the team, recording a 6.03 average in his very first season. The *Speedway Star* thought, 'Barry certainly looks a likely prospect for very big things. He could be another in the

Canterbury's first team in 1968. From left to right: Tyburn Gallows, Lex Milloy, Barry Lee, Neville Slee, Barry Crowson (captain, on bike), Martyn Piddock, Chris Raines.

Tyburn Gallows, real name Raymond Humphries, rode for Canterbury in their first season in 1968.

Brian Crutcher-Ronnie Moore-Barry Briggs mould.'

At the top end of the score chart, Peter Murray continued to show what he had showed at the end of the previous season and that was that he was really too good for the Second Division. His average went up even higher to 10.36, but behind him Martyn Piddock was improving out of all recognition to become the Crusaders number two on 9.80. Vale continued as third heat leader until a dislocated shoulder put him out towards the end of the season and his place was taken by the ever-improving Graham Miles. Once again, Hoskins chopped and changed the lower orders as a number of different riders put in appearances at reserve or second string, including Dave Percy, Neville Brice, Graham Banks, Brian Foote, Alan Kite, Chris Raines, Jake Rennison and Frank Wendon. There was a marginal improvement in the team's position as it went up 1 place to finish 6th, though it should be pointed out that there were now 16 teams in the league. They could not hold on to the cup and went out in the second round to Crewe.

At the end of the 1969 season, Canterbury lost all three of their heat leaders as Peter Murray returned to First Division Wimbledon, Martyn Piddock went to First Division West Ham and Ken Vale retired. Hoskins managed to replace two of them, firstly by enticing Barry Crowson back and secondly by signing up Graeme Smith from Rayleigh. But he could not find that elusive third heat leader and it looked as though Canterbury might have to settle once again for a mid-table position or maybe even worse. What happened however, was beyond Hoskins' and the supporters' wildest expectations as Barry Thomas turned into a top star in his first full season, averaging 9.11 to become that third heat leader behind Crowson on 9.17 and Smith on an unbelievable 10.49. Not only did Thomas become a star but not far behind him were the two Grahams, Banks on 7.53 and Miles on 7.44. With these top five riders, Canterbury did much more than achieve a mid-table position. Unbeaten at home and with 7 wins and 1 draw away, the Crusaders incredibly went on to win the league. The other regulars in that title-winning team were Alan Kite, Jake Rennison, Dave Smith and Mike Barkaway. Also coming in for five rides at an average of 4.22 was a young man by the name of Ted 'Hurricane' Hubbard. It was a good year for Thomas and Crowson individually as well. Thomas won the Junior Championship of the British Isles as well as a contract with First Division

Frank Wendon was in and out of the Canterbury team during 1968 and 1969.

Hackney, the team he was to stay with for the next twenty years. Crowson was Canterbury's representative at the Division Two Riders' Championship Final, coming second with 12 points.

1971 started the same way as 1970, almost. Thomas had gone to Hackney and Crowson had gone to King's Lynn, while Graeme Smith was still recovering from a broken leg which he sustained in a crash the previous September. The Crusaders were three heat leaders down again. This time however it was worse, as Graham Miles had gone with Thomas to Hackney. Only Graham Banks was left of the Famous Five that had taken the Crusaders to the 1970 League Championship. This time, Hoskins was not able to find the replacements and he started off the season with Banks and a team of juniors. The opening meeting was a disaster as the Crusaders went down by 38 points to Eastbourne. Worse still was the fact that Banks scored zero. Hoskins then pulled off a masterstroke by talking former Poole, Eastbourne and Romford favourite, Ross Gilbertson, out of his short-lived retirement following his two successful seasons with Romford. Gilbertson proved to be an inspiration to the team and became its number one. Banks improved after that first disastrous meeting and both of them scored at 8 plus for the season. The biggest disappointment of the season was Graeme Smith. When he did come back, he was nothing like the rider he had been and his average dropped by something like 4 points per match to 6.32.

It was definitely a year of consolidation for the Crusaders as several youngsters were brought into the team and given extended runs in the hope that they would form the basis of the team in future years. Dave Piddock averaged 6.75, Graeme Stapleton 6.29, Hubbard, 5.44 and Barney Kennett, 4.09. But the league title was lost as the Crusaders plunged to 14th place in the league. They were also knocked out of the Cup in the second round, having been given a bye in the first. Banks did have some individual success as he took the Silver Helmet from Ipswich's John Louis on 8 May and successfully defended it three times before losing it to Teeside's Bruce Forrester on 27 May.

Most of the regular 1971 team stayed together for 1972 and while there was a slight overall improvement it was very much a standstill year as the Crusaders finished 13th in the League. In spite of their disappointing league position they did achieve one record with their 63-15 thrashing of Scunthorpe equalling the biggest victory ever in Division Two.

Martyn Piddock was Canterbury's only ever-present rider in their first season.

Gilbertson continued as top man. In fact he improved his average by over 1 point a match to 9.46. Behind him Banks dropped slightly, while Hubbard improved enough to become the third heat leader on 7.26. Piddock's average also rose to over 7. Newcomers this year included Bob Hughes, Les Rumsey and Ipswich loanee, Trevor Jones. Gilbertson finished 4th in the Second Division Riders' Championship with 11 points.

Before the 1973 season started, discussions took place between the City Council, Johnnie Hoskins and the Control Board over possible noise problems at the stadium. Eventually these were settled amicably and speedway was allowed to continue at Kingsmead. Once again the season started with a more or less settled team and the hope that this year the juniors would come good to back up Gilbertson. After the first meeting the juniors were all they had as Gilbertson crashed out with a broken nose and jaw and never appeared again. Although during the season, Canterbury signed up Derek Cook from Eastbourne and welcomed back Peter Murray from Wimbledon, they never recovered from the loss of their number one. Graham Banks' form inexplicably collapsed and he finished up just managing to stay out of the reserve spot. Top scorer of the year and number one man at Kingsmead was a much improved Barney Kennett with an average of 7.38, but for any team with title aspirations, 7.38 is not the sort of average for the number one man to have. The rest of the team was close behind, Murray on 6.90, Hubbard, 6.75, Cook, 6.41, Jones, 6.33. In effect, it was a team of good second strings and it dropped down the League to 15th place, Canterbury's worst position since joining the League six years previously.

On 16 June, the Junior Championship of the British Isles was held at Kingsmead. During the meeting some supporters took the opportunity to confront Wally Mawdsley, the Division Two chairman, to ask why Kennett had not been chosen to represent England in the Division Two Test match against Poland which was due to take place at Canterbury on 30 June. Mawdsley replied that as Kennett and favourite for the Junior Championship, Peter Collins, were due to meet in heat 13 he would see how Kennett got on in that race. Although Collins eventually went on to win the Championship, Kennett beat him in heat 13 in the fastest time he had ever recorded at Kingsmead. Before the meeting was over, Mawdsley informed Kennett that there had been a 'revision' to the England Test team and that he would be riding. Kennett went on to score 4 points in the Test match.

Graeme Smith joined the Crusaders in 1970 and shot to the top of the averages with 10.49. He returned in 1971 following a serious injury at the end of 1970 but was unable to find his form again. He left at the end of the season.

Before the 1974 season started, Graham Banks decided he wanted to leave and was replaced by Roger Johns from Eastbourne. Other than that change and the fact that Peter Murray did not make the opening meetings as he was still out in Rhodesia, the same team (that had come 15th the year before) stayed together. Kennett continued from where he had left off but then, for some reason, lost form mid-season and from being the number one struggled to stay in the team. Fortunately, three of Canterbury's youngsters began to show real improvement this year as both Jones and Hubbard moved up to 8 plus averages and Dave Gooderham, who had had a few outings in 1973, became the third heat leader on 7.28. It was a much better year for the Crusaders as they moved up the table to 6th place. Hubbard was Canterbury's representative at the Second Division Riders' Championship where he scored 13 points and came second after a run off for first place with Boston's Carl Glover.

It looked at one time as though Canterbury would not be running in 1975. As usual, the City Council had extended Hoskins' planning permission but a member of the council referred the matter back to the planning committee following objections from about twenty local residents led by a Mr M.H. Wise who lived near the track. At the planning committee a decision was taken to recommend to the next full council meeting that speedway cease immediately at Kingsmead. Hoskins, of course, had been aware of the noise problem and had already tested several types of silencer and had offered to erect a sound barrier, but this was all to no avail. Immediately, as the planning committee's decision was known, the supporters' club swung into action and organised a 3,000 signature petition to hand in to the full council. When the council met on 5 March, the final vote surprised everyone as it went in favour of speedway continuing at Kingsmead by 33 to 13, a much larger majority than anyone had predicted. There were some provisos. One was an embargo on any music and the toning down of the public address, the other was that the speedway had to examine further ways of reducing noise.

With speedway at Kingsmead saved there were some big changes in the team for 1975 which was the first year of the New National League, as the Second Division had now been renamed. Ted Hubbard had gone the way of Thomas and Miles to try his luck at First Division Hackney, while Roger Johns had returned to Wimbledon. In came Graham Clifton, Bob Spelta, Gerald Purkiss and Terry Casserly. But it was to be three long-standing Crusaders who were to catch the eye this year. Firstly, Les Rumsey suddenly broke out of his accustomed reserve spot to become number one with a 9.90 average and then both Gooderham and Kennett chased him up the score chart with 8.64 and 8.23 respectively. If these three had had some better backing it could have been a good year for Canterbury, but number four man, Clifton, could only manage 5.31 and so the team dropped slightly to 10th place in the league. Rumsey qualified for the New National League Riders' Championship, scoring 10 points and finishing 4th after coming 2nd in a three-man run-off for 3rd place. As the season finished, he too announced his intention to move up to the British League.

The programme cover from the meeting on 22 April 1972 showing Dave Piddock and Graham Banks presenting Johnnie Hoskins with his eightieth birthday present.

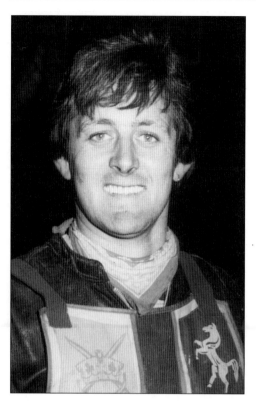

Canterbury's most loyal servant, Barney Kennet, rode for the Crusaders for 14 seasons from 1971 until 1984.

At the end of the year, Canterbury were once more in trouble with the council as the planning committee again voted against a further extension of speedway's planning permission. Supporters' Club chairman Reg Funnell decided to make a direct appeal to the Mayor. He said, 'Speedway is a wonderful public amenity ... In the eight years the track has operated we have shown ourselves to be most public-spirited too.' He cited many examples of this public-spirit, mentioning financial aid towards equipping a St John Ambulance Brigade ambulance, support for Canterbury's Hospital League of Friends and donations to most mayoral charity appeals. Once again the full council vote surprised everyone as it was even more emphatic than the previous year, 35 votes to 7 in favour of speedway continuing. It was thought that the recent FIM ruling on the compulsory introduction of silencers for all speedway machines had played a decisive part in the vote.

Before the start of the next season, the eighty-three-year-old Johnnie Hoskins decided it was time he started to take things a bit easier and so he concluded an agreement with Wally Mawdsley for the latter to come in with him as co-promoter. Maurice Morley arrived with Mawdsley to take over as general manager. There were changes in the team's colours as well. Gone were the crossed swords and in came the new quartered strip. Following Rumsey's move to British League Exeter, Gooderham and Purkiss also decided it was time to move on. In their places came the experienced Reg Luckhurst, the returning Graham Banks and the Australian, Steve Koppe, in his first year in this country. Later in the season, Rumsey returned following a difficult spell with Exeter, and, even though he slotted back in as a heat leader, his scoring was down on 1975. It was a good all-round team performance, spearheaded by Banks with 8.06, with the result that the Crusaders moved up the table to take 4th place.

The start of the 1977 season was postponed as once again Canterbury ran into difficulties with the council's planning committee. This time it was over a £15,000 improvement scheme for spectator accommodation, the pits area and noise baffles. At its meeting in March, the planning committee decided that details of the scheme had not been advertised properly and would have to be reconsidered at its April meeting and may even have to go to full council. In the end the plans were passed and Kingsmead opened for speedway on 16 April. The promoters also had to defend the speedway yet

Mike Ferreira was Canterbury's top rider from 1979 to 1981. In 1981 he recorded 15 maximums and an average of 10.87.

again from local residents, this time in court, as a Nuisance Order was brought against them. On this front too, Hoskins and Mawdsley were successful, much to the relief of the local supporters.

The late start to the season meant that Canterbury had to race 9 of their first 11 fixtures away from home, which put them in something of a false league position going into the middle of the season. By the end of the season they had put that right and finished up in 4th place. Top of the team averages for the year was Steve Koppe with Graham Banks his number two. Les Rumsey, who had once again left only to return again during the season was the third heat leader. The most improved riders were Bob Spelta and Brendan Shilleto who averaged 7.37 and 6.07 respectively. Meanwhile, Barney Kennett continued to give strong support with 6.44.

By the time the 1978 season started, Canterbury had managed to achieve a new agreement with the council which gave them five-year planning permission. With more stability, the management were able to plan better for the future. 600 new seats had already been added in the stand and Wally Mawdsley was now looking to improve spectator conditions on the back straight, although a plan to erect the stand from Romford had to be abandoned because of foundations problems.

Maurice Morley took over as co-promoter on behalf of Wally Mawdsley Productions and set about building up a team good enough to challenge for the title. First he had to overcome two tragic blows to the team. The first was that Bob Spelta, who had injured his neck late in the previous season had returned home to Australia and seemed unlikely to ride again. The second was even worse as Graham Banks was killed in a grass-track crash just after the start of the season.

Morley's first new signing proved to be an inspired choice as he obtained the transfer of the young Rhodesian, Mike Ferreira, from Coatbridge for just £350. Then he talked David Piddock into returning to Kingsmead and Brendan Shilleto out of retiring. Now with strong backing for the top two, Morley felt he had a team that could go all the way. Steve Koppe and Les Rumsey competed with each other throughout the season to see who would be number one. At the time the averages were drawn up for the National League Riders' Championship representation, Koppe was narrowly in front of Rumsey

Veteran Nigel Boocock had one season with Canterbury in 1979.

and so became the representative. Although they were rivals for the number one spot, they were great friends and Rumsey travelled to Wimbledon as Koppe's mechanic, helping him score 14 points to take the title. Crusaders' fans, who went to cheer on Koppe, also saw 'old boys' Hubbard and Gooderham come in 3rd and 4th. Ironically, at the end of the season, Rumsey just topped the averages with 9.80 to Koppe's 9.68.

The team performed as well as Morley had hoped, winning 12 away matches, the same number as Newcastle, with whom they fought a hard duel all season. With just one match to go for Canterbury, Newcastle had finished their season and were top of the league with 60 points. Canterbury had 58. With their superior race points, the Crusaders knew that all they had to do was to beat Mildenhall in their last match to take the league championship for the second time in their history. Although Rumsey and Koppe were the top scorers it had been an all round team effort to get the team into contention for top honours, so it was fitting that in that final all-important match with Mildenhall, the top three scorers were Mike Ferreira (10 points), David Piddock (9) and Graham Clifton (9). The rest of the team on that glorious night, when the Crusaders beat Mildenhall by 48 points to 30 to become National League champions, were Les Rumsey, Steve Koppe, Barney Kennett and Brendan Shilleto. It should not be forgotten that the late Graham Banks had also played his part. He had begun the season with 11 points in his first match and a maximum 12 in his second. At the time of his tragic death he was Canterbury's third heat leader, averaging 8.11.

As if winning the league wasn't enough for the Grand Old Man of Speedway, it was announced in the 1979 New Year's Honours List that Johnnie S. Hoskins would now be Johnnie S. Hoskins MBE. He received his award for services to speedway at the investiture on 27 February 1979.

The recall of Steve Koppe to his parent club Exeter came as no surprise following his outstanding year at Canterbury, but what Maurice Morley had not reckoned with was Les Rumsey also departing Kingsmead after 7 years and 206 appearances. To lose his number one and two was bad enough, but when Brenda Shilleto broke an ankle after just four matches while guesting for Wimbledon things began to look very bad for the League champions. Mike Ferreira, Barney Kennett and David Piddock tried their best. In fact, all of them improved on their 1978 averages, but there was no Koppe or Rumsey – let alone both – to help them remain at the top of the tree. The veteran forty-two year old Nigel Boocock was signed up to try and add that extra something. As usual 'Booey' gave 100 per cent effort for his new club, ending the season as the club's number one with an 8.54 average just 0.01 ahead of Ferreira. Tim Hunt and Roger Abel came into the side to bolster up the middle order, while Graham Clifton filled the reserve spot. It was a reasonably good side, but got nowhere near retaining the title as, in the end, they finished the league in 10th place.

It was Boocock who represented the Crusaders at the National League Riders' Championship. He only just missed out on a rostrum place as he scored 11 points, which was equal to third-placed Andy Graham of Milton Keynes. However, Boocock lost in the run-off.

The usual comings and goings at Canterbury over the close season meant that 1980 started without Nigel Boocock, Tim Hunt and Roger Abel, their places being taken by old favourite, Ted Hubbard and teenager Denzil Kent. Kent's signing was the subject of some controversy at the beginning of the season as Oxford had paid his air fare from South Africa but had failed to get him to sign a contract. When Maurice Morley discovered this error on the part of the Oxford management he stepped in sharply and signed the young Mr Kent up for the Crusaders. Kent's form in his first season was to show just what a mistake Oxford had made in letting Morley snap him up from under their noses. His average at the end of the year was 6.63. Apart from Ferreira however, Kent was

Denzil Kent in action for Canterbury in 1982.

about the only success story Canterbury had that year. Kennett continued to score at his usual 7-point average, but to be second heat leader with that score was not good news for the Crusaders. Hubbard was down on scoring power and seemed to lose form after a reasonable start to the season. The one man who did get even better was Mike Ferreira whose average shot up to 10.32. But two success stories were not enough to save Canterbury from dropping to their lowest ever position in the league as they finished 18th out of 20 teams. One of the teams below them was Workington who finished bottom with just 2 wins all season. One of those wins was over Canterbury. In some ways it summed up what a poor season it was for the Crusaders.

The news at the beginning of 1981 was that Kingsmead Stadium had been sold and that the buyer wished to build a hotel and leisure complex on the site. Maurice Morley told supporters this would mean that the council would have to rehouse them and the outcome of this would be that they would probably move to a new stadium with better facilities.

1981 proved to be much the same as 1980 only Mike Ferreira and Denzil Kent got even better. Kent's average improved to 7.75 to make him number two behind Ferreira. Barney Kennett was there as usual hovering around the 7-point mark, this time as third heat leader, but behind those three, the Crusaders were very weak. Ted Hubbard had retired over the winter and the next highest scorer was Mark Martin on 4.69. The team finished the year in 14th place, only a slight improvement on the year before.

In the end, 1981 was mostly about Canterbury's twenty-five-year-old Rhodesian star, Mike Ferreira. He took the National League by storm. He topped the league averages

The Canterbury pair, Barney Kennett and Jamie Luckhurst, in 1983.

Nigel Couzens rode for Canterbury from 1981 to 1982. This photograph dates from 1982.

with an incredible 10.87. In 138 official rides, he was first 112 times recording 15 maximums. He was unplaced on only 7 occasions and came 3rd just once. He took the Silver Helmet from Glasgow's Steve Lawson in July and retained it against Edinburgh's Neil Collins before relinquishing the title. With Denzil Kent he took the National League Pairs Championship and to top it all off, he won the National League Riders' Championship with a faultless 15-point maximum.

At the end of the season, the City Council refused to renew permission for speedway to continue at Kingsmead. Consequently, Wally Mawdsley submitted plans for a new stadium to be built on a ten-acre site at Marsh Farm, Sturry Road, Canterbury. The promoters hoped to build a stadium for 5,000 spectators. The Council's Policy Committee Chairman, Cllr Arthur Porter, thought there would be few, if any, objections to speedway on this site. After months of discussions over the winter, the Canterbury City Council at its meeting in March decided to defer planning permission for the new development and instead agreed that Canterbury could have one more season of speedway at Kingsmead.

While discussions were going on about where they would race there were also many discussions about who would be racing. Not surprisingly, Ferreira left to try his hand in the British League with Swindon. Morley hoped that Kent's progress would continue to the point where he would take over from Ferreira as Canterbury's number one. As cover, he signed up Ian Clark from Hackney and Nigel Couzens from Peterborough. Clark in particular did his job of covering well, turning in a 7.64 average, but, unfortunately Kent didn't progress. His average stayed almost identical to the year before at just about 7.5. The real surprise packet of the year, if you discount Les Rumsey's reappearance for 4 matches and 51 points at the tail end of the year, was Barney Kennett. Kennett had been at Canterbury for 12 years and had settled down to a regular 7-point man, but the departure of Ferreira seemed to have spurred Kennett on and he took over the top spot with an average of 8.66. It didn't save the team from dropping to 16th place but it gave many long standing Crusaders' fans great pleasure to see Kennett at last make it to number one.

At the end of 1982, Wally Mawdsley wound up Wally Mawdsley Speedway Promotions and launched a new company, Canterbury International, which took over control of Canterbury Speedway. The company was under the sole control of Mawdsley with

Teenager David Mullett joined Canterbury in 1981. By 1985 he had become the Crusaders' leading rider. He announced his retirement from Reading at the end of the 2002 season.

Darrell Mason becoming responsible for the commercial side of the business and Maurice Morley general manager. Reg Luckhurst took over as team manager. Mawdsley also stressed that 'Speedway's undisputed Grand Master, Johnnie Hoskins MBE, will very much continue to play an active part in our speedway proceedings and will be flying the Canterbury International flag in his usual inimitable style.' Canterbury International's first coup was to sign a sponsorship deal with Invicta Motors.

The usual uncertainty about Canterbury's future surfaced again during the winter as the Council once again refused permission for speedway at Kingsmead and once again, following an appeal by Mawdsley, saw its refusal overturned, this time by the Government inspector, who gave permission for speedway to continue at Kingsmead until the end of 1984. At that time the council were to make a decision on whether to allow speedway to remain at Kingsmead or whether to give permission for a new site.

With Kelvin Mullarkey joining the Crusaders at the start of 1983 to link up with Kennett and Kent there was great hope amongst Canterbury supporters that this might be the year when the team got away from hovering around the bottom of the table. Kent did improve slightly this year to become top man on 8.20 but Kennett dropped back to his usual 7.5. Mullarkey disappointed slightly with 7.43. During the season other riders came in to try their best including Andy Hibbs, Jamie Luckhurst, David Mullett, Laurie Etheridge and Keith Pritchard, but it was all to no avail as Canterbury failed to win one single away match and remained in the bottom quarter of the table in 15th place.

Once again it was a case of all change at the top for Canterbury in 1984 as Denzil Kent left just before the end of the 1983 season and Kelvin Mullarkey returned to his parent club, Rye House, after only one match amid bitter controversy. Morley claimed that he was given notice of Mullarkey's recall just five hours before the Crusaders were due to meet Weymouth and put an injunction on him to prevent him riding the next day for Rye House. Mullarkey said he was surprised by Morley's move, 'I have nothing against Canterbury whatsoever,' he said, 'but it was no secret that I wanted to move to another track to save the clash of Saturday night racing with my business commitments.'

Canterbury moved quickly to replace Mullarkey, bringing in twenty-year-old Alan Mogridge on loan from Hackney. Mogridge proved to be an excellent replacement as he became Canterbury's number two with a 7.69 average. Either side of him, as the other two heat leaders, were another two youngsters who had improved greatly on their 1983 performances. First there was twenty-year-old Jamie Luckhurst, who shot to the top of the Crusaders' score chart with 8.11 and second there was eighteen-year-old Dave Mullett who recorded 7.61. The ever-faithful Kennett was slightly down on his scoring this year, but he nevertheless gave good support to the three heat leaders. Rob Tilbury, who had been around the team for the past couple of seasons was given an extended run and did well for his 5.72 just outscoring Kevin Brice, now in his fifth season with the Crusaders. Yet again though, it was not a good year for the team as a whole. Given their experience the youngsters were good, but Canterbury needed

Left: *Keith Pritchard rode for Canterbury from 1982 to 1984.* Right: *Alan Mogridge was at the centre of controversy on 2 August 1986 when he effectively rode for both Canterbury and Rye House in the same match.*

127

another Mike Ferreira or Les Rumsey or Steve Koppe if they were to climb up that table. For the second year running they failed to win one single away match and finished the table in 12th place out of 16 teams.

Three of the top four from the 1984 team left the Crusaders before the start of the 1985 season. Luckhurst moved on to Wimbledon, Mogridge moved back to Hackney and Kennett decided to hang up his leathers after fourteen years as a Crusader. Canterbury's most loyal servant had ridden for the team in fourteen out of their seventeen years of existence making a record-breaking 494 appearances. To replace them, new manager Dick Searle brought in Mike Spink, Lawrie Bloomfield and Steve Bryenton. Rob Tilbury, Neville Tatum and Kevin Brice stayed on along with David Mullett, the only one of the previous year's top four to remain. It was not a side of world beaters, but Searle hoped for the best. His hopes were rudely shattered in the very first home meeting when Middlesbrough thrashed them 46-32. After beating Mildenhall by just two points they lost again to Arena Essex, 41-36. Once again it was a poor season for Canterbury, though they did at last manage to win an away match, three in fact, over Arena Essex, Long Eaton and Rye House, and once again they finished up languishing near the foot of the table in 16th place out of 19 teams. Mullett moved up to become the number one with an average of 8.78. The third heat leader was Rob Tilbury with just 6.44, which goes some way to explaining why the Crusaders finished up where they did.

Alan Mogridge returned for the 1986 season to join Mullett, Spink and Tilbury, all of whom stayed on and there was a new signing – Alan Sage. By August, the season was going the same way as the previous six seasons with the Crusaders looking destined to finish near the bottom of the league. But on 2 August it was all change at Kingsmead as Chris Galvin and Terry Waller took over from Wally Mawdsley and Canterbury International although it was not a case of all change right from the start. On the same day that Galvin and Waller took over, Canterbury met Rye House at Kingsmead. In the Rockets team was Alan Mogridge who, until three weeks earlier, had been a Canterbury rider. He had fallen out with the then promoters and asked for a transfer. As a result of this, Canterbury had been given special dispensation to use rider replacement as Mogridge was deemed to be 'withholding his services.' With Mogridge riding for Rye House and Canterbury using rider replacement for Mogridge it meant, in effect, that Mogridge was riding for both teams. If this wasn't enough of a baptism of fire for Galvin and Waller, Canterbury also lost the match 41-36. With Poole and Eastbourne winning at Kingsmead in the next two weeks, the new promotion had to wait until the visit of Stoke on 23 August before it chalked up its first win and even that was only as the result of a last race engine failure by Stoke's Paul Thorpe. But then came the transformation as the Crusaders won 5 out of their 8 fixtures in September, including 2 away. This had come about mainly because Chris Galvin had gone out and bought Paul Evitts from Birmingham. The team might have had an even better finish to the season if Mike Spink had not broken his collarbone on the same day that Evitts was signed.

Evitts finished the season as top rider with an average of 8.87, just ahead of Mullett on 8.69. Spink was the number three with 7.60. At the end of the 1986 season, Dick Searle reflected on the poor run of success the Crusaders had had in the 1980s and

Left: *Rob Tilbury first rode for Canterbury in 1982 and stayed until its closure in 1987.* **Right:** *Kevin Brice rode for Canterbury from 1980 to 1985.*

said, of the 1987 campaign, if we don't get success on the track, I think it could be the end for Canterbury.' A decade of mediocrity had taken its toll at Kingsmead and gates had fallen dramatically over the last few seasons. If what Dick Searle was saying was true, the start of the season did not augur well for Canterbury's chances of staying in business as they lost their first six matches. It wasn't until mid-May that the Crusaders' chalked up their first win at home to Glasgow. Ironically, this match was later expunged from the records as the Tigers withdrew from the League.

Over the winter the track had been reshaped and Paul Evitts could not get to grips with it. His scoring fell alarmingly and the man who had given hope to Canterbury at the back end of 1986 saw his scoring fall by over 2 points per match to a lowly 6.33. Mullett returned to the top of the averages with 8.62 followed by Spink and Tilbury as the other two heat leaders. But once again it was a dismal season for the Crusaders and they finished up in 13th place out of 16 teams.

At the end of November the news that all Canterbury supporters had dreaded came at last. The council informed Chris Galvin that they were not prepared to renew his licence to stage speedway at Kingsmead. The promoters would either have to find a new track or it would be the end of speedway in Canterbury. Galvin began immediately to look around for a new site, while at the same time making a last ditch appeal to the council to allow speedway for one more season to provide time to find somewhere else. But in the end neither option came off and Canterbury was forced to close down, never to return. At the time of its closure, Canterbury was one of only two clubs to have participated in the Second Division every year since its formation in 1968, the other being Middlesborough.

Canterbury's last team in 1987. From left to right, back row: Paul Evitts, Rob Tilbury, Dick Searle (manager), Carl Chalcraft, David Mullett. Front row: Paul Whittaker, Mike Spink (on bike), Richard Pettman.

The last match at Kingsmead was against Rye House in the second leg of the Kent-Herts Trophy on 31 October 1987. Rye House held a 42-36 lead from the first leg but that had been whittled away by heat seven. In the end Canterbury ran out easy winners, beating the Rockets 49-29 on the day and 85-71 on aggregate. David Mullett finished with a maximum.

It should come as no surprise to learn that Barney Kennett holds the record for the most appearances for Canterbury with 494, ahead of Les Rumsey on 210 and Graham Banks on 206. Kennett also holds the record for the most points scored with 3,691, again ahead of Rumsey on 1,652 and Banks on 1,535. Top of the tree for best average is Mike Ferreira on 9.34, followed by Ross Gilbertson on 9.20 and Martyn Piddock on 9.01. Ferreira also scored the most maximums in Crusaders' colours with 35, 29 full and 6 bonus, ahead of Rumsey on 34, 23 full, 11 paid and Steve Koppe, 25, 8 full, 17 paid. As befits the team man that he was, Barney Kennett holds the record for the highest number of paid maximums with 18.

6

CRAYFORD

Speedway racing first took place at Crayford's London Road Stadium as far back as 1930, though in the early days it was really grass-track racing. The track was converted to a proper dirt track in 1931. It was very much an amateur affair with meetings being held on Sunday afternoons in 1931 and between 1935 and 1937. *Homes of British Speedway* quotes Wilf Plant (later to ride for Wimbledon, Middlesborough and Fleetwood) as saying, 'There were no grandstands. I can remember the railway line running past the track. I was a junior in those days and got much of my early training at Crayford.'

The stadium returned to full-time speedway in 1968 when the Wolverhampton promoters, Mike Parker and Bill Bridgett, opened it up and entered Crayford as founder members of the British League Division Two. The pair spent something like £15,000 preparing the stadium, upgrading spectator facilities and laying down a track. They explained that they had chosen Crayford 'because we're thoroughly convinced that speedway has a big future at Crayford. Kent has long been a hotbed of motorcycle enthusiasm, and we're certain that support for this most exciting of all short circuit motorised sports will not be lacking.' The Highwaymen was chosen as the team's nickname following a competition held in the local paper as the area between Crayford and Bexley had been notorious in the eighteenth and nineteenth centuries as a haunt for highwaymen. The Highwaymen's opening meeting, on 12 June, was a league match against

Racing gets underway at Crayford.

CRAYFORD STADIUM

BRITISH LEAGUE MATCH DIV. II
CRAYFORD v NELSON
WEDNESDAY, 12th JUNE, 1968 AT 7.45 P.M.
First Season—1st Meeting   PROGRAMME 1'-

The programme cover for Crayford's opening meeting on 12 June 1968.

Nelson. The team for that first meeting was Tony Childs, Geoff Ambrose, Mick Handley, Stuart Riley, Derek Timms, Dai Evans and Dave Parry. The Highwaymen ran out easy winners by 50 points to 27. Mick Handley won the first race in a time of 74.6.

Handley had arrived on loan from the promotion's other team at First Division Wolverhampton and was to spend the season commuting between the two. During that season with Crayford, his class as a First Division man really showed and he finished the season with an average of 10.48. To a large extent he carried the team as the next highest scorer, Tony Childs, could only manage 7.68. The experienced Derek Timms was the third heat leader on 6.54. Timms retired towards the end of the season and his place was taken by Archie Wilkinson. In his first two matches he scored maximum points. With just one match to go, everyone wanted to see whether he could complete the season unbeaten. Unfortunately they had over a month to wait as on the date the final match was due to take place, the track was under three feet of water. When the match was eventually staged, Wilkinson could only manage a mere 10 points, being pushed back to 3rd in one race.

It was not a great season and they finished 6th in the League. But at least they could console themselves with the fact that they had come one place above their local rivals, Canterbury, who were also making their debut in league speedway. Unfortunately for the Highwaymen, however, they lost to Canterbury in the Cup by 37 points to 56. Handley was one of the strong favourites for the Division Two Riders' Championship but on the night he could only manage 4th place. Strangely enough the winner was Graham Plant, the son of the same Wilf Plant who had ridden at Crayford 33 years previously.

For the next season improvements were made to the track, following criticism that it was like 'taking a bike around the Belle Vue bobs with the tide in.' The track was taken back to its foundations prior to installing a new racing surface of grey quarry dust similar to the one used at Canterbury to replace the original silver sand and the bends were reshaped to give more sweeping angles. Following the floods, a new drainage system was installed. A new set of racing colours featuring three black pistols on a red background with white trimming was also introduced. Crayford's second season began without Handley, who was recalled to his parent club, Wolverhampton. After his debut in Highwaymen's colours at the end of the previous season, great things were expected of Archie Wilkinson and he did start off well, but a fall in mid-season resulting in a broken wrist seemed to affect his scoring on his return, though he still finished the season with an 8.56 average. The three heat leaders rode well for Crayford, with Ambrose scoring at just over 10 and Tony Childs at 8.24. There was good support from Chris Harrison, Mick Steel, Colin Clark and Tony Armstrong and the team moved up one place in the League to finish in 4th place and were only 1 point behind the runners-up, Reading. It was the only team in the League to boast a 100 per cent home record. As if all that wasn't enough for its second season it also broke the then British League record away winning score with a 54-22 defeat of Berwick. Unlike Handley the year before, Ambrose did live up to expectations and won the Division Two Riders' Championship at Hackney.

Before the start of the 1970 season, the track was once again remodelled and reduced from 300 to 270 yards, making it the shortest in the country. With Ambrose recalled to Wolverhampton, Crayford were hoping that captain Archie Wilkinson would move up to take over the number one spot. In his first ten matches he scored 100 points. In 44 rides he was unplaced just once. But then a stomach complaint put him out for the rest of the season while the doctors decided how to deal with it. This left Tony Childs as number one but with an average of 7.97. Behind him came new signing, George Devonport. With his never-give-up, full-action style, Devonport made himself very popular with the Crayford fans. The third heat leader, after Wilkinson had gone, was Derek Timms who had returned to help his old team out. Timms' average was 5.19,

Crayford's first team in 1968. From left to right: Stuart Riley, Dai Evans, Geoff Ambrose (captain on bike), Tony Childs, Mick Handley, Derek Timms, Tony Armstrong.

Mick Handley, Crayford's leading rider in its first season.

Geoff Ambrose, Crayford's leading rider in its second season, 1969.

reasonable for a second string, but nowhere near good enough for a heat leader. In fact with that average, he wouldn't even have made it to the number 8 place in the Eastbourne team! Without Wilkinson, the season was something of a disaster and the team slumped to 14th place in the League.

During the season there were rumours that Crayford would not return for the 1971 season. At the beginning of July, Parker and Bridgett announced that the meetings scheduled for 15 July, 5 August, 20 August and 16 September had all been cancelled and would be replaced with banger racing. Parker denied that this meant he was looking to end speedway at Crayford but it was well known that crowds at the London Road track were poor and that the promoters were having to pump in their own money to keep the team going. In a bid to overcome their financial difficulties, Parker advocated that in future, Division Two be run on regional lines. Although the BSPA turned down his proposal, Parker nevertheless committed Crayford to running the following season and even as late as February 1971 was planning the fixture list. The news of their withdrawal from the League didn't come until the very eve of the season, in March. In a statement to the press, Mike Parker said, 'We have relinquished our licence at Crayford ... As you know, the Crayford position on speedway was very questionable and we didn't try to hide the fact. We had to plough £2,000-£3,000 into the venture to keep it going last season. We waited until negotiations were completed on pay and then made our decision that Crayford would carry on. But I understand that the riders' pay-scale has still not been decided and I don't feel willing to blow further money on Crayford speedway. Therefore we have reluctantly decided not to operate this season.' Incidentally, the pay rise the Speedway Riders' Association was demanding was for an increase to £1 a start and £1 a point. Crayford became the first Second Division club to pull out of the League.

The London Road stadium continued to host greyhound and stock car racing. Towards the end of 1974 there were rumours that speedway might return to the track. Rayleigh had been forced to close at the end of the season and promoter, Len Silver, on behalf of Allied Presentations Ltd., was looking around for a suitable alternative site for the Rockets. One of the problems with Crayford however was that, of the 30-week summer season, stock cars wanted to run on 20 weeks, leaving just 10 for speedway. Following the local council's restrictions on the number of motor sport meetings that could be held at the stadium being lifted however, these difficulties were overcome and it was agreed that speedway could run every Tuesday night from April through until October. It meant that Silver could announce that Crayford would run in the New National League in 1975. Although, by this time, the Rayleigh team had moved on to Rye House, a number of riders under contract to Allied Presentations at Rye and Hackney formed the basis of the new team. Peter Thorogood was installed as the new promoter and Crayford were ready to go.

The team nickname was changed to the Kestrels and the colours changed to red, gold and black. Thorogood explained that, although he hadn't put the changes to a meeting of the Supporters' Club, the decision was not an arbitrary one. 'Great consideration was given to former Crayford followers, already equipped with red and black favours' he said and added, 'of the many letters received a vast proportion suggested Kestrels as the Crayford nickname.' In spite of Crayford having to close in 1971 because of poor crowds, Thorogood was optimistic about the return of speedway, 'The area has built up a lot and has developed a lot since Crayford closed down. Another factor is the regular race-night as we no longer have to share it with the stock cars.'

The track was reshaped yet again with each bend being altered and a new white line being laid down. The new track was even shorter than the old one, measuring just 265 yards. The former Rye House and Hackney team put together by Thorogood consisted of Laurie Etheridge, Pete Wigley, Trevor Barnwell, George Barclay and Les 'Red' Ott, with Bob Young joining later in the year. To this nucleus was added former West Ham and Ipswich rider, Alan Sage and later on Alan Johns, who arrived from Eastbourne. During his time with Crayford, Johns was to suffer the indignity of having

Laurie Etheridge, Crayford's inspirational captain from its return in 1975 until 1982.

to have special cleansing fluid treatment from the track doctor after an enormous piece of bubblegum exploded in his beard.

Right from the start of the season Etheridge proved to be an inspirational choice as captain. Not only was his own form excellent but his enthusiasm and experience encouraged the rest to give 100 per cent effort for the team. With Sage, Ott, Barnwell and Wigley all making a tremendous start to the season, the Kestrels rocketed to the top of the league and looked as though they might take the title in their first year back. Unfortunately, fate was not kind to the Kestrels, as first Ott broke his wrist and was out for the season and then Barnwell went out, first with a blood disease and then with a broken scaphoid. The loss of Ott and Barnwell upset the balance of the team and in the end it could only finish 8th in the League. A good comeback, but without the injuries it could have been even better. Etheridge topped the averages with 9.74, followed by Sage on 8.51. Wigley, who took over as third heat leader during Barnwell's absence, proved to be a real team man, as he turned in a magnificent total of 46 bonus points.

Etheridge's outstanding contribution to the rebirth of Crayford was rewarded when he won the New National League Riders' Championship at Wimbledon following a dramatic run-off with Glasgow's Brian Collins who fell at 30 yards.

As the season approached its close, Bexley Council asked Crayford to submit a new planning application for permission to stage speedway at the stadium on a permanent basis. It had received objections from local residents and although it appeared more sympathetic to speedway than Canterbury Council did, it nevertheless felt it needed to impose sound restrictions. Discussions continued until the following February when Bexley finally gave permission for speedway to continue at the London Road Stadium. 'Without doubt, the new silencer regulations swung the decision our way,' was Peter Thorogood's comment on the decision.

With Red Ott moving back to Hackney and Trevor Barnwell retiring, Thorogood looked round to find a rider to complement Etheridge, Sage and Wigley at the top of the Kestrels' order. He found him in forty-three-year-old Mike Broadbanks.

Alan Johns, who rode for Crayford from 1975 to 1980.

Pete Wigley in action. Unlucky with injuries, Wigley rode for Crayford between 1975 and 1978.

Broadbanks brought with him a wealth of experience including seven World Finals, over 40 international appearances and a riding record that stretched back to 1954 at Rye House, where, for seven years, he had also been responsible for running the training school. Once again, the season started very well for the Kestrels. The top four were in good form and they were joined by Alan Johns, who was having a better season than 1975. Once again, Crayford's chance of taking the title was hit by injury, this time to Wigley, who sustained a serious neck injury. Even so, the Kestrels improved on their 8th position, finishing in 6th place. Etheridge and Sage continued as the numbers one and two with 9.87 and 8.79 respectively, while Broadbanks weighed in with 7.33. At the New National League Riders' Championship, Laurie Etheridge became the first holder of the title to defend it. All the other winners had moved up to the First Division after their success. Unfortunately he did not have such a good time this year, managing just 6 points.

With Wigley retiring because of his injury and Broadbanks moving on at the end of the season, Thorogood signed up another experienced rider, someone even older than Broadbanks. Colin Gooddy had first set wheel on track back in 1951 when he had two practice rides at Aldershot. But once again it was to prove an inspired choice as Gooddy did even better than 'Broady', finishing the season with an average of 8.53. Two further signings were Garry May from Weymouth and Mike Bessent from Eastbourne. 1977, however, was not like the two previous seasons. Etheridge and Sage continued to score well and, with Gooddy, proved to be a formidable heat leader trio, but the support was not there. Johns scoring dropped to 5.47. Behind him John Hooper improved from 3.09 the previous year to 4.63 this year. His riding also improved. Never the most

Below: *Trevor Barnwell rode for Crayford from 1975 to 1976 and again from 1980 to 1982.* Right: *Paul Gilbert rode for Crayford in 1979 and 1980.*

The Crayford team in 1975, the year of its revival. From left to right, back row: Bill Archer, Alan Sage, Pete Wigley, Les (Red) Ott, George Barclay, Trevor Barnwell. On bike in front: Peter Thorogood (manager), Laurie Etheridge (captain).

delicate of riders, Hooper's all action-style started to show results but Crayford needed a good 6 or 7 point second string if they were to make any impression in the League and they just didn't have one this year. It meant a fall in the League to 10th place.

With yet another season in which he rode in every official fixture, Alan Sage broke the record for the number of consecutive appearances. He had now ridden for 7 years without missing any matches, 1 year for West Ham, 3 for Ipswich and now 3 for Crayford. In all, he had ridden in a total of 265 matches without missing any.

Towards the end of the season, the stadium owners, Ladbrokes, decided they wanted to run the speedway themselves and bought out Allied Presentations' promotion at the stadium. Their first move was to kit the team out with Ladbroke Leisure leathers and to introduce a series of special offers to attract more people to the stadium. Peter Thorogood agreed to stay on as speedway manager but the start of the 1978 season was not a happy baptism for Ladbrokes as Crayford lost 7 and drew 1 of its first 11 matches. Thorogood was not pleased with this start so he ordered the team to go to the training track at Iwade for an extensive training session.

The only real changes to the team had been the signing of Tony Featherstone to take the place of Colin Gooddy and the return of Pete Wigley in place of Mike Bessent. After the training session things did start to improve a little. Much of this was due to the fact that, unlike previous seasons when they had experienced injury problems, the Kestrels were able to track an unchanged team week after week. In fact, five members of the team, Etheridge, Sage, Johns, Hooper and Richard Davey appeared in every official fixture and Wigley missed only two. It was only when Featherstone injured his shoulder and missed seven matches that Crayford were able to experiment with their juniors. As before, Etheridge and Sage proved themselves to be very able heat leaders, but it was the lack of a third heat leader that once again ended their chances of moving up the League, which they finished in 10th place, exactly the same position as the previous year. Etheridge once again represented Crayford at the National League Riders' Championship and also appeared in 4 National League Test matches, 2 against Australasia, averaging 13.50 and 2 against Denmark, averaging 6.86.

An amazing event took place on 22 July 1979. For the first time since 1970, Alan Sage missed a match after breaking his leg while guesting for Canterbury. It brought to an end one of the most remarkable records in the history of speedway, a run of 327 consecutive appearances in official fixtures. It also finished off Crayford's chances of breaking out of that mid-table role to which it now seemed perennially doomed. It was doubly unfortunate because for once Crayford had found that third heat leader in Steve Naylor, signed up at the beginning of the season on loan from Eastbourne. In fact, not only had it found its third heat leader, but Naylor went straight in at number one replacing Etheridge who dropped to number three behind Sage. It had even found a useful top second string in Paul Woods, although there was very little support after that with Johns dropping to 4.57.

At the end of the season, Crayford finished in 12th place, a fall of two places from the last two seasons. With the arrival of Les Rumsey at Crayford to join Naylor, Woods, Sage and Etheridge for a fee of £6,000, things looked very promising for the Kestrels as the 1980 season got underway. Unfortunately their challenge for the league title never materialised but they did win the National League Four Team Championship, to bring

Steve Naylor signs for Crayford in 1979. From left to right, back row: Stan Wolfe (stadium manager), Johnny Hooper, Alan Johns, Pete Wigley, Laurie Etheridge, Alan Sage. Front row: Steve Naylor, Peter Thorogood.

them their first-ever title victory of any sort. There was also one outstanding moment in the League when they thrashed Workington by 65 points to 12. Every one of the Crayford seven was unbeaten as they scored 5 points in each race. Workington were so poor they couldn't even manage to provide two finishers in every race. The score was an all-time record for a match that was actually raced.

By their standards, both Etheridge and Sage had poor years, scoring 6.00 and 6.89 respectively and it was left to Woods, Naylor and Rumsey to make up the heat leader trio. Woods, in particular, had an incredible season, averaging 10.55 in league fixtures. The new line-up did mean a slight improvement for Crayford as they moved up the table to 9th place. Paul Woods was having a good year individually. He took the Silver Helmet from Mike Ferreira in September, successfully defended it against David Gagen in October and ended the year as holder. His luck however ran out in the National League Riders Championship Final. In the race against his chief rival for the title, Wayne Brown, the two clashed on the fourth bend resulting in a fall for Woods. The race was stopped and the referee, Stan Mellish, ordered a re-run without Woods. His announcement led to a chorus of disapproval from the crowd who thought that Brown had been in the wrong. To the cheers of the crowd, Woods threw his helmet on the track and refused to leave, but Mellish was unmoved and Wimbledon promoter, Cyril Maidment, had to persuade Woods to leave. Brown went on to win the Championship with Woods finishing in 4th place.

The worst thing about the season from the Crayford management's point of view however was the weather. They lost so many matches during the season that they were unable even to complete their fixtures. Several attempts were made to race against Weymouth but continual postponements prevented it from ever taking place. It was

Paul Woods rode for Crayford in 1979 and 1980.

probably this as much as anything that led to Ladbrokes giving up its experiment in running the speedway as well as everything else at its London Road Stadium and shortly after the end of the season, Thorogood was made redundant and the speedway rights put up for sale. Ironically, in spite of the poor weather and lack of real success for the team, Ladbroke's sale came at a time when attendances at London Road had risen by about 20 per cent. It was a time of uncertainty for the supporters but help was at hand, as, just four weeks after the sale notices went up, Kestrels' supporter and Kent-based businessman, Terry Russell, came to Crayford's rescue and bought the club. His first act was to reinstall Peter Thorogood as team manager.

The first problem the new management team faced was the loss of its top three riders as Eastbourne recalled Woods, Rye House bought Naylor off his parent club, Eastbourne and Rumsey left for Wolverhampton. To replace these three, Russell signed up Barry Thomas and first-season junior, Keith Pritchard. Thomas was, of course, a masterstroke. The ex-England international and former Hackney captain was a rider of real quality and a crowd pleasing entertainer with a never-give-up attitude to his racing. But, good as Thomas was, he couldn't cover for three heat leaders. Amazingly, after the first meeting, it looked as though National League debutant, Pritchard, might make it to heat-leader class as he had a sensational baptism, scoring a paid 10 points from 5 rides away at Canterbury. Unfortunately he was never to repeat this performance, though he did well enough for a first-year junior, finishing the season with an average of 4.15. It was left to old hands, Sage and Etheridge, to back Thomas up as the other two heat leaders, but, with averages of 7.88 and 6.90, it was not really what Crayford wanted. Thomas himself scored at just over 9. Amazingly, Sage was once again ever-present. Crayford's mid-table run continued as they finished 10th in the league.

At the end of the season, Peter Thorogood was sacked. Terry Russell issued a statement saying, 'Today I have reluctantly relieved Peter of his duties as team manager of Crayford and in wishing him well in the future may I thank him for his past efforts on behalf of Crayford ... Next season I will act as team manager in addition to being promoter ... I'm confident we can make Crayford into a more progressive and positive-thinking promotion. Looking at everything, I had to cut costs to bring myself within the budget I had set aside for 1982 and employing a team manager meant expenses we could ill afford.' Thorogood's response was, 'I am really sick and have no further comment to make at this time.'

Russell then set about making improvements to the track. He was very aware that Crayford had suffered more than its fair share of rained-off meetings and felt much of this was down to poor drainage at the track, so he spent a large amount of money installing a new electric pump to clear away water on the Tote bend. In spite of Russell's statement when sacking Thorogood, he then appointed George Barclay as team manager.

The team that started the 1982 season was basically the same one that had finished the 1981 season with the exception of Pritchard. Russell had taken a conscious decision that he wanted his own team and did not want riders on loan who would be trained up at Crayford and then, when they were good enough, would leave and go back to their parent clubs. What this meant though was that once again, Crayford went into battle with just one recognised heat leader in Barry Thomas and even his average was down this year to 8.75. Mike Spink improved enough to become the second heat leader, but his average was only 6.83 and, in any case, he was injured and missed several matches. His replacement was Trevor Banks, who rode in 10 matches and averaged 7.62. The third permanent heat leader was, once again, ever-present, Alan Sage. Etheridge was still battling gamely but his average was now down to 5.67. It was a very poor year for the Kestrels and, for once, they broke out of their mid-table position, but, unfortunately it was in the wrong direction as they dropped to 15th place out of 19 teams.

During the season, Russell brought off a sponsorship deal with McDonald's, who was making its first foray into speedway sponsorship. This deal led to the *Speedway Star* running the headline, 'There's a difference at McCrayford'. At the end of the season, Russell once again decided that he would take over as team manager, saying that he could not afford to keep Barclay on as a paid team manager, though he would continue

Opposite: *Alan Sage in full flow for Crayford. Sage rode for the Kestrels for nine years, being ever present in seven.*

Right: *A young Ben Howe riding on a special bike sponsored by McDonald's in 1982.*

to help train the juniors. In a statement, Russell said, 'I'm taking over and, although I know it won't be easy, it doesn't worry me.'

Team changes at the beginning of 1983 meant that for the first time since Crayford had reopened in 1975, Laurie Etheridge was not a member. Along with Mike Spink he said farewell to the club that he had done so much for and captained over the past eight seasons. In all he had turned out 293 times for the Kestrels scoring 2,533 points at an average of almost exactly 8 points per match. Into the team came Kevin Teager and, as for the rest, Russell just trusted to luck and hoped that some of his juniors would make the grade. His trust in his juniors was rewarded with some outstanding performances. While Thomas continued as number one man with a much improved average of 9.69, second heat leader place went to Paul Bosley, whose improvement over the year before was startling. He increased his average by well over two and a half points from 5.22 to 7.88. Unbelievably another of the juniors did even better as Andy Galvin increased his from 2.4 to a magnificent 6.7, over four points a match better. With Teager scoring at over 7 and Sage at over 6, this team that had been put together more in hope than anything else ended the season with a 100 per cent home record and won 6 matches away. They shot up the table to finish in 3rd place. It was Crayford's best ever position in the League. For good measure they also reached the final of the Supernational where they lost to League champions, Newcastle, 100-91 on aggregate.

Thomas also had a good year in the Silver Helmet. He won it from Berwick's Steve McDermott on 7 May and successfully defended it on 6 occasions before losing it to Scunthorpe's Julian Parr on 27 June. He regained the Helmet on 23 August by beating Glasgow's Jim McMillan, defended it successfully once and then lost it to Oxford's Nigel Sparshott on 1 September. Incredibly, he won it for a third time, beating Sparshott on

Crayford's team and supporters after winning the National League Four Team Championship in 1980. On the extreme right is a young Bryn Williams.

6 September and defended it twice before finally losing it to Boston's Steve Lomas on 25 September.

For the third year running, Alan Sage was ever-present again. He had been with Crayford since its return to league speedway. Out of those 9 seasons, he had been ever-present in 7 of them. In all he had ridden 315 times for the Kestrels out of a possible 347 matches.

Just over four weeks after the season ended, Russell announced that he would be closing Crayford and moving the team to Hackney. Doubts had arisen over the future of London Road Stadium and Russell had been told that a planning application had been put in for redevelopment. If it was approved it would have meant the stadium being pulled down in July 1984. Russell felt he had no option but to look round for a new home for the Kestrels. It was ironic that just as Crayford seemed to have found a winning team it was forced to close down.

The name Crayford did appear once more in 1985, as a testimonial was held at Arena Essex for the Kestrels' former faithful servant, Alan Sage. Arena Essex took on a team labelled Ex-Crayford which included Sage himself plus Paul Woods, Barry Thomas, Andy Galvin and Kevin Teager with George Barclay as the team manager. But there was to be no more speedway at London Road itself. The very last meeting had been the Supernational Final First Leg on 26 October 1983, narrowly won by Crayford 48-47. The Kestrels team on that night was, Barry Thomas, Paul Bosley, Alan Mogridge, Alan Sage, Trevor Banks, Andy Galvin and Kevin Teager. By winning heat 16, Paul Bosley wrote himself into the record books as the last rider ever to take the chequered flag at Crayford.

Top right: *Barry Thomas joined Crayford in 1981 and was their top scorer in their last three seasons, 1981 to 1983.*

Below left: *Peter Thorogood hands Newcastle's Tom Owen the Kentish Times Trophy for the 5th time. The trophy was only held from 1975 to 1979 with Owen winning it every time.*

Below right: *A young Ben Howe looks on in amusement as Crayford promoter, Terry Russell, suffers a dire fate at the hands of the riders at Crayford's last ever meeting at the end of the 1983 season.*

145

7
ROCHESTER & ROMFORD

From having no league teams in Kent in 1967, at the beginning of 1969 it looked as though there would be three. Canterbury and Crayford had already started in 1968 and now it seemed that Rochester would be joining them. When Weymouth folded up at the end of 1968, promoters Wally Mawdsley and Pete Lansdale looked round for a suitable spot to move their team to and they thought they'd found it at Rochester. There was great enthusiasm in the Medway town. The local papers, the *Chatham, Rochester and Gillingham Evening Post* and the *Kent Messenger* both gave over acres of space to the announcement that speedway was to be staged at the City Way Stadium and promised that they would give the team full coverage. In fact, speedway had been staged at the City Way Stadium in the 1930s with a dirt track being constructed there in 1931. Towards the end of that year, a few trial meetings were held and then in 1932 two open meetings took place. The first, on 1 August, featured the Chatham Scratch event, won by Lea Bridge's Alf Foulds. After just one more meeting on 9 August, speedway ceased at the stadium.

Due to speedway having been staged at the stadium before, Mawdsley and Lansdale were given to understand that they did not need to seek full planning permission, merely that they had to give official notification to the City Council that they intended to re-open the track. After discussions on this point however, it was decided that a full planning application should be submitted. They planned to construct a 340-yard track inside the greyhound circuit. While this was being done, Mawdsley and Lansdale, together with Maurice Morley, set about signing up riders to ride for the new team and in January 1969 they were able to announce their first signing, Barry Duke. Duke's signature was followed by Chris Yeatman and Tony George.

As an ex-RAF gunner, Lansdale suggested that the team should be known as the Bombers and a competition was held through the *Evening Post* to design the body colours. There were 23 entries for the competition. On 14 March, Mawdsley and Lansdale staged a demonstration race at the track for council officials. The race was won by Martyn Piddock from Reg Luckhurst, Judd Drew and Rob Stewart.

On 25 March, Rochester Council gave the go-ahead for Speedway Enterprises Ltd (Lansdale and Mawdsley's company) to promote speedway at the City Way Stadium for a one-year trial period. There were conditions attached to the approval, namely that effective silencers had to be fitted and that noise at a distance of 140 yards from the centre of the track must not rise above 65 decibels. Mawdsley and Lansdale were confident that these conditions could be met and that, although the decision had to be ratified by the Kent County Council, this was seen as a formality and work continued at the stadium.

At the beginning of April, the colours for the new team were finally chosen, the winning entry being the RAF roundel on a white background. And, on 17 April,

Lea Bridge's Alf Foulds rode at Rochester in 1932.

Rochester raced their first match, a British League Division Two match away at Ipswich. The team for that first night were Barry Duke, Phil Woodcock, Mick Steel, Tony George, Frank Wendon, Chris Yeatman and Charlie Benham. It was a great start for the Bombers as they won 42-36, Duke and Woodcock both scoring maximums. After one more away meeting at Long Eaton, which they again won, this time by the even bigger margin of 46 to 32 with another maximum from Barry Duke, the Rochester promotion were shocked to hear that Kent County Council had refused to ratify Rochester Town Council's recommendation that speedway be allowed at the City Way Stadium. Speedway Enterprises Ltd immediately submitted an appeal.

While the appeal process was taking place, Mawdsley thought it prudent to look round for another home for the Bombers. As it happened, the Speedway Enterprises office was situated in Romford and Mawdsley thought that maybe the football stadium at Brooklands, home of Romford Football Club, might fit the bill, so he went over to speak to the stadium owners. He immediately came to an agreement to stage speedway there and within nine days, Maurice Morley had laid down a track ready for the Bombers to move in to their new home. As a result of the pressure of time, no base had been laid, instead the top surface of turf and soil round the outside of the football pitch had been cut away and red shale and granite dust laid on top of what was left. The track length was 375 yards and part of the safety fence consisted of a concrete wall.

Interestingly this was not the first time that speedway had been proposed at Brooklands. In October 1961, the *Speedway Star* reported that a 'mystery man' with £10,000 backing had offered to promote speedway at the stadium. The secretary of the football club, Mr Herbert Muskett, said that the 'prospects of speedway racing here are virtually nil. A track would ruin the football pitch. We can never have both at Romford.' When it was pointed out to him by Dave Lanning that football and speedway ran at other stadiums without any problems, Mr Muskett replied, 'My board will improve this stadium when necessary.' The idea was subsequently dropped.

The Bombers had raced two more fixtures as Rochester before the opening night at Brooklands, on 29 May, which was a challenge match against Crewe. The team for that opening meeting was Ross Gilbertson, Frank Wendon, Tony George, Charlie Benham, Phil Woodcock, Chris Yeatman and Judd Drew. Barry Duke had moved on to First Division Swindon following his sensational start for the Bombers of 8 rides, 8 wins. The first race at the Brooklands Stadium resulted in a 5-1 win for the new Romford Bombers as Gilbertson and Wendon headed home Crewe's Dave Parry and Pete Saunders. The gate for that opening fixture was around the 3,000 mark. With Duke gone, team manager, Pete Lansdale, had looked round for a rider who could come somewhere near to his scoring power. With all the best riders already firmly in place with other teams, he turned to Ross Gilbertson and enticed him out of retirement. Gilbertson showed that he had lost nothing during his lay-off and returned to his winning ways immediately. He finished the season with a 10.10 average.

The start of the season proved to be sensational for the Bombers as, after just 6 matches, 5 of them away, they had already chalked up 4 wins. For a while it looked as though they could do the unthinkable and win the League Championship at their very first attempt. As so often happens however, they were struck with injuries as first Tony George and then Chris Yeatman both broke legs. Brian Foote was drafted into the team and then Ian Gills.

Romford's first team in 1969. From left to right: Tony George, Phil Woodcock, Judd Drew, Ross Gilbertson (captain on bike), Chris Yeatman, Frank Wendon, Charlie Benham.

The programme cover for Romford's first meeting on 29 May 1969.

Des Lukehurst had a phenomenal first season with Romford in 1969, averaging 11.52 in 11 matches.

The addition of Foote and Gills to Wendon and Benham gave Romford a very strong second string and reserves combination but what they were lacking was a third heat leader to go with Gilbertson and Woodcock. Brian Davies arrived from West Ham to take the third heat leader position, but he didn't save them from two home defeats at the hands of Rayleigh and Ipswich. The crowds were exceptionally good, averaging 5,000 per week, but Lansdale and Mawdsley were concerned that, after its bright start, the team was beginning to lose too many matches and that this could lead to a drop in support. Their next move, obtaining the signature of Des Lukehurst, turned out to be a masterstroke of massive proportions. Lukehurst rode for Romford for the first time on 3 September. That night Romford made British League history by becoming the first team to beat Belle Vue Colts on the latter's own track in the two years that Division Two had been running. The following night, in the return at Brooklands, the Bombers won again. From the time Lukehurst joined the side until the end of the season, Romford rode in 11 matches, of which it won 10 and drew 1. It was a tremendous end to the season which saw it finish in 3rd place in the league, equal on points to runners-up Reading but just behind on match points. Lukehurst's form was nothing short of phenomenal. Out of 42 races for the Bombers, he came first in 39 of them, second in 2 and unplaced in 1. His average at the end of the year was 11.52.

The supporters responded to Romford's late run of form by turning out in even bigger numbers. For the last meeting of the season, the Boro Individual Trophy, there was a record crowd, which was reckoned to be in the top ten of speedway attendances anywhere in the country that year. They saw a superb meeting too, as Crayford's Geoff Ambrose took the trophy, albeit after Des Lukehurst had been stretchered off and taken to hospital following a crash in his first race. Ambrose's strongest challenge came from Romford's own Phil Woodcock and Canterbury's Martyn Piddock. Ambrose and Piddock met in heat nineteen in what should have been the deciding heat but it proved to be anti-climactic as Piddock fell on the first bend. Many of the crowd felt that Ambrose should have been excluded for boring as he and Piddock came out of the first bend. It was a wheel-to-wheel incident where neither man was going to give way, but someone had to give and it proved to be Piddock. Overall, Woodcock finished runner-up with Piddock 3rd. Lukehurst had arrived too late to qualify for the Division Two Riders' Championship. This honour went to Gilbertson, who scored 13 points to finish in 3rd place.

Although the first year at Romford had been an undoubted success both in terms of results and crowd numbers, Speedway Enterprises nevertheless pressed on with its appeal at Rochester, hoping to be able to open the City Way Stadium in 1970. The hearing before a Ministry of Housing and Local Government official was eventually heard on 2 February 1970. After hearing from the promoters, Kent County Council, local residents and experts on both sides, the appeal was turned down. The official in

Phil Woodcock rode for Romford in all three seasons, 1969-71. He was top scorer in 1970.

Brian Davies rode for Romford in its inaugural season, 1969.

Kevin Holden in action at Brooklands in 1971. The concrete safety fence is clearly visible in the foreground.

his summing up said it had been a finely balanced decision which was 'a difficult one when it was clear that the public interest on both sides had to be taken into account.' He did acknowledge however, that 'Motor-cycle racing was progressively extending its crowd attraction…'

With the appeal at Rochester behind them, Mawdsley and Lansdale were able to concentrate on their Romford team, but then, in May, came another bombshell as a local householder, Mr William Stretch, went to court to serve an injunction on them in an attempt to prevent any further speedway racing at the stadium. While the judge considered the position he placed noise restrictions on the promotion including a total ban on music between races and sought an assurance that meetings would finish no later than 9.30 p.m. They were also ordered to erect a baffle wall at the rear of the terracing which backed on to Willow Street, the street in which Mr Stretch lived. Eventually, after further consideration, the judge agreed to allow speedway to continue as long as the conditions were met.

As for the team itself, Lukehurst and Davies left at the end of 1969 to be replaced by Geoff Penniket and Colin Sanders. They were also hoping for great things from novice rider, Kevin Holden. After just seven matches, Penniket decided it was time to move on which left the Bombers with only two recognised heat leaders in Gilbertson and Woodcock. The rest of the team, Foote, Sanders, Gills, Benham and Holden, gave strong support but without that third heat leader they were unable to hold on to their third spot in the league. It did make for exciting racing, with plenty of close results, such as the meeting on 9 July, when Romford went down at home by just two points, 38-40 to Eastbourne. The meeting was described as 'superb' and one that would 'fill speedway stadiums everywhere', but it did mean that Romford dropped to 8th place in the League. Lukehurst did return late in the year and once again scored well – not quite as prolifically as the year before, but by then it was too late anyway. Individually, Woodcock had a good season, topping the team's averages with 8.87 and taking the Silver Helmet on 9 April from Long Eaton's Malcolm Shakespeare. He defended it successfully against Workington's Lou Sansom before losing it to Mike Vernam at Reading on 27 April.

At the start of the 1971 season, even the two heat leaders Romford had had disappeared. Gilbertson retired again, though he was to be talked out of retirement by Johnnie Hoskins over at Canterbury and Woodcock decided, after two matches, it was time to go full-time in Division One. There were hopes that some of the juniors might make good, especially Holden, who had had a good first year in 1970, recording an average of 4.65. Hopes were fulfilled as Holden moved up from Romford reserve to become the number one heat leader with an average of 8.95. Behind him, Brian Foote also came good. He had had two average years with the Bombers, but in 1971, he moved up to record an 8.00 average. Once again though, there was no third heat leader and even the two they had were not on a par with Lukehurst, Gilbertson or Woodcock, so the team suffered. Bob Coles was brought in to try and improve their lot and in his

thirteen matches he did make a difference with his 8.06 average. Stan Stevens also came into the team towards the end of the season. As solid and reliable as ever, Stevens could have been a life-saver if he'd been signed up earlier. But, overall, it was not a good year for the Bombers as they dropped down to 12th place in the league, losing 4 matches at home and only picking up full points away from home once.

Then there was even worse news for Romford, as Mr Stretch had continued his one-man campaign against speedway being staged at Brooklands and on 30 April a judge agreed to his request for an injunction preventing speedway being staged at the stadium, though he agreed a stay of execution until the end of the season. The last meeting ever held at Brooklands, the first leg of the Essex Gold Cup against Rayleigh, took place on 30 September 1971. It was an emotional night on what had been one

Ian Gills was a regular for Romford in all three seasons.

Charlie Benham was the only Romford rider to ride in both its first and last matches.

of the best supported tracks in the whole of British speedway but the Bombers were unable to go out in a blaze of glory as they lost the match 41-36. Romford's last team was Kevin Holden, Charlie Benham, Brian Foote, Stan Stevens, Ian Gills, Ted Spittles and Ross Gilbertson, who had returned one last time to Brooklands as a guest for the injured Ian Gills.

The last race of the night was the second-half final of the Brooklands Farewell Trophy. It was won by Brian Foote in a time of 72.2 seconds. In the final night's programme, Mrs Grace Gower, secretary of the supporters' club said, 'The night that we would rather not have shared has arrived and we must say a sad farewell to Brooklands Stadium ... our one consolation is that we have seen three years of great speedway, made many good friends and shared the ups and downs of the greatest team in the country.'

At the end of three years racing, Romford boasted three riders who had stayed with the team throughout its short career, Charlie Benham, who appeared in 88 matches, and was the only rider to figure in both the first and last match, Brian Foote (80 matches) and Ian Gills (56 matches). Romford's top scorer of all time was Ross Gilbertson with 655 points, followed by Phil Woodcock on 600 and Foote on 522. Apart from Duke's two match average, giving him the perfect 12.00 average, Des Lukehurst's average of 10.14 was the best, with Gilbertson next on 9.3. Woodcock finished with 9.06. But it was Woodcock who had scored the most maximums for the Bombers with 12 full and 2 paid, just ahead of Gilbertson on 6 full and 7 paid.

The Romford Bombers had three more away meetings to race, coming second in a four-team tournament at Rayleigh on 3 October losing the second leg of the Essex Gold Cup at Rayleigh on 9 October, and losing a challenge match at Canterbury on 30 October. And then it really was all over. It is said that shortly after the end of the season, Mr Stretch moved away from the area.

8

IWADE & SITTINGBOURNE

The first mention of the possibility of speedway at Sittingbourne came at the end of 1969 when Bill Chesson, sports promoter at the successful Lydden motor-sport circuit in Kent, announced that he was seeking permission to develop a former brickyard at Sittingbourne into a multi-sport area. It was hoped that speedway might be included in this new development. But it wasn't until 1970 that Barry and Ivor Thomas actually opened a speedway track in the area at Marshbank Farm, Iwade. Originally a training circuit, it was built and operated by the Thomas brothers on the site of a Second World War gunnery school. They had to get a bulldozer to level off the ground, dig out a track and then put down chalk and brick dust. This didn't bed down too well, so they got some redstone dust, like they had at Canterbury, and put that on top. The track was originally 250 yards in length and used straw bales for a safety fence. On their opening day, just three hopefuls turned up, but the numbers soon increased.

The track was increased in size to 352 yards in March 1971. During this reconstruction it is said that 'Barry Thomas, in an effort to dry out the track, spread 85 gallons of used engine oil over the track, prior to setting fire to it.' (*Homes of British Speedway*, page 140). For

most of 1970, 1971 and 1972 the track was used purely for training purposes mostly by members of the Kent Youth Grass Track Racing Association and the Kent Youth Motor Cycle Club. The school operated on Sundays to fit in with Barry Thomas's racing schedule.

In February 1972, Barry Thomas said that he felt the school had been a success and that although, 'we've nothing like a Peter Collins, there are one or two lads coming along most Sundays who could certainly make a Division Two team place.' Nearby Canterbury Crusaders were interested in this training school on their doorstep and sent along scouts to watch the local talent. The first open meeting took place on 5 November 1972 when a training school championship was held. This was won by Paul Dowdall with Rocky Coutts second and Mick Camier third.

A photograph of the young Barry Thomas taken in 1970 at about the time he and his brother founded Iwade.

Homes of British Speedway also has this to say about conditions in the early days at the track, 'Visitors to the track had to stop at a bungalow by the entrance where the old lady who owned the land lived. All visitors had to shut the gate behind them in order to stop the chickens and goats from wandering into the main road.'

Iwade continued to hold training sessions and meetings throughout the winter months. It was hoped that team matches between Iwade juniors and trainees from other tracks could be arranged, but, in the winter of 1973, it ran into planning problems. Being only a practice circuit it was not licensed to run matches and a scheduled match against Poole juniors on 11 November had to be cancelled after the Control Board threatened to suspend any riders taking part. In its place the Thomas brothers ran a The Rest *v*. The Colts match. The most impressive juniors on show were Pip Austen, who scored 14 points from 5 rides, and Rocky Coutts, who scored a maximum 9 points from his 3 rides.

By late 1973, anything up to 35 hopefuls were turning up on Sunday to use the facilities on offer. When the track had first opened there were seldom more than six or seven. Training began at around midday and continued until it got dark. The normal agenda for the afternoon was 90 minutes of general training, followed by specialist training in areas such as starting and then finally proper race experience with either individual races or a match between two made up sides of juniors. Sometimes full individual meetings were held, such as the annual Eddie James Trophy which was won in 1973 by Rocky Coutts with a full 15-point maximum.

The 1975 Iwade team. From left to right, back row: Dave Ross, Paul Dowdall, Gary Keown, Ray Allen, Ivor Thomas (manager), Kevin Garcia. Front row: Roy Barwick, Paul Heller (captain, on bike), Alan Diprose.

To try and overcome the problem of licensing, the Thomases erected a proper board safety fence around the shale track. They hoped this would enable them to apply for and obtain a licence to run team matches as they felt the reason they had been unable to get one was down to insurance cover as Iwade had been unable to obtain any; all trainees had been made responsible for finding their own.

On 15 September 1974, a team of Iwade Juniors took on Mildenhall's Fen Tigers. This was in fact a return leg as the Fen Tigers had entertained Iwade at Mildenhall the week before. With Iwade winning 41-36 it was felt the return at Marshbank Farm would be a walk-over. Iwade's Paul Heller had scored a maximum at Mildenhall and he repeated the feat at Iwade. He was ably supported by Paul Dowdall who scored 9 points and established a new track record in his opening race of 69.0 seconds for the slightly reshaped circuit. He equalled the time in heat ten, but, in heat eleven, a fifteen-year-old Fen Tiger took a massive 1.5 seconds off that record. The name of the fifteen-year-old was Michael Lee. Far from having a walk-over, Iwade only just managed to hold off the Fen Tigers winning by the almost identical score of 41-37. Mildenhall's best riders were Paul Davey and Michael Lee, who scored paid 7 from his 3 rides.

With matches against other teams being introduced the facilities at the track were also improved. There was now a proper starting gate, a good pits area with changing facilities, a well-sited officials' box and natural banking for spectators. Sometimes, even refreshments were provided. Over the winter of 1974/5 an informal Training Track League was inaugurated between Iwade, Crewe and Mildenhall. Crewe was due to visit Iwade for a league match on 5 January but asked for a postponement following a 56-18

Andy Galvin, on the right, and his father, Chris, on the left, at Iwade in the early 1980s. Note the gun emplacement still standing in the background.

defeat at the hands of Mildenhall. Crewe's manager, Charlie Scarborough, felt that his team needed 'a little more time' before they would be ready to tackle Iwade.

Early in 1975, Peter Thorogood came to an arrangement with Iwade to enable the newly-revived Crayford to have first call on any promising juniors and to give them second-half rides. He also arranged for a regular Tuesday evening coach service from the Sittingbourne area so that supporters of the local juniors could visit Crayford. On 9 February, Iwade's Kentish Colts met Mildenhall again in the Training Track League. It was an extremely close run match which resulted in a narrow victory for the Fen Tigers by 39 points to 38. Iwade's captain and top rider, Paul Heller, suffered machine trouble all afternoon, as did two other up and coming juniors, Roy Barwick and Alan Diprose, while Paul Dowdall was involved in a nasty looking crash in heat eight and had to receive medical attention which left Ray Allen and Dave Ross as top scorers for Iwade. Top scorers for the Fen Tigers were Michael Lee and Kevin Jolly. In the return match at Mildenhall, Heller had a much better match, top scoring with 11 points. Unfortunately, the rest of the team didn't and they lost by 56 points to 21. Once again that man, Lee, top scored for the Fen Tigers, this time with a maximum 12 points. Following the match, Heller was offered a chance to join Coatbridge in the Second Division. During the 1975 season he raced 10 times for the Coatbridge Tigers, averaging 4.00. Paul Dowdall also had one outing for them as well as one for Wimbledon.

On 1 June a new refinement was added to the Marshbank Farm track when, for the first time, race starts were controlled from an electrically-operated gate. Until then they had been powered by clockwork and elastic. The new gate was donated by one of the track's supporters, the appropriately named Mr Tony Springate. Other work being carried out included improvements to the safety fence and better track grading thanks to new equipment purchased from Mildenhall as well as a new tractor. With Mildenhall having been accepted into the New National League, the Thomas brothers were beginning to think that this route could be a long-term possibility for Iwade.

The 1975/76 season started with a visit from Barry Thomas's Hackney team-mate and Polish international, Zenon Plech. For the new season, the Thomases had organised their own training league team competition to be raced for by four teams all drawn from Iwade's own trainees. The teams, called Reds, Yellows, Blacks and Whites, were captained by Pip Austin, Colin Clark, Dave Ross and Fred Stubberfield respectively. Ivor Thomas chose these four because, 'these, we feel, are the "hard" men who'll be able to get the best out of their teams.' Austin, formerly with Long Eaton, was returning to the track after an absence of just over a year, during which time he had been a regular visitor to Iwade, often acting as starter. During his year away from riding he had worked as an engineer and as a member of a troupe of clowns in his cousin's circus.

The new league was launched on 28 December when the Whites defeated the Reds 47-37 and the Blacks defeated the Yellows 44-39. Crayford junior, Roy Barwick, was the inspiration behind the Whites' success as he rode to a 12-point maximum. Best rider for the Reds was Ian Williams who scored 14 from 5 rides. For the Blacks, Graham Knowler lost his chance of a maximum when he fell in heat four, but other than that he remained unbeaten, while for the Yellows, it was their captain, Colin Clark who top scored with 8.

A 1984 view of Iwade showing its desolate setting. The rider is Jason Taylor.

Roy Barwick continued his run of good form at the next meeting when he unluckily missed out on another maximum because of an exclusion under the two-minute rule. Knowler, however, made up for his lapse in the first meeting by completing his maximum without mishap this time. One young rider who made his debut for the Yellows that afternoon was a fifteen-year-old schoolboy by the name of Brendan Shillito. His score of 9 points in his first-ever competitive match impressed everyone watching. He later went on to become a heat leader with Canterbury. Others to impress were John Douglas, Duane Kent, Dave Basson and Dave Cullen. The mini-league was so successful that the Thomas brothers decided to keep the track open during the summer both for training purposes and to continue running open meetings, the mini-league, matches against other tracks and individual meetings.

On 25 July, Iwade took on a team from Crewe and thrashed it by 53 points to 24. Iwade's top riders were Steve Davey and Dave Ross, both of whom scored full maximums, while reserve Duane Kent scored paid 9 from 3 rides. There was one moment of controversy in the match when Kevin Garcia was excluded for being lapped. This brought a strong complaint from the Speedway Riders' Association vice-chairman, George Barclay. 'I'm all for sticking to the rule', he said, 'but it made no difference to the match result and didn't affect Garcia's pay. He'd worked hard preparing his equipment and saw it as his duty to remount after falling to finish.'

Training Track League matches were stopped at Iwade at the end of 1976 as the Control Board announced that to compete, tracks would have to have an officially recognised Training Track Licence, something Iwade did not actually have. Specific requirements were laid down by the Control Board to meet minimum safety and insurance standards, including a full safety fence, and, on the occasion of races being staged, proper measures to ensure that a race can be stopped in the event of an accident. Ivor Thomas felt that with a little work, Iwade would meet these requirements as they had long had the provision of flag marshals situated at both bends and on the straight to display red flags on the instruction of the referee and the safety fence was almost continuous, the only gap being at the entrance to the pit area. Thomas said it would not take too much effort to build a wooden swing gate to complete the run. Consequently, the Thomases applied for the necessary licence. It was over a year before they heard that they had become the first officially-licensed training track operating under the auspices of the Speedway Control Board.

In the meantime, Barry and Ivor Thomas had been continuing to run mid-week individual tutorial sessions and 'open-to-all' Sunday sessions with regular competitions between the best of the trainees. One of these competitions, the Eddie James Trophy, was won in November 1977 by sixteen-year-old Nigel Sparshott, who had just been offered a contract by Crayford.

Iwade continued under the control of Barry and Ivor Thomas for the next seven years, with the same diet of training, open meetings, inter-track matches and matches between four teams of their own trainees. During that time they threw up a number of riders who were subsequently to make a name for themselves. For example, the four teams in the 1983 season, which had by then changed their names to Mustangs, Shires, Stallions and Colts included Chris Mulverhill and Ray Morton for the Mustangs, Paul Whittaker and Mark Fordham for the Shires, Terry Mussett and Paul Tillman for the

The programme cover from Iwade's first attempted season as a league team in 1994. This is for the first match of the season, a challenge match against Middlesbrough on 2 May.

Stallions and Mark Loram and Paul Muchene for the Colts. Andy Galvin was another to get some of his early experience at Iwade, though he unfortunately broke his ankle there in 1982. But this did not deter the Galvin family as in 1984, his father Chris, together with Terry Waller, took over the track and continued the good work started by the Thomases.

In 1987 Terry Whiberley took over the promotion of the track with Eddie James as general manager. Early in 1988 they took on Eastbourne in a junior-team match. The *Speedway Star* reported that 'Eastbourne's team will include the highly-rated Joseph Screen. He will ride in place of David Norris.' Both Screen and Norris were sixteen-year-old novices, who had yet to make their league debuts.

At the end of 1988, Iwade applied for a licence to run in the National Junior League. Dick Bracher, the Control Board manager visited the track and saw a demonstration race between the fourteen-year-old Justin Elkins and the twenty-year-old Steve Brady. Bracher was very impressed with both the facilities and the demonstration race. As well as obtaining a Control Board licence, there was another obstacle to overcome before they could join the league. Alan Hodder, the National League's Director of Operations, said that the riders Iwade would be permitted to use did not have to be under contract but, if they were signed on, it would have to be to an existing promoter. To obtain an open licence so that they could sign on their own riders, James felt that they would have to do more work on the track making it a bit wider on the straights. In the end, they were unable to obtain the necessary licence and had to continue as a training track only.

Kevin Teager on the outside takes on Linlithgow's Stuart Coleman in a 1994 challenge match.

This view from Sittingbourne's first Academy League match on 7 May 1995 shows the Crusaders' Kevin Teager leading from Kevin Little of Berwick with Sittingbourne's Daniel O'Brien in third place.

At the beginning of 1990, James said that he hadn't ruled out the possibility of introducing junior league racing on a regular basis at Iwade and the Speedway Control Board carried out another inspection with a view to granting the necessary licence. James had arranged for a friendly against a Cradley Junior Select. This was held in February and resulted in a thumping win for Iwade by 61 points to 34. Justin Elkins and Ben Howe starred for the Colts, both scoring 15-point maximums. Once again however, Iwade were unable to take part in the Junior League. The next serious attempt to get into league racing came at the beginning of 1993. The BSPA had agreed to start a Third Division in 1994 and were looking for applications from interested tracks. James invited Tim Swales, the chairman of the BSPA, to have a look at the track. Swales told James he was very impressed with the facilities.

The 1993 season started with the Nunhead Spring Trophy, which was won by Jason Green from David Mason and Dean Chapman. This was followed by the annual Eddie James Trophy, won this year by Nathan Gaymer. Once again, Mason had to be content with the runner-up spot, with Mark Smith coming 3rd and Dean Garrod 4th.

At the beginning of 1994 there was tragedy at Iwade when, in January, twenty-year-old Karl Nicholls was killed in a crash. The track closed for a week as a mark of respect. James said that it was 'a tragic loss and all at Iwade send their condolences to his family and friends.'

In spite of the tragedy, James said that Iwade were still pressing ahead with their plans to join the proposed Third Division, 'That's our goal, and prospective team members are welcome to attend this Sunday or any weekend.' Preparations continued throughout the year, with the track being lengthened from 270 metres to 322 metres, and, at the beginning of 1994, the track was accepted by the BSPA and was ready to appear in the newly-formed Division Three. Kevin Teager was appointed captain and coach and then, after 24 years of operation, Iwade opened on 2 May for the first time as a fully-fledged league team. The opening fixture was a friendly against Middlesborough. An estimated 1,100 spectators saw their team win by 58 points to 17. The Iwade team, now known as the Kent Crusaders, was Kevin Teager, the captain, who scored a 12-point maximum, Scott Swain, who scored a paid maximum, Mark Fordham, J. Green, David Mason, Dean Chapman and Nathan Gaymer, who scored 9 paid points from three races. The season continued with a series of challenge matches. Teager and Swain continued their magnificent form in these early matches.

There was a delay in starting the new Third Division and by July, Eddie James was beginning to wonder what had happened to it. He said he was not prepared to go on holding an indefinite number of challenge matches. 'We have already staged a series of challenge matches,' he explained, 'and are as ready as we'll ever be for league action. We feel sure that this is what the supporters want too, and we are given to understand that an announcement regarding the launch of the Third Division is expected within a fortnight.'

The announcement finally came as promised within the next two weeks and Iwade's first-ever league match was away at Stoke. Before the Crusaders had a chance to race the match however, Terry Whiberley made it known that, for personal reasons, he was putting the club up for sale. The historic league match with Stoke took place on 30 July and resulted in a hammering for the Crusaders by 50 points to 27. Kevin Teager was once again the top scorer with 9 points but he had very little support from the rest of the team which was Mark Fordham, Nathan Gaymer, David Mason, Dean Chapman, J. Green and Keith Yorke. Following this match, Iwade withdrew from the League. The clerk of the course at Iwade, Graham Arnold, had hoped to put together a rescue package to keep the team going but was unable to do so.

At the end of 1994 there was better news for the team's supporters as Arnold at last managed to get together a local consortium, which included David Mason's father Peter, to rescue the Crusaders and the track was back in business as a training track on 20 November. Arnold and Mason were named as the new promoters and their first major decision was to change the name of the team to Sittingbourne. Their reasons for doing so were set out in a press release, 'We felt that the time was right for a change and we are sure it will help to generate even more publicity for the return of the sport to Kent. We obviously hope to be part of Division Three, or whatever it will be called next season.' In fact, the league was renamed the Academy League and Sittingbourne's application to take part in 1995 was accepted.

The Crusaders second attempt at league racing began on 7 May 1995 with a home match against Berwick. Unfortunately, Berwick did their best to wreck the party atmosphere at the Marshbank Farm track by running out winners 56-39. Teager was once again the star for Sittingbourne, scoring 17 points from 6 rides. He was well supported by Mason, who scored 11 paid 12. The rest of the team, which was managed by former Canterbury, Rye House and Hackney rider, Ted Hubbard, was Dean Chapman, John Jefferies, Ben Osborn, Daniel O'Brien and Nick Upton. Although this was a disappointing beginning, the next home league match raised the team's spirits as they overcame Devon 61-35 with no less than three Crusaders, Teager, Mason and Jefferies, scoring maximums.

The season progressed reasonably well for Sittingbourne and they did not lose another home match all season. They lost Upton after just five matches through injury and Jefferies was not always able to turn out because of other commitments. Being a training track, Iwade used the opportunities presented by missing riders to give other youngsters a chance. Probably the highlight of the season came with the 49-47 victory over Stoke. Stoke had arrived at Marshbank Farm with a team of mostly experienced riders. This did not sit well with Sittingbourne's philosophy of what the Academy League was all about and, in fact, they had just called in sixteen-year-old Bobby Eldridge to replace the injured Upton. The win gave Arnold and Mason great satisfaction, especially as Eldridge scored paid 10 points from 5 rides on his debut. Although they were winning at home they were having difficulty picking up points away from home and a mid-table position always looked likely. In fact, the team finished 4th out of 7, exactly half way. As the only old hand, Teager performed exceptionally well, setting a good example to the youngsters with a final average of 10.63. Mason finished with 9.35 and Jefferies with 7.57. Eldridge, in his first league season, scored 4.87. Towards the end of

The 1995 Sittingbourne fours team. From left to right, back row: Darren Andrews, Graham Arnold (promoter), Daniel O'Brien. Front row: Nick Upton, Kevin Teager, David Mason.

the season, another sixteen-year-old, Paul Lydes-Uings, was drafted into the team. In only four matches he managed to average 6.35.

The season ended with the Nathan Gaymer Memorial Trophy won by Tommy Palmer. Gaymer, who had been a member of the abortive 1994 team, had been killed in a road crash before the 1995 season started. Sittingbourne was back in league action in 1996 in the Conference League, the third change of name in as many years for the Third Division. The only riders to continue from the 1995 team were Mason and Chapman, the rest had all found team places elsewhere or, in Jefferies' case, had decided to concentrate on grass tracking. The departures left the Crusaders waiting for a time when they would be able to put out a competitive side. That time never came and Sittingbourne finished rock bottom of the league, having won only 1 match all season. A total of 21 riders were tried in just 18 matches.

Mason was by far and away the best rider in the team. His end of year average was an amazing 11.38. He won 68 out of a total of 77 races and came last just once. The second best average was Chapman's with 5.68. The third heat leader, Mark Czyz, managed just 5.37. A couple of youngsters came and went for a few matches with better scores, Bobby Eldridge for example, who averaged 6.25 from three matches, Simon Wolstenholme, 8.80 from two and Keith Yorke, 7.20 from two, but none of them were there long enough to save the team.

At the end of the season, a local resident objected to proposals by the club to build a smaller training track at Marshbank Farm. The club had been operating on temporary planning permission but this did not extend to building a new track. Arnold said that he wanted a lease on the track rather than renting and that they couldn't get that unless they had full planning permission. Arnold also revealed that the club was having financial problems, not because of the attendances, but because there had been a series of break-ins at the club. It all made participation in the league in 1997 seem very doubtful. Arnold was also very unhappy about the number of experienced riders being allowed in the Conference League as he saw it mainly as a training league for young-sters. In the end, he decided not to enter Sittingbourne into the league and the track returned to a diet of training and open meetings for juniors including the Under-16 Championship, won in 1997 by David Howe and in 1999 by Chris Harris. The last meeting under the aegis of proper league racing to take place at Iwade/Sittingbourne was the Nathan Gaymer Memorial Fours which took place on 13 October 1996 when Sittingbourne took on the victors, Peterborough, Eastbourne and Reading.

There was one further twist to the Sittingbourne saga in 2001 when Terry Russell applied for planning permission to stage speedway at the town's Central Park Stadium. His intention was to enter the team in the Elite League, but the local council turned down planning permission.

9

ARENA ESSEX

Since the closure of Rayleigh at the end of the 1973 season, Essex had been without a speedway track. One man who wanted to put this right was Peter Thorogood. In 1983 he was working for Wally Mawdsley at Canterbury, acting as team manager on away trips. Mawdsley suggested to Thorogood that he might like to have a look at a stock-car circuit called Arena Essex situated near Purfleet in Essex. As it happened, Thorogood knew the owner of Arena Essex, Chick Woodroffe, from his days as manager at Crayford, as Woodroffe had run the stock cars there. He had once said to Thorogood that if he was ever looking for another speedway track he would be able to get one inside the stock-car track at Arena. Woodroffe had in fact made a few brief appearances himself on the speedway track in West Ham second halves just after the war.

Following discussions between Mawdsley, Thorogood and Woodroffe it was all agreed and Arena Essex applied to join the National League with Mawdsley and Woodroffe as joint promoters and Thorogood as team manager. At first Terry Russell objected, as he thought this new track would affect attendances at Crayford. Crayford however was just about to close and when he moved the Kestrels to Hackney, he withdrew his objection and the National League accepted its newest member with open arms. Arena Essex was, in fact, the first new speedway track to open in six years. Following this the Arena Essex management signed up a sponsorship deal with Essex Radio.

One of the first decisions taken was to call the new team the Hammers and to have body colours of white crossed hammers on a red and blue background, reminiscent of the old West Ham team. The West Ham theme was carried on in the first night programme which reproduced photographs of several old-time West Ham favourites, including Bluey Wilkinson, Jack Young, Aub Lawson and Ken McKinlay. A more controversial decision which followed was the one to dispense with a safety fence. As the 253-metre track was inside the stock-car circuit it was hoped that the width of that would act as a sufficient barrier. The outside line was therefore marked by white flags and the outside post of the starting gate had to be taken down and carried to the centre green during the first lap of every race. The fact there was no fence around the circuit led to a number of exclusions for riders leaving the track.

The first meeting at the new circuit, the Essex Radio Championship, was held on 5 April 1984. The winner was small-track specialist, Bob Garrad, who beat Alan Sage in a run-off after both had scored 14 points. The first rider to win a race was Sage, who won the first heat in 61.5 seconds, which remained the fastest time of the night. The crowd was estimated at between 2,500 and 3,000. While all the preparations for the first meeting were going on, Thorogood had had to put together a team from scratch. His first signing was Alan Sage from the defunct Crayford outfit. Laurie Etheridge signed but

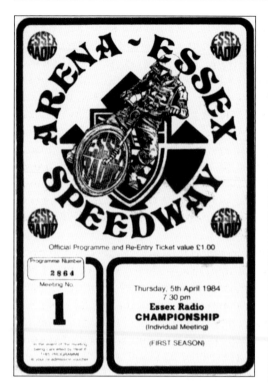

Above: *The programme cover from the first meeting at Arena Essex on 5 April 1984.* Right: *David Smart rode for Arena Essex from 1984 to 1986.*

then thought better of it. Bob Humphreys was persuaded to come out of retirement. These two were supported by Martin Goodwin, David Smart, Peter Johns, Jeremy Luckhurst and Kevin Price.

Kevin Price was injured before the league season even got started and was replaced by the Australian, Bill Barrett. The Hammers made a poor start to the season losing their first two home matches but things started to look up when they defeated Peterborough in the Knock Out Cup on 26 April. From then on the team did reasonably well at home, but was unable to pick up any away wins. A bad patch at the end of June and beginning of July when it lost two home matches and drew one convinced Thorogood that he needed to sign up another rider and he found what he was looking for when another Australian, Dave Cheshire, agreed to join the team. Cheshire scored 8 points on his debut on 2 August as the Hammers recorded their biggest win of the season, 51-27 over Berwick. Cheshire's addition bolstered the middle order and even led to one away victory, again at the expense of poor old Berwick and one away draw at Glasgow. It wasn't a great season by any means as Arena Essex finished the League in 14th place – Berwick incidentally finished 5th and reached the final of the Knock Out Cup – but Arena Essex had definitely established itself and was drawing in large crowds.

The Hammers' real problem in their opening season was the lack of a top-class heat leader. Bob Humphreys was top of the averages with 7.189, fractionally ahead of Alan

Sage on 7.188. Third was Martin Goodwin on 7.104. Thorogood got the man he was looking for just as the 1985 season was about to start when Neil Middleditch signed from the defunct Poole Pirates British League team. With Humphreys, Sage, Goodwin, Smart and Cheshire all staying on, hopes were high that the Hammers would improve on their 1984 position. Junior, Ian Humphreys, was promoted into the team, but he did not have a happy time and was dropped in favour of another youngster, Gary Chessell.

With Middleditch as the outstanding number one, Arena Essex's fortunes picked up and they finished the league in a healthy sixth place which could have been even higher had they not been defeated by a single point, 39-38, in their opening fixture to Middlesborough and then lost one more match at home to Canterbury by just two points, 38-40. Middleditch's final average was a healthy 9.47. Goodwin and Humphreys were the other two heat leaders. Cheshire showed a good improvement, up from just over 5.5 to almost 7.

It was a good year individually for Middleditch and Goodwin. Middleditch romped home in the National League Riders' Championship Final. The night of the Championship was a triumph for Arena Essex in other ways as well. Kate Woods, Miss Arena Essex, won the National League beauty competition, while the Arena supporters' coach picked up the best-decorated coach award! Middleditch also won the Silver Helmet during the season, beating Hackney's Alan Mogridge on 30 August. Goodwin won the inaugural National League Grand Slam at Peterborough on 20 July beating Andy Galvin into second place with Middleditch taking the bronze.

A view in the pits before the start of the first race in the match against Long Eaton on 9 August 1984. The Arena Essex riders are Alan Sage and Dave Smart, the Long Eaton rider is Paul Stead. The Hammers' manager, Peter Thorogood is talking to Alan Sage.

1985 was Alan Sage's testimonial year and, as already mentioned in the Crayford chapter, a special testimonial meeting was held on 3 November. It will come as no surprise to learn that during his two years with Arena Essex, Sage had once again raced in every single official fixture. In his 15 years in speedway, he had been an ever-present for his team in 13 of them.

At the end of 1985 Mawdsley left Arena Essex, leaving Woodroffe in charge, with Thorogood stepping up to become advisory non-executive co-promoter. Of the riders, Alan Sage left to become an ever-present with Canterbury, extending his record to 14 out of 16 years. Cheshire also left, to join Birmingham. To replace them, Thorogood brought off a real coup when he signed the league's hottest prospect, Andrew Silver, from Rye House for a reported £9,000. The Hammers now had three top-class heat leaders in Middleditch, Goodwin and Silver with strong second-string support from David Smart. Unfortunately, Smart was unable to start the season and his absence really exposed the lack of back up to the top three. Nevertheless, it was a much better season for the Hammers as Andrew Silver fully lived up to his potential by averaging 10.40 and Middleditch's average was slightly up on the previous year to 9.56. Goodwin's was also up to 8.87. Arena Essex finished in its highest position so far, coming 4th. It also had a good cup run. In reaching the semi-finals, it had maintained an unbeaten record, home and away. But Mildenhall proved just too strong for the Hammers, running out winners 79-77.

Andrew Silver represented Arena Essex in the National League Riders' Championship, finishing 5th. He also reached the British Final of the World

Championship and won the Silver Helmet from Edinburgh's Les Collins and successfully defended it once against Canterbury's Mike Spink.

When Middleditch and Smart left before the start of the 1987 season, Arena Essex supporters' feared the worst. Their places were taken by Nigel Leaver and Steve Bishop. Mark Chessell was also brought in to boost the lower end. Unfortunately, the supporters' fears proved to be only too realistic as the team lost home match after home match. In all, it was defeated 7 times at home and drew 1. Silver and Goodwin maintained their form, in fact both of them even improved on their 1986 averages with 10.66 and 8.91 respectively, but Leaver proved to be no

Andrew Silver rode for Arena Essex in 1986 and 1987, scoring over 10 points per match both seasons.

Martin Goodwin rode for Arena Essex from 1984 to 1990 and returned as team manager in 2000.

Middleditch and, as third heat leader, could only manage 6.76. Gary Chessell certainly did the job that was asked of him and was only just behind Leaver, but after that the tail was far too long. The result was that Arena Essex dropped from their best ever 4th place to 12th in the League. For the second year running, Arena Essex reached the semi-final of the Cup, only to go out to Mildenhall again.

The season was saved from being a complete disaster by the incredible form of Andrew Silver. Top of the National League averages, he put on a magnificent performance in the National League Riders' Championship Final, taking the title with a faultless 15-point maximum. He also reached the World Championship British Final for the second year in succession, scoring 9 points to qualify for the Overseas Final. Towards the end of the season, he lowered World Champion Hans Nielsen's Arena Essex track record by 0.4 seconds to 57.6. One week later he knocked a further 0.2 off that.

There was, of course, not the slightest chance that Silver would stay in the National League in 1988 and sure enough he left for Swindon. With the two Chessells and Steve Bishop also moving on, it left the Hammers with a lot of team building to do. As part of the deal which took Silver to Swindon on loan, David Smart rejoined Arena Essex and then Chris Cobby joined from Edinburgh. This still left the Hammers under the minimum 38-point limit however, and it was only on the very eve of the season that Thorogood finally got his last man in Rob Tilbury. It was a bit of a surprise choice as Tilbury had not exactly endeared himself to the home fans on previous visits with Canterbury because of his robust style of riding. He had even been involved in a fight with both Gary and Mark Chessell following one race the previous season. Goodwin was moved to the number one spot and juniors Simon Wolstenholme and Ian Humphreys were given their chance in the team. It did not look a great team on paper, and there was a more than a hint of blind faith about it, especially that the juniors would be able to make big strides during the season.

One thing that did turn out in the Hammers' favour was the fact that the septet were able to stay together for all but three matches. Tilbury, Leaver, Cobby, Humphreys and

Malcolm Simmons only rode in 16 matches for Arena Essex in 1989 before he was injured. His later non-appearance was steeped in controversy.

Wolstenholme were all ever-presents, while Goodwin missed just one match and Smart two. Humphreys and Wolstenholme did all that was expected of them, both recording averages of over 4.5, while Goodwin rose to the challenge of being the new number one at Purfleet with great relish, finishing the season with a 9.68 average. During the year he even broke Silver's track record, recording a time of 57.2. The problem for the Hammers was that Goodwin had no real heat-leader support, the rest of the team recording averages between 5 and 7. It all resulted in a mid-table spot as Arena Essex finished 9th in a league of 16 teams. One bit of good to come out of the season was that Tilbury won the hearts of the fans.

A number of changes took place at Purfleet that year including a change of race night from Thursday to Saturday which resulted in an increase in crowd numbers, and a change of announcer from Dave Lanning to Bob Miller. 1988 was an interesting year for the number of young faces the Arena Essex crowd saw that year. The traditional opening night fixture, the Essex Radio Championship, was won by the seventeen-year-old Mark Loram, while in the second half of the match against Eastbourne, the Eagles brought along some of their juniors for a demonstration. These Eaglets included an eleven-year-old David Mason, a thirteen-year-old Ben Howe and a nine-year-old Lee Richardson!

Towards the end of 1988, Woodroffe announced that, owing to ill health, he wished to relinquish the day-to-day running of speedway at Arena Essex and wanted a new promoter to take over. With no-one immediately forthcoming, however, Woodroffe agreed to continue for another season rather than see Arena Essex close.

1989 was to prove to be the year of Malcolm Simmons, initially for the right reasons, but towards the end of the season for all the wrong reasons. The close season was not a happy time for the Hammers as they lost three of their top five riders in Smart, Leaver and Cobby. Wayne Garratt came in on loan from Cradley as did Troy Pratt, but right up until March 1989, Thorogood had no-one to take Smart's place as heat leader. Then, literally just days before the season started, he pulled a rabbit out of the hat, announcing that he had talked the forty-three-year-old former world number two, Malcolm Simmons, out of retirement. The last time Simmo had worn crossed hammers was as a member of the West Ham team, a quarter of a century earlier.

At first, Simmons was a great success, linking up with Goodwin and a much-improved Tilbury to become a formidable heat leader trio. With strong backing from Garratt and a much improved Wolstenholme they had, by the start of July, taken Arena Essex to the top of the League. By then, however, Simmons had ridden his last race for the Hammers. He had injured his ankle when kick-starting a trials bike before the Arena Essex-Hackney Lomex Cup tie on 29 June. It appeared to be a very minor injury and Simmons was expected back every week. For Hammers' supporters, the situation became very exasperating. Every week Thorogood had to make a different excuse for his absence and there were a number of occasions when the rider himself said he would turn up and then didn't. As if the situation with Simmons wasn't bad enough, Goodwin and Tilbury also missed a number of meetings through injury and the brunt of the scoring fell on Garratt, Pratt and Wolstenholme. The final straw was when Garratt broke his shoulder and also missed a number of matches.

The Hammers' season turned into a shambles. From having been top of the League they nose-dived down the League as nothing went right for them. This was forcibly illustrated when Long Eaton managed to take the match points away from Purfleet even though Arena Essex had won the match 49-46. Long Eaton had ridden the match under protest because Arena Essex had used rider replacement for Simmons without declaring his medical certificate. At the subsequent hearing, Long Eaton were vindi-

Andy Galvin rode for the Hammers in the early to mid-1990s, making a comeback in 2001.

With the exception of just two years, 1995 and 1996, Troy Pratt rode for Arena Essex from 1989 to 2001.

171

cated as neither the Hammers nor Simmons were able to produce the certificate. The victory on track turned to a 51-43 win for the Invaders as all rider replacement points were expunged from the record. Arena Essex finished the season in 12th place. Thorogood immediately announced that Simmons would not be in the Hammers line-up in 1990. 'I think you can just forget about Malcolm riding for Arena Essex next year,' he said, 'the supporters just would not accept it. It was embarrassing enough for me to tell the fans every week that I didn't know what was happening. They always gave me the bird, and most weeks someone used to shout out, "Simmo's still in the Dartford Tunnel."'

In spite of expressions of discontent over the close season from Goodwin, Tilbury and Wolstenholme, all three signed up for the 1990 season. Simmons, of course had gone and Humphreys also left. In their places, Thorogood signed up Adrian Stevens from King's Lynn and Kevin Brice. It was hoped that Stevens could provide the third heat leader support to Goodwin and Tilbury, but, in the end, no-one provided that support. Stevens could only manage a disappointing average of 4.48. Third best rider in the team was Garratt with an average of 5.77. When Goodwin suffered serious injuries during a World Championship round at Cradley, and missed twelve meetings, they were down to just one heat leader. Rider replacement proved useless. It was another poor year for the Hammers as they slipped to 14th place in the League.

By the end of the season, Woodroffe's ill health had become too much for him to carry on and, in an announcement at the penultimate meeting of the season, the Supernational Marathon, he said that he was putting the club up for sale for £70,000. He made it clear that if no buyer could be found for the club then 1990 would prove to be its last season.

Arena Essex was saved on 31 January 1991, when former Crayford and Hackney promoter, Terry Russell, stepped in, and with his partner, Ivan Henry, bought the promoting rights at the Purfleet track. Peter Thorogood stayed on as speedway manager. 1991 was also the year of the amalgamation of the leagues as the British Leagues Division One and Two came into existence with promotion and relegation between the two. Russell looked forward to the challenge of his new club in a new league with relish. 'We're not here to make up the numbers,' he said, 'our aim is to win the league and gain promotion at the first time of asking.'

His first act was to install a safety fence round the outside of the track. After that he set about building up his promotion-winning team. Andy Galvin was the first to arrive at Purfleet to be followed shortly afterwards by Bo Petersen; both had been big stars at Hackney and great things were expected of them. Next new signing was schoolboy, Paul Hurry. Another former Hackney rider in the form of Alan Mogridge was next and then Jan Pedersen. Of the failed 1990 team, only Troy Pratt retained his place. The new era at Arena Essex opened on 29 March with a thrilling 45-44 win over Rye House in front of a 3,000 plus crowd.

Petersen and Mogridge proved themselves to be excellent heat leaders, but Galvin did not quite live up to hopes and in mid-June he was rested for a while. At this point, Russell and Henry pulled off the coup of the season when they signed up Brian Karger. His made his debut away against Peterborough in the Knock Out Cup and scored 10 points. In the return leg the next night, he scored a maximum. Karger never looked

Below: *Bo Petersen rode for Arena Essex from 1991 to 1993.* **Right:** *Jan Pedersen rode for Arena Essex on and off from 1994 to 2000.*

back. At the beginning of July, Arena Essex went on a northern tour, coming away with maximum points from 3 wins over Glasgow, Middlesborough and Edinburgh. Karger and Petersen dropped just 6 points between them in thirty races.

On 21 July, Arena Essex picked up its first team trophy when it won the BSPA Fours at Peterborough with maximums from Petersen and Karger. In the League and Cup, Arena Essex stormed to victory after victory. Between 29 June and 26 August, the Hammers raced in 17 matches and won them all. One loss at Eastbourne on 30 August was followed by 6 further wins, including one amazing 46-44 victory at Exeter after they'd been down by 27 points to 9. The great night came on 12 September when Arena Essex beat Stoke by 60 points to 30. Although there were still three league matches to race, it was the victory over Stoke that finally assured the Hammers of the League Championship and with it promotion to Division One thus becoming the first club in speedway history to be automatically promoted.

Arena Essex's season was far from finished however. On 18 September the Hammers beat First Division Coventry by 48 points to 42 in the BSPA Cup in one of the greatest matches ever seen at the Arena Essex Raceway. Arena's heroes that night were Alan Mogridge and Brian Karger, both with 11 points. And as if all that wasn't enough, the Hammers went on to clinch the League and Cup double by defeating Glasgow after a draw in the first two legs. Terry Russell, Ivan Henry and Peter Thorogood had transformed one of speedway's Cinderella sides into one of the best teams ever seen in the

The 1992 Arena Essex team. From left to right, back row: Ivan Henry (co-promoter), Bo Petersen, Andy Galvin, Alan Mogridge, Peter Thorogood (manager), Troy Pratt, Brian Karger, Terry Russell (co-promoter). Front row: Josh Larsen, Wayne Russell (mascot, on bike), Allan Johansen.

Second Division. It had been a magnificent achievement. Petersen and Karger both finished the season with ten plus averages, Petersen with 10.54 and Karger with 10.23. Mogridge played his part as third heat leader with 8.85, while the rest of the team, Troy Pratt, Andy Galvin, Jan Pedersen, Paul Hurry and Colin White, also put on outstanding performances. It was a team and a year Arena Essex would never forget.

Although they were now in the First Division, Russell and Henry kept faith with the team that had taken them there. The only changes were Josh Larsen and Allan Johansen coming in to replace Colin White and Paul Hurry. In their opening home Gold Cup fixture, the Hammers thrashed King's Lynn by 22 points, Petersen scoring a maximum 15 points and Karger paid 14. It looked as though the promoters had been right to stick with the 1991 Championship-winning team. After five matches it topped its section of the Gold Cup.

Unfortunately, the rest of the season was not to prove so easy as Mogridge found life difficult in the higher division and Johansen struggled away from home. When Galvin tore ankle ligaments at Ipswich and Pratt suffered a similar injury, Arena Essex found itself in trouble. Johansen returned home to Denmark at the beginning of August and was replaced by Peter Ravn. By now, the Hammers had reached their lowest point of the season and found themselves propping up the League. When Pratt returned at the end of August he injected a bit of life into the tail end and the Hammers began to pick up a few wins. Just enough in fact to avoid bottom spot and automatic relegation back to where they'd come from. In the end they finished 11th in the League, two points above Eastbourne and three above Swindon.

On the plus side for the Hammers, both Karger and Petersen had shown that they could live with Division One pace, recording averages of 8.73 and 8.25 respectively. Pratt also came on in leaps and bounds to finish the season with an average of 6.10. Karger had a good year individually, qualifying for the World Championship Final.

Now an established First Division club, Russell and Henry invested in improving the standard of spectator accommodation and a £1 million clubhouse complex on the first bend was opened. The promoters intended that this would be the first in a series of improvements for the stadium. The major new signing for the 1993 season was Dane, Claus Jacobsen. He was brought in to replace Bo Petersen who had decided it was time to retire. Following practice day at Arena Essex, Russell was happy that he had found a worthy replacement for the flying Petersen. Unfortunately, the Hammers' faithful never got to find out if he was right or not as Jacobsen crashed in the Star of Anglia meeting at Ipswich before ever setting wheel on track in anger at Purfleet and was out for the season. Immediately on the look out for a replacement, Russell and Henry followed the negotiations between two times Australian Champion and World Under-21 Champion, Leigh Adams, and Poole with great interest. With Adams' final refusal to return to Poole,

Arena Essex's two new signing for 1992, Allan Johansen (left) and Josh Larsen (right) shake hands.

he was put up for sale for £20,000 and was snapped up by the Arena Essex promotion. Adams scored 11 points on his debut at Purfleet. With Adams and Karger spearheading the team, Russell thought the Hammers now had a real chance of moving up the League and escaping forever the possibility of dropping back into the Second Division. When, on 12 April, they went to Reading and beat the defending champions by 57 points to 51, thanks to 15 points from Peter Ravn, Russell began to think that maybe even the League Championship was within their grasp. Two nights later they won away at Poole. After that however, things didn't go quite as well as they might, as they began losing matches at home and were not picking up enough points away to make them serious championship contenders. Injuries to Pratt and Karger did not help either. Even worse was to come, when Andy Galvin was involved in a high-speed smash at the end of July, suffering multiple injuries which put him out for the rest of the season. At the beginning of August an injury to Ravn put him out for the season too. With the loss of so many riders, Russell and Henry pleaded with Petersen to make a comeback. He reluctantly agreed. Petersen's return stabilised the team and he slotted back as though he'd not been away. A small revival saw the team finish the year in 4th place in the League. The Hammers managed to battle their way through to the final of the Speedway Star Cup against Bradford, but just before it was due to take place, Karger dislocated his shoulder and was out for the rest of the season.

Above: *The sixteen-year-old Leigh Lanham first rode for Arena Essex in 1993. He returned in 1998 and has been a leading member of the side ever since, apart from 2000 when a horrific injury put him out at the start of the season.*

Right: *Three times World Long Track champion, Kelvin Tatum, first rode for Arena Essex in 1994. He returned in 2002.*

World Under-21 champion and twice Australian champion, Leigh Adams signed for Arena Essex in 1993 and stayed until 1995.

The final itself was nothing short of a farce. At home for the first leg, Bradford won by 8 points. Due to injuries, Russell drafted sixteen-year-old Leigh Lanham into the team on loan from Ipswich. Bradford had also recently drafted two new riders into the team, Paul Pickering, who had just scored 36 points in two successive nights' racing, and Paul Thorp. When the Bradford team arrived at Purfleet, its promoter, Allan Ham, protested at the home side's use of Lanham. He cited the rule which said that the movement of riders after 31 August was banned except at management committee discretion. The referee, Paul Ebdon, would not take a decision without first consulting the BSPA. It was a bitterly cold evening and the crowd was left for over an hour waiting for a final decision to be made. In the end, Ebdon ruled that Lanham and Thorp would have to be withdrawn but that Pickering could ride. With Pickering in the side, Bradford was able to restrict Arena Essex to a two-point victory and thereby win the Cup on aggregate.

The arguments over the ruling continued for weeks. Russell said, 'Undoubtedly Paul Pickering was the man who swung the Cup Final Bradford's way, there is no question of that. Bradford won, but had we been able to use Leigh Lanham I feel we would have won.' Russell and Henry were so disgruntled with the outcome that they both considered giving up speedway altogether which would have thrown Arena Essex into turmoil. In the end however, after reflecting on their achievement over the last three years of pulling a poor Second Division club up to one of the best and most feared First Division teams in the country, they relented and agreed to stay on.

Adams had an outstanding year with the Hammers. His end of year average was 9.49 and he qualified for the World Championship Final, scoring 4 points. Later, during the British close season, he made it a hat-trick of Australian Championship victories with a 15-point maximum. Pratt also had a good year, qualifying for the British Final and making his international debut at Arena Essex against the USA.

Arena Essex faced a winter of team rebuilding as Karger and Jacobsen both decided to stay in Denmark for 1994, Larsen decided to stay in America, Petersen retired again and Galvin and Ravn were uncertain starters due to their injuries. The chequebook came out again, this time for former World number three Kelvin Tatum, a £20,000 signing from Bradford, and Paul Hurry was recalled from Peterborough. The closure of Rye House over the winter enabled Terry Russell to bring in his brother Ronnie as team manager. Ronnie brought Rockets' Jan Pedersen and Mikael Teurnberg with him. Adams, Pratt and White stayed on from the 1993 team. It was hoped that Pratt would join Adams and Tatum as the third heat leader. Pedersen was injured after four matches and replaced by Sweden's Christer Rohlen. Never the best of gaters, Rohlen was to become a crowd favourite as he chased after, and often passed, the opposition. He won his very first ride at Arena Essex having come from behind to pass Belle Vue's Jason Lyons.

Russell's hopes that Pratt would become the third heat leader were not fulfilled, which left too much for Adams and Tatum to do on their own. Adams had another magnificent year, finishing 3rd in the League averages with 9.86, sandwiched between three World Champions in Per Jonsson, Hans Neilsen and Sam Ermolenko. Unfortunately for his own World Championship chances, he broke a finger just before the semi-finals and was unable to progress any further. Tatum started well, but he seemed to be concentrating more and more on his long-track activities and did not finish the season well. He announced at the end of the season that he would not be returning to Purfleet. The Hammers' biggest success story was Paul Hurry. Like Rohlen, he was not a good gater, but would thrill the crowds with his charges from the back. It was Hurry who eventually became the third heat leader with an average of 6.28. It was not a great year for the team as it dropped down the League to finish in a mediocre 8th place out of 11.

In a major coup for the Arena Essex management, the FIM. announced at the beginning of 1995 that Arena Essex had been chosen as the venue for that year's British Grand Prix. Many improvements had been made, or were in the process of being made, to make the stadium worthy of a Grand Prix. The track had been widened and lengthened to 285 metres. New floodlights were being installed and covered seating for 5,000 people was being laid on as well as customised Press facilities. Russell, Henry and Woodroffe all said they were prepared to sink a great deal of time, effort and money into providing a facility of which speedway could be proud. The choice was not popular with everyone. The three times World Champion, Hans Nielsen, said he was not impressed. He felt the alterations to the track had actually made it more dangerous. 'Now all you have is a narrowed, longer track which will give riders more speed into tighter corners. They haven't really widened the straight and if they have it can only be by a yard which won't make any real difference,' he said. Russell's response to this criticism was that, 'The FIM

Left: *The American Josh Larsen rode for Arena Essex in 1992 and 1993, returning in 1995.* Right: *The Swede Mikael Teurnberg rode for the Hammers in 1994.*

have laid down specifications for tracks and we have worked within those specifications. There is a minimum width, and a minimum length, we are over both.' Neilsen continued his campaign of opposition and claimed he was seeking support from his fellow GP riders.

Following his outburst, there were rumours that Russell himself and other BSPA members were considering switching the Grand Prix venue to Waterden Road, the former home of Hackney Speedway and now a luxurious sports arena called London Stadium. The rumours were confirmed as true at the beginning of July when it was announced that the venue for the British Grand Prix had indeed been switched to the London Stadium. With Russell now associated with the old Hackney venue, supporters were fearful that he would move the Hammers team to Waterden Road and close the Arena Essex Raceway to speedway.

But all that was still to come as the 1995 season dawned. Russell and Henry had moved quickly over the close season and were the first management to announce their full-line up for the newly formed Premier League. As expected Tatum had left speedway altogether to concentrate on long-track racing, Rohlen said he could not return as he could not risk losing his job in Sweden and Pratt left for King's Lynn. In their places, three former Hammers, Josh Larsen, Jan Pedersen and Alan Mogridge returned. Together with Adams, Hurry, Teurnberg and Robert Ledwith, Ronnie Russell felt he had a team which could challenge for the title.

The 1994 Arena Essex team. From left to right, Troy Pratt, Paul Hurry, Mikael Teurnberg, Leigh Adams (on bike), Ronnie Russell (team manager), Kelvin Tatum, Jan Pedersen, Peter Thorogood (general manager).

It certainly seemed Ronnie was right, as the Hammers romped to 6 wins out of 6 in their opening fixtures. Adams started like an express train recording an average of 10.13 in those six matches. He received strong backing from Larsen and Hurry, but then Larsen was injured in Germany and out of the team until late July. For a short while he was replaced by the return of Christer Rohlen, who did reasonably well, especially in his second meeting back when he scored paid 12 to help the Hammers to an away victory at King's Lynn, but generally he was not quite up to Larsen's standard. Adams continued in good form throughout the season and Larsen once again gave good support on his return to finish with an average of 8.09. Hurry rode well as the third heat leader for his 7.45, but, after its strong beginning, the injury to Larsen affected the team's form and it finished up 10th out of 21 teams.

As the season finished, the fears that Russell would move the team to Hackney resurfaced. In December, Russell and Henry announced that they were in dispute with Chick Woodroffe who, of course, was still the stadium owner although he had given up his interest in the speedway promotion. It was never made clear what they were in dispute about. The next announcement came from Woodroffe who said that he had given Russell and Henry notice to quit Arena Essex, who then announced that they would be taking the team, lock, stock and barrel to their new promotion at London Stadium to become London Lions. As the BSPA January deadline for the declaration of intent to run in 1996 passed, no one came forward to take over at Arena Essex. It looked as though the worst fears of the Hammers supporters had been realised and that there would be no more speedway at the Arena Essex Raceway.

It was a telephone call from Tony Mole (charged by the BSPA management committee with the responsibility of expanding the number of teams in the proposed Conference League) to Chick Woodroffe that brought hope that perhaps there would be speedway after all at Arena Essex in 1996. Woodroffe immediately asked former promoter and manager, Peter Thorogood, whether he would be interested in such a proposition and in late February Thorogood confirmed that an application had been submitted to the BSPA for the Hammers to join the Conference League. Thorogood said, 'everyone, including Chick, Terry, Ivan and the BSPA were very keen to retain the sport at Arena Essex.' At the beginning of March, Thorogood was able to confirm to the Supporters' Club that the application had been accepted and speedway would definitely continue at Arena Essex.

In sole charge of speedway at Arena Essex for the first time, Thorogood had the problem of building up a completely new team. His first signing was Russell Etherington, a former junior at Arena Essex who had not ridden since 1992. Next was grass-track specialist, Nathan Morton. They were followed by Australian, Darren Bolger, former Rye House and Hackney junior, Phil Ranson, Peterborough junior, Gavin Pell and novice Andy Carfield. Roland Pollard was also signed up but he had made it clear he couldn't commit himself to the team full-time because of his work commitments.

The first meeting was the Essex Individual Championship and was won by Paul Lydes-Uings, a rider Thorogood had been after but who had signed for Eastbourne instead. The best Hammer on show was Pollard, who was the only rider to head Lydes-Uings all night before an engine failure stopped him. Seven hundred Hammers spectators braved the cold for their first glimpse of Conference League racing. During the meeting one of the riders, Bobby Eldridge, crashed and had to be taken to hospital. As there was only one ambulance on duty, the crowd had to wait 45 minutes for it to take Eldridge to hospital and return. After this incident, Thorogood vowed to make sure that there were always two ambulances on duty.

With Etherington as captain, the team rode its first match in the Spring Gold Cup against Mildenhall. Its defeat by 52 points to 26 led to great concern that it was too weak. However in its first actual

Robert Ledwith first rode for Arena Essex in 1989 and stayed with them until 1995.

181

Colin White came into the Arena Essex side as a member of the 1991 Second Division championship winning team. He remained with the team until 1994.

Conference League match against Reading on 10 May, Arena Essex won by 43 points to 35, Etherington scoring paid 14 from 5 rides and Bolger 11 from 5 and from then on they rode reasonably well to finish 6th out of 13 teams. With the league being decided on a percentage basis, the Hammers were always at a disadvantage as they were the only ones to run all their fixtures.

After his victory in the Essex Individual Championship, Thorogood continued to pursue Lydes-Uings in the hope of signing him up. He eventually got Eastbourne to agree to loan him in early July and there is no doubt that he added a bit of class to the team. Former Hammer, Simon Wolstenholme, turned out in a few matches towards the end of the season. Etherington played his part as captain well to finish the season as top scorer with an average of 8.11, just ahead of Lydes-Uings' 7.91. But probably the best performance came from the grass-tracker Nathan Morton, who had had no real experience of speedway before the season started. He finished with an average of 6.82 and was voted 'Rider of the Year' by the Supporters' Club. Thorogood was able to reflect on his first season back in control with some satisfaction. He had maintained an average of 500 spectators per week and had also managed to make Arena Essex a profit.

At the end of the season, Thorogood and Woodroffe decided to apply for Premier League status in 1997. With London folding after just one season, Thorogood was able to take back some of the riders signed to Russell and Henry, most of whom were, of course, former Arena Essex riders. From this source came Jan Pedersen, Colin White and David Mason. Thorogood also kept on Paul Lydes-Uings from his Conference team. Troy Pratt was welcomed back as captain and Tommy Palmer signed up on loan from Peterborough. After just eight matches, Lydes-Uings found the going much more difficult than in the Conference League and was loaned out to the Isle of Wight, his place being taken by John Wainwright. Apart from that change, the team stayed together all year.

The opening meeting as usual was the Essex Championship, won this year by Jan Pedersen. It was his first-ever individual meeting win in this country. The first-team match was against Exeter in the new Premier League Cup (South). It resulted in a 23-point win for the Hammers, with White scoring a 15-point maximum. As the season wore on,

Pratt proved to be an excellent captain and number one, finishing the season with an 8.65 average. Pedersen was just behind him on 8.42. Palmer couldn't quite get to grips with his home track and actually finished the season with a better away average than home, 7.16 to 6.99. It was a reasonable return to the Premier League for Arena Essex as they finished the season 7th out of 14 teams. Attendances at the track were boosted during the season when the BBC soap opera Eastenders filmed some racing at the track for a storyline they were developing. Troy Pratt doubled for Walford Lions' Ricky Butcher (Sid Owen).

Thorogood's real concern going into the 1998 season was to strengthen the heat leader section of the team. He hoped he'd found his man when he signed up Ipswich's Leigh Lanham on loan. Matt Read, a grass-track rider from Kent, was also signed up and with the 1997 team all staying on (with the exception of Palmer and Wainwright) together with Lydes-Uings returning as well as Nathan Morton (another of the 1996 Conference team), Hammers' supporters were optimistic about the coming season.

But it started to go wrong even before a match had been raced, as Read broke his hand on press and practice day. Things got even worse at the first meeting. The traditional opener, the Essex Championship, had attracted a very large crowd but had to be abandoned when the track doctor failed to turn up. The next two meetings were both rained off and then the Hammers suffered a heavy defeat at Peterborough. There was a further problem in April when Lanham crashed heavily during the British Under-21 Championship, but, as it happened, the fears that he would be out for a while proved groundless.

Gradually however, things began to improve. Pedersen scored an 18-point maximum against Newcastle in May and he and Lanham gradually pulled the team round. But Pratt was having his worst season for some time and when he failed to improve he decided it was to time to retire. The news of his impending retirement stunned everyone, Thorogood and supporters alike. Pratt had been a tower of strength for Arena Essex since he had signed for them ten years previously and it was such a shame that his career seemingly ended on such a low note when he failed to score in an away match at Reading. Thorogood was unable to find a replacement for Pratt and resorted

It was Matt Read's inspirational ride in heat five of the second leg of the Premier League Cup Final against Edinburgh in 1999 that gave Arena Essex hope that they could pull off a surprise victory.

to rider replacement. When that facility ended and Thorogood still had not found a new rider, the supporters began to get restless and when the Hammers lost 49-40 at home to Reading their patience snapped and Thorogood was roundly condemned for the defeat. Thorogood himself was incensed by the fans' attitude and told the crowd that he had been trying to sign someone but there just was not a suitable replacement available. The new captain, Colin White, came out to back him up, but the supporters were not convinced. Shortly afterwards, Thorogood signed up David Mason who went some way to filling the gap left by Pratt.

1998 was not a happy season for the Hammers and they finished 11th out of 13 in the League. There were some bright spots however. Colin White, for example, after taking over as captain, managed to play a big part in keeping the team together and he showed some tremendous form at home, averaging 9.52. Pedersen went even better, scoring at 10.16 at home, better even than Lanham. But in general, Lanham was Arena Essex's star of the season. He finished top of the club's overall averages with 9.03. In addition to that he took the Silver Helmet on 15 August and successfully defended it twice before losing it to the Isle of Wight's Ray Morton on 31 August. He won it again on 24 September by default when Peterborough's Glenn Cunningham was unable to defend the title. After one successful defence against Philippe Bergé of Peterborough, he ended the season as the holder. Lanham also finished 6th in the Premier League Riders' Championship Final.

By Christmas 1998 it looked as though Arena Essex had settled its team for the following year. Three of the previous season's top four, Pedersen, White and Read,

looked like certainties to return. The fourth, Lanham had let it be known that he wanted to continue on loan with Arena Essex and Gary Corbett, who had ridden in a number of matches in 1998, was ready to sign up. By February 1999, only Corbett seemed certain. Ipswich were prevaricating over the continued loan of Lanham, White put in a transfer request, Pedersen asked for more money and Read had still not definitely signed. Suddenly everything happened in February. Ipswich relented and Lanham was back, Read finally signed up, White re-signed after a new sponsor was found for him and Pedersen left. The most amazing news of all though was that Troy Pratt wished to return to the saddle with Arena Essex. Roger Lobb was signed from Exeter and former Hammer John

Gary Corbett rode for Arena Essex from 1998 to 2000.

Wainwright was brought back. With five days to go before press and practice day, seven Hammers were ready to go.

Pratt started the season better than he had finished the previous one. Unfortunately a broken collarbone put him out for two months and he missed sixteen matches. Lanham continued from where he had left off the previous season and White showed a marked improvement. With Lanham and White riding in every one of the Hammers official fixtures, along with Corbett and Wainwright, the Hammers had a good solid stability about them that had been missing the previous season, and it showed. The team showed much improvement over the one that had ridden in 1998, moving up the League to 9th place. But its biggest triumph was in the Premier League Cup where it reached the final. Having lost the first leg in Edinburgh by 54 points to 36, few people gave the Hammers much chance of pulling back such a deficit. Nevertheless, the biggest crowd since the 1996 return of Peter Thorogood turned out to watch the second leg of the final at Purfleet. It turned out to be a night of real passion which had everything except the fairy tale ending of a Hammers' victory, but there is no doubt that they went down fighting. After four heats, the score was 12-12, and it looked all over. In the next heat, Pratt streaked off from the gate with Edinburgh's James Grieves just behind. At best, it looked as though the Hammers could go into a 2-point lead but Read had other ideas as, in the ride of his life, he rode flat out round the outside to take Grieves from behind and help the Hammers to their first 5-1 of the night. It gave Arena Essex more than a 5-1 – it gave them motivation and the belief that they might actually do it after all. Heat six saw another 5-1 to the Hammers. Two 3-3s followed and then came heat nine and another 5-1. By the time heat thirteen arrived, Arena Essex needed three 5-1s from the last three heats to win the Cup. White was away but Lanham got caught at the back behind Edinburgh's two top riders Grieves and Peter Carr. Coming out of the fourth bend on the first lap, Lanham drove round the outside, keeping his foot off the footrest for extra grip and because he was so close to the fence. With Grieves already on a very wide line, Lanham had to squeeze through the tiniest of gaps, but he did it and joined White for the first of the 5-1s they needed. Their cup hopes were still alive but unfortunately, heat fourteen ended the Hammers' hopes as the Edinburgh pair of Kevin Little and Ross Brady scored a 5-1 of their own. The final heat was academic but it ended in victory for Lanham and Pratt with a 4-2, making the final score on the night 49-41 to the Hammers.

Arena Essex also finished second in the Premier League Pairs with Lanham and White, and reached the final of the Premier League Four Team Tournament. Lanham had another good season, averaging 9.10. He started the season as holder of the Silver Helmet and successfully defended it three times before losing it to Sheffield's Sean Wilson in June. After his problems of 1998, it was pleasing for Peter Thorogood to have such a good year in 1999 with gates up by something like 25 per cent, or 200 people, on average.

Soon after the Cup Final, the seventy-five-year-old Chick Woodroffe announced that he was pulling out of running speedway at Purfleet and was in negotiations with a new consortium who wished to take over. Eventually, a long-time sponsor of Troy Pratt, Colin Brine, linked up with Alan Sargent and Adrian Kearney to take over the reins.

Roger Lobb joined Arena Essex from Exeter in 1999.

Peter Thorogood said, 'I was sad at the end of the season when Chick decided he could no longer be promoter, but the time would always come. He is not in the best of health and age is not on his side. I enjoyed working for him all the years I did, so it was sad for me.'

The new promotion had a horrific start to the season as before the season was even a week old, both Leigh Lanham and new reserve, Nick Simmons, had broken their legs and were out for the season. With Peter Thorogood still on board, and the former Hammer Martin Goodwin appointed team manager, it had looked like being a good season. Lanham, Pratt, Corbett, Read and White had all agreed to stay on. The only two positions remaining to be filled were the reserve berths and these were taken by David Mason and Nick Simmons. Things were looking good and then, in heat ten of their very first match of the season against the Isle of Wight, Lanham and Phillipe Bergé locked together on the home straight and both were propelled into the safety fence. With both ambulances being used to take the two to hospital the meeting was abandoned. In their second match, Nick Simmons broke his leg in a crash while trying to avoid a fallen rider.

Old favourite Jan Pedersen was signed up to replace Lanham, while a number of different riders were used to cover Nick Simmons and later on Pratt and Mason, who were both dropped. Pratt eventually returned to the side a different rider and showed what he could do, becoming almost unbeatable at home. Amongst the other riders used were Savalas Clouting, Justin Elkins and Barrie Evans. The two injuries however, knocked the stuffing out of the side and although there were some good performances, it was mainly a year to forget as the Hammers struggled, finishing one from bottom. White took over as top heat leader with 8.12 and Pratt's comeback pushed his average up to 7.72. Clouting made an immediate impact at Purfleet with a 12-point maximum in his first match, but he too missed some matches through injury and wasn't the same on his return, although he finished with a reasonable 6.44 average.

Arena Essex did have success in the Southern Counties (Junior) League, which they won, losing just one match all season. Top junior was Mark Thompson, who rode in every match and averaged 10.67. His main support came from Matt Etherington.

There was sadness at the end of year at Arena Essex as the man who had started it all, Chick Woodroffe, died. Woodroffe had, of course, been ill for some time, but he had remained a spectator right through the 2000 season, watching the speedway from his office at the Purfleet Raceway. His final gift to the club had been to personally sanction £50,000 worth of work resurfacing the bumpy entrance road.

There were a number of changes to the line-up for 2001. Lanham, Pratt, White and Evans were back with Shaun Tacey, Andy Galvin and Luke Clifton replacing Pedersen, Corbett and Clouting. It looked a strong line-up on paper and the team started off well at home although they were finding it difficult to muster points away. Tacey and Galvin in particular had not started well, Galvin even dropping down to reserve. Goodwin resigned as team manager after just a couple of meetings due to pressure of work and Thorogood took over. But this was to be the last year, after many years of enthusiastic and devoted service, that Peter Thorogood was to be involved with the management side of Arena Essex.

With injuries and loss of form playing a part, several different combinations were tried at reserve level with Brent Collyer, Lee Dicken and Lee Herne being brought into the team at various times in place of Galvin and Evans. Lanham returned to the top of

A 1997 Arena Essex programme cover.

John Wainwright signed for Arena Essex in 1997 and returned in 1999.

the Hammers' tree, averaging 8.44, with Colin White and Troy Pratt the other two heat leaders, but there wasn't really the depth of strength available for the Hammers to worry the league leaders and they finished the table in 10th place. During the season, Troy Pratt, appropriately in his testimonial year, took over from Martin Goodwin as Arena Essex's highest points scorer of all time. The Juniors did not do quite so well this year, finishing in 3rd place in the Southern Junior League. Carl Downs, Russell Paine and Chris Mills were the pick of the team's juniors.

As 2002 got underway, there was news of yet another management change at Arena Essex as Ronnnie Russell became joint promoter with Colin Brine and Martin Goodwin returned to become joint team manager with Russell. The major change in Arena Essex's line up for 2002 was the loss of Troy Pratt, a Hammer since his debut for the club in 1989, with the exception of just two years, 1995 and 1996, making a total of eleven years service to the club. His replacement, former Hammer and three times World Long Track Champion, Kelvin Tatum certainly made plenty of headlines. Brine and Russell hoped that he would become one of the top stars in the Premier League able to take on and beat the likes of Workington's Carl Stonehewer and Sheffield's Sean Wilson to give the team a real chance of at least reaching the Premier League play-offs. He joined Lanham. White, Tacey, Galvin and Herne with Scott Courtney coming in as reserve. Although Tatum had a reasonable year, averaging 8.54, he was outscored by Lanham, who topped the Hammers' score chart at 9.17. It was not a great year for the team and it finished in 11th place in the League. The season did end on a high note however as Leigh Lanham finished in 6th place in the Championship of Great Britain after scoring 10 points which gave him the tantalising possibility of a shot at securing a Grand Prix place in 2004.

Although the club lost money during the season, Russell made it clear that the team would definitely be running in 2003, but whether in the Premier League or whether it is going to take the plunge and move up to the Elite League is uncertain at the time of writing.

10

ISLE OF WIGHT

The idea for a speedway track on the Isle of Wight was the brainchild of former Eastbourne promoter, Gareth Rogers. After discussing the matter with Mark Firmin, the owner of Ryde Football Club's Smallbrook Stadium, the pair of them decided to go ahead with the idea of introducing speedway to the island. Firmin felt that the island was 'crying out for sport and activities' because tourism had been on the decline for some time. Consequently the pair applied to the Newport Council (Isle of Wight) for permission to run twelve meetings. The stadium, which boasted a 1,500-seater grandstand as well as a two-storey clubhouse for sponsors and the press, was a well-appointed stadium which had a disused athletics track running round the outside of the football pitch. It was on this circuit that Rogers oversaw the building of a rough 396-metre track with no fence or banking just so that they could give a demonstration to councillors and officials from the Newport Council. Poole's Martin Willis and Justin Elkins were the riders chosen to give the demonstration. When Firmin saw Willis go out for the first time he thought their chances of obtaining permission were finished. 'He seemed to be going so fast he couldn't possibly turn,' Firmin said, 'I felt a catastrophe looming large in front of our invited guests that would end speedway before it had even started! I was left thinking that I'd have an injured rider in front of all these people, but he turned the bike – and they all applauded. That was a vital moment for us.' Although Firmin and Rogers only asked for two years' initial permission, the council granted them permission for five years to run up to twelve speedway meetings a year between the hours of 7 p.m. and 10 p.m. The Newport Council planning officer, Paul Stack, said the council had approved the plan with the intention of boosting tourism on the island. He explained that the stadium was about one mile from the Ryde town centre and therefore far enough away from the centre of population not to constitute a noise nuisance.

At first the Poole promoters, Mervyn Stewkesbury and Pete Ansell, looked likely to be involved in the promotion but Firmin decided he would promote the sport himself with Rogers and the Poole pair dropped out. The following spring, Firmin and Rogers attended the meeting of chairmen for the new Conference League that was to come into existence in 1996 and they were welcomed with open arms.

Former Birmingham captain, George Major, a resident of the Isle of Wight, was appointed team manager and the job of building up a team from scratch started. The first two targets were the two riders who had taken part in the demonstration rides, Martin Willis and Justin Elkins. Both of them agreed. While this was going on, Isle of Wight Radio was running a competition to find a name for the new team. In the end, the name Wight Wizards was chosen.

Elkins became the first rider to sport a Wight Wizards racejacket when he appeared at the Arena-Essex Essex Championship on 26 April, and finished a creditable second.

The programme cover from the first speedway meeting ever held on the Isle of Wight, 13 May 1996.

Unfortunately for the Wizards, after this meeting Elkins was called up by Eastbourne to cover for the injured Neville Tatum. His average was higher than that of the Eagles' reserves, so he was put in at number five. The Conference League rules did not allow anyone riding in a Premier League team above the number six spot to ride in it, which meant that Elkins' debut in the Wizards team was delayed until June.

The Isle of Wight's opening meeting was the Island Individual Championship held on 13 May 1996 and won by Martin Willis in front of a crowd of 1,800. Arena Essex's Darren Bolger set the new track record with a time of 79.5 seconds and also made the first first-hand examination of the safety fence, which he said was 'first class.' The first Conference League match was held a week later and resulted in a 42-36 victory over Sittingbourne. The team for that first-ever league meeting was Mark Chessell, the captain, who scored a 12-point maximum, Martin Willis, Colin Crook, Chris Simpson, Mike Bowden, Barry Bishop and Paul Oughton. Chessell continued to score well, but in early June he damaged his knee and the Wizards' management brought in the Czech, Vaclav Verner, to cover for him. Normally, being a Czech, he would have needed a work permit, but as the Conference League was for amateurs he did not need one. This did not stop the other tracks from making uncomplimentary comments about the situation.

By the 24 June, the Wight Wizards had ridden six matches and won them all, but their last match in June was their first one away, and they were heavily defeated at Sittingbourne by 52 points to 26. This was no surprise really as their top three riders, Willis, Elkins and Verner were all missing. However, this did highlight the main problem with the Wizards team in their initial season. They had a trio of excellent heat leaders but there was no-one who could be relied on to give them strong support at second string level. Colin Crook finished the season with the best average of the second strings, but that was only 5.25.

Chessell attempted a number of returns during the season, but only rode in four more matches altogether. Verner was eventually banned following a new rule brought in by the Conference League chairmen that only British riders would be allowed to ride in the League. Without these two for most of the second half of the season, the team suffered away and although it maintained its unbeaten home record to the end, the lack of away points meant it was unable to challenge effectively for the Conference League title. In the end, though, 4th place out of 13 teams was a very creditable performance for the Wizards in their first year of existence.

The three main heat leaders finished the season with incredible figures. Willis was third best with 10.35! Verner averaged 11.38, having ridden in a total of 26 heats and not come last once – he only came third twice. Elkins finished with an average of 11.17. He started in 63 races and won 53 of them. He only came last once. In the matches he did manage, Chessell recorded a 7.87 average.

Elkins and Willis represented the Wizards in the Conference League Riders' Championship. Willis scored 8 points but Elkins topped the score chart with 14 points. Unfortunately, in the one-off final he came second to Mike Hampson. It had been a successful season for British speedway's newest venue. The first club ever to operate on the Isle of Wight had regularly attracted crowds of over 2,000. Firmin and Bolger thought it was time to apply for permission to run 20 meetings a year. Newport Council had no hesitation in approving the application.

Chessell and Crook expressed their wish to stay on for the 1997 season as did Dean Garton, who had had two outings with the team in 1996. Rogers brought in Bobby Eldridge and Paul Lydes-Uings, both from Eastbourne. Willis had hoped to step up to Premier League racing but agreed to stay on with the Wizards following a dispute over adjusting his average for the Premier League. The new season opened on 31 March when an unlucky Lathallan came up against the full force of the Wizards. In a 59-19 thrashing, Eldridge, Willis, Chessell, Garton and Crook all scored full or paid maximums. The early season form of Eldridge and Willis was outstanding, Eldridge scoring 36 points in three matches and Willis 35 paid 36. Unfortunately, their brilliant form was a double-edged sword as Premier League teams snapped up both of them, Willis going to Newport and Eldridge to Reading. Eldridge returned later in the year, but Willis never did. With their departure, Chessell was left to carry the high-scoring burden almost alone. Crook had some good meetings but also some bad ones, although generally his performance was up on the previous year. Greg Daniels and Andy Kerrison came into the team in place of

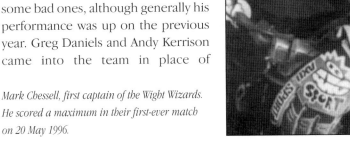

Mark Chessell, first captain of the Wight Wizards. He scored a maximum in their first-ever match on 20 May 1996.

Eldridge and Willis but their scoring was well down on those two. Lydes-Uings came back into the team at the beginning of June. He started well but fell away a bit before finishing the season with three double figure scores.

Without Eldridge and Willis, the Wizards went through a five-match sequence in May and June losing the lot, including two at home. After this however, the team seemed to pick up a bit with Crook and Daniels scoring solidly, if not spectacularly. With the return of Eldridge and the good end to the season from Lydes-Uings, the Wizards finished with 4 wins and 1 draw out of their last 6 meetings. It was enough to move them up the table to finish in 3rd place, one position better than the previous year. Chessell topped the team's averages for the year with 10.65, with Eldridge just behind on 10.18. Lydes-Uings finished as third heat leader on 8.13. Eldridge was the Isle of Wight's representative at the Amateur League (as the Conference League had been renamed for 1997) Riders' Championship. He was joint top-scorer on 13 points but lost out to Jon Armstrong in a run-off for the title.

Amateur League racing was not the only racing the crowds at the Smallbrook Stadium saw that year. In July it was announced that Skegness was to move its Premier League operation to Ryde and become known as the Isle of Wight Islanders. Peter Oakes' gamble of opening a new track in Lincolnshire had not paid off as crowds did not live up to expectations. Rather than withdraw from the League altogether, Oakes looked round for another home for his team and found it at Ryde, where Firmin offered the stadium rent free.

Most of the Skegness team moved with the club. This included Brett Woodifield, Nigel Sadler and Gavin Hedge. At first, Wayne Carter did not want to move, but later rejoined the team. Paul Clews was unable to transfer across as the Isle of Wight's Monday race night clashed with his job. He was replaced by Shaun Tacey. Another newcomer was Jason Bunyan, dropped by Oxford, but who became a revelation for the Islanders. In the match away to the Cheetahs on 19 September he showed Oxford just what a mistake they had made in letting him go by scoring 10 points from 5 rides. Mark Simmonds was the last rider to join the team, coming aboard at the end of August.

When they arrived at Ryde, the Skegness team was in the lower half of the League and looked unlikely to reach the Young Shield play-offs for the top eight. However some good victories in September put them in contention. It was probably the match on 25 September that did as much as anything to put the team in the play-offs. Edinburgh had won the first encounter on its own track by 17 points (53-36), so it was a mammoth task that faced the Islanders if they were to capture the bonus point. But while Edinburgh were getting used to the track, the Isle of Wight went in to a 14-point lead. Edinburgh gradually fought its way back and in the end it all came down to the final heat. A 3-3 draw was needed by the Islanders to force a run-off for the bonus point. Tacey and Carter were out against Edinburgh's Peter Carr and Robert Eriksson. The Isle of Wight pair gated well and came out of the first turn in the lead. It looked as though they might even win the match and the bonus point outright, but Carr managed to get past them and the match finished 53-36 to the Isle of Wight. A run-off was needed to settle the destination of the bonus point. This time, Tacey made no mistake as he led Carr home. This unlikely bonus point gave the Islanders hope that they could reach the

Brett Woodifield arrived at Ryde with the Skegness team in 1997.

play-offs. The final home match of the season had to be raced on a neutral track as Smallbrook could not fit the fixture in. So the Isle of Wight took on Long Eaton at Alwalton, home of Peterborough. Although the Islanders lost, they took the bonus point, which was just enough for them to finish the season in 8th place and qualify for the Young Shield. It was not a fairy tale ending however, as their opponents in the first round, Reading, defeated them home and away. Nevertheless the move to the Isle of Wight had been beneficial and it gave the fans and Mark Firmin a taste of Premier League racing.

Tacey ended the season as the number one with an average of 8.23, followed by Woodifield on 7.63 and Sadler on 6.73. It was this lack of a really top-class heat leader that prevented the Islanders from finishing higher in the League.

After the season had finished, Firmin announced that he was looking to form a consortium to run Premier League racing at Smallbrook in 1998. He felt that, having seen Premier League racing in 1997, the supporters would not want to go back to a pure diet of Amateur League racing. He said that crowds for the Amateur League matches had dropped in 1997 and he understood that the league was to become even more youth orientated in 1998. If that would be the case, the Isle of Wight would not be interested and may have to close.

In November, Firmin announced that a meeting for prospective investors had been held and that about 25 to 30 supporters had come forward willing to become shareholders in the club. 'It will be a co-operative and very much a club where the local people contribute at a practical level, as well as on the financial front.' The arrangement made the club unique in British Speedway in being owned by its own supporters. Martin Newnham, who along with Dave Pavitt, was named as one of the new co-promoters, chaired the new co-operative. The meeting had also confirmed that the team would definitely be entering the Premier League. With the new consortium in place, Firmin gave up his promoter's licence.

The new promoters kept on Wayne Carter and Jason Bunyan from the 1997 team and signed up Ray Morton as captain. Morton was followed by Neville Tatum, Philippe Bergé and Danny Bird. Bergé left after five matches through injury to be replaced by Scott Swain, though he returned later in the season.

Before the 1998 season started, the track was remodelled and reduced to 382 metres. The new captain, Ray Morton, tried it out on press and practice day and was very impressed. 'The track is absolutely brilliant and will be the fastest and best racing strip

The Isle of Wight team in 1998, the year they won the Young Shield. From left to right: Philippe Bergé, Anthony Barlow, George Major (manager), Ray Morton, Neville Tatum, Wayne Carter, Jason Bunyon. Kneeling: James Major (mascot).

in the country in my opinion. Those people who have worked so hard on it during the winter deserve so much credit it's not true.' It was to prove a remarkable year for the Islanders as once again they hovered around the cut-off point for the Young Shield play-offs. The race for the final place lasted right through to the very last week of the Premier League season. Even then it looked as though it might have to come down to a ruling due to be given by the management committee as to the validity of Edinburgh's two outstanding home fixtures which had been arranged for after the 24 September cut-off date. The only team that could prevent the management committee having to make a ruling necessary was the Isle of Wight. It had one last match to race away at Sheffield. To qualify irrespective of what happened to Edinburgh it needed to get within four points of Sheffield. The Islanders had only won one away match all season, so it did not look too promising, but, in an amazing match, the Isle of Wight not only got within four points of the Tigers but actually won by an incredible 50 points to 40. The hero of the evening was Scott Swain who scored 13 points.

Having just qualified for the Young Shield at the last gasp, no one expected the Islanders to do much in the tournament itself. When they went down by 18 points in the first leg of the first round at Exeter, it seemed certain that they were out. But in a rain-affected match at Smallbrook, they came back and astonished everyone with a 49-22 win. Exeter were not happy that the referee had allowed the match to go on in atrocious conditions, but it was allowed to go to the 12th heat at which point it was abandoned with the score standing. Glasgow were their next opponents and, once again, the Islanders were thrashed in the first leg, this time by 12 points, 51 to 39. In the return leg, Glasgow increased its lead and after four heats were a further 2 points in front. Successive 5-1s in heats five and six put the Isle of Wight back in with a chance. In heat eleven, they scored a 4-2 and went in front for the first time. Amazingly, Glasgow just seemed to give up at this point and the Islanders scored 3 maximums in the last 3 heats to win the match 58-31 and the tie 97-82. The Islanders were now through to the final where they were up against League and Cup champions Peterborough. Once again, the Isle of Wight were away for the first leg. This time they managed to hold the Panthers to a 10-point lead. Back at Smallbrook, the Islanders gradually made up the deficit. By heat ten, they were 6 points up overall, but Peterborough hit back and going into the last heat either team could have taken the trophy. However, a 5-1 to Steve Master and Ray Morton for the Isle of Wight ensured that the Islanders won their first title.

In winning the Young Shield the team paid a fitting tribute to its supporters' co-operative that had kept it going during 1998. With crowds falling below break-even level, they had put in time and money to keep the Islanders afloat. They had also made representations to the council, who had responded magnificently by agreeing to offer an interest-free loan and licensing the speedway company to take over the running of the entire Smallbrook Stadium complex. It was a generous gesture which resulted in the long-term future of speedway on the island being assured. The victory in the Young Shield brought further rewards as the publicity generated by this on the island brought in an additional £15,000 sponsorship.

At the start of the 1999 season, Pavitt switched the race night from Friday to Tuesday in an effort to bring back the crowds. At the end of the season he had the satisfaction of seeing numbers increase by 20 per cent. Tatum, Swain, Bergé, Bird and Carter stayed on from the 1998 team while Morton and Bunyan moved into the Elite League. In their places came Tommy Palmer and Nick Simmons who had raced in a handful of matches for the Islanders in 1998.

The Islanders had a poor start to the season, losing their first 5 matches but, as 4 of these were away, they were not too concerned. This was followed by 4 wins in succession. It was another season of hovering round the mid-table seeing if they could make the Young Shield play-offs. Once again, they just made it finishing in 8th place. But there was not to be the same happy ending as in 1998, as they were knocked out in the first round. The Islanders' best competi-

Adam Shields powers away at the start. The Australian, Shields, joined the team in 2000. By 2002 he was the Islanders' top rider. His ability was such that he was much in demand by Elite League teams as a guest.

tion this year was the Four-Team Tournament as Tatum, Bergé, Carter and Swain took them to the final where they came equal 3rd.

Tatum proved to be the top rider in 1999, averaging 8.54, just in front of Swain on 8.02. Bergé was the third heat leader on 7.46. The most improved rider for the Islanders was undoubtedly Danny Bird, who doubled his average to 6.39. He also secured his first Young England cap. Not surprisingly, Bird was retained for 2000 along with Palmer, Bergé and Swain. Ray Morton was re-signed and teenager Glen Phillips was given a chance at reserve. This left one place open, which was eventually taken when Adrian Newman was signed from Conference League St Austell. It was a strong-looking team and gave the Ryde faithful some hope that this year it might rise above 8th position in the League. But disaster was to strike in the first meeting, a challenge match at Arena Essex when Bergé was involved in the horrific smash that put both himself and Leigh Lanham out for the season with Bergé suffering a broken neck. After using guest riders for a while, Pavitt signed up a long-term replacement in Australian, Adam Shields, a man who was destined to become a huge favourite at Smallbrook. Pavitt actually knew nothing about Shields when Shields telephoned him asking if there was any chance of a team place. Pavitt arranged to see him in a second-half event at Swindon and the rest, as they say, is history. Richard Juul joined the team in mid-season after Adrian Newman had not shown the promise it was hoped he would and was dropped.

Ray Morton's return was nothing short of triumphant as he headed the Islanders' averages with a superb 10.09, the 3rd best in the League as a whole. Unfortunately, he was out on his own and although, Bird, Swain and Shields all did enough to show they could be stars of the future, their averages, all between 6.5 and 7, were not enough to carry the team at heat-leader level. The Islanders lost four matches at home and did not win one away. It took them away from their accustomed mid-table spot, but unfortunately, in the wrong direction, as they dropped to 11th place.

A typical all-action shot of Isle of Wight favourite Ray Morton.

Adam Shields (left) and Danny Bird (right) with their Premier League Pairs trophies, which they won in 2002.

Dave Pavitt retained his young hopefuls, Bird, Shields, Swain and Phillips for the 2001 season and, along with Morton, they formed the basis of the team. They were joined by David Watt and Frenchman Christophe Cayre. Cayre had a disastrous start, failing to score in three matches and then breaking two vertebrae to put him out for the season. His place was taken by another French rider, Seb Tresarrieu. With the continuing improvement of Bird and Shields, the team had its best season since entering the Premier League. Bird moved up to be the number two behind Morton, with an 8.79 average, while Shields was just behind him on 8.61. Morton finished on 9.42. The second strings also played a big part as Watt, Tresarrieu and Swain all scored at over 6 points per match.

For the first time, the Islanders qualified for the Young Shield in 4th place, with a 100 per cent home record. It wasn't such a surprise this year when they went on to take the Young Shield for the 2nd time in their history, beating Edinburgh in the final by 103 points to 77 after a mammoth home leg win of 61-29. The team also did well in other events, coming 3rd in the Premier League Pairs with Morton and Bird and 4th in the Premier League Fours with Swain, Watt, Bird and Shields.

Adam Shields proved to be the rider of 2002. His rise to the top continued without a hitch as he moved ahead of Ray Morton. Both Shields and Morton finished the season in the top four of the Premier League averages. Danny Bird continued to provide excellent backing and with such a strong heat-leader trio, the Islanders stayed near the top of the League all season finally finishing in 3rd place just 1 point behind the champions, Sheffield. Shields represented the Isle of Wight at the Premier League Riders' Championship winning the title after a tremendous final in which he and Newport's Craig Watson passed and repassed before Shields managed to get away. It was Shields, and the Islanders' second title of the year, as he and Danny Bird had already won the Premier League Pairs Championship. Bird also recorded a remarkable achievement by winning the semi-final round of the Championship of Britain.

At the end of the 2002 season, Pavitt summed up what it was like to be part of the Isle of Wight scene when he said, 'If we had to rely on admission money alone, we wouldn't still be in existence but it is a glowing testimony to our shareholders that we are and that we are having such a successful season. It's a unique club in every sense and one that I'm delighted to be part of.'

PART II
MINOR LEAGUE TRACKS

11

DAGENHAM

Speedway came to Dagenham in 1932 when a 320-yard track was opened in Ripple Road. As was the norm with these early amateur operations, the usual diet during the early part of the 1930s was the individual scratch races, handicap races, match races and so on. Some meetings were also billed as challenge matches, as teams from Dagenham, riding under the name Romford, took on teams from other local amateur tracks, such as Barnet and later, Rye House as well as teams just made up for the occasion, such as Cambridge. In 1934, Hawk Speedways ran speedway meetings, but in 1936, the Amateur Dirt-Track Riders' Club took over, under the stewardship of Arthur Warwick. The opening meeting that year, on 21 June, was opened by West Ham star, Tiger Stevenson.

Warwick set up a training school at the track. His original school consisted of 25 novices, three of whom had never been on a motorbike in their lives, but all of whom wanted to be World Champion one day. Each Monday was spent in theory and lectures with Warwick explaining how to build an engine, the mysteries of tuning or some other technical matter. On Thursday the novices were put through their paces on the practical side. There was also a keep-fit routine with no smoking, no drinking, plenty of exercise and early to bed being the order of the day. Eventually the great day would come when some of the novices were considered good enough to ride in public. Warwick instituted a Silver Cup in 1936 to be raced for throughout the season by the juniors, with points being accumulated each week. By the end of the season, Frank Hodgson had proved to be easily the best with Roy Duke trailing well behind in second place. Other juniors to take part in the Silver Cup races included Jim Baylais, Freddie Wiseman, Ken Tidbury and Crusty Pye.

Hodgson was born in Middlesborough but in 1935, with jobs being scarce in the North East, had come down to London. His first job was to paint the scoreboard at Hackney Stadium. As he painted, he was able to watch the Hackney riders at their morning practice. Although he was an expert motorcyclist, this was his first glimpse of speedway. He was so impressed that he decided to try it out and joined the Amateur Dirt-Track Riders' Club, which led him to Dagenham. He very soon got the hang of

speedway and by the time of his fourth meeting had already become Arthur Warwick's star pupil. By the end of the season, he was unbeatable and continued in this vein throughout 1936 and 37.

In fact Hodgson's form in 1937 was such that he was criticised by Dagenham's own supporters for continuing to ride for them! Their complaint was that he was too good. He was now riding for First Division Hackney Wick and Second Division Nottingham as well as turning out at Dagenham on Sunday afternoons. One supporter, Mr W.T. Smith, wrote to the *Speedway World* in May to say, 'I think, like a good many others, that when these boys get about 2/6 per point, it is a disgrace to allow this man to come here and take it away from these lads just as he likes.' Mrs Gladys Thornton, secretary of the Amateur Dirt-Track Riders' Club, defended the decision to allow Hodgson to continue at Dagenham by saying, 'just because this boy has succeeded where others have failed, it is no reason for people to maintain it is unfair to allow him to ride at Dagenham … it is hardly fair to bar a man from the original source of his success. I should also like it to be known that when the "Coronation Cup" was won last week by Frank Hodgson at Dagenham, he sportingly gave it back for the runner-up. A better instance of club spirit I should like to hear of.'

Another youngster to take some of his first rides at Dagenham in 1937 was Malcolm Craven. Malcolm was spotted by Colin Watson, who then took him to see Alec Jackson at Wembley. Jackson put the young Craven through his paces and signed him up immediately. After the war, Craven moved on to West Ham where he became one of the country's leading riders until he retired at the end of the 1953 season.

In 1938, Dagenham entered two teams, Dagenham and Romford, in the Sunday Dirt Track League. To get it ready for league matches a considerable amount had gone into improving the track. All the old cinders were removed; the base was rolled with a steamroller and then re-laid. The cinders used were identical to those being used at Hackney. It was hoped that their larger size would stop the dust nuisance that had been so prevalent the year before. It was also felt it would provide more spectacular racing as it had a 'better gripping quality' enabling the riders to ride into the bends faster.

The opening meeting on Easter Sunday was attended by the largest crowd, up to that time, at the Ripple Road track. The first league match was held on 1 May when Dagenham took on Romford and defeated them by 44 points to 39 in spite of losing unlucky heat thirteen, 5-0. In spite of the criticism of Hodgson, and the fact that he was now captain of Hackney Wick, he was nevertheless appointed captain of the Dagenham Daggers. The other leading riders were Baylais, Pye and Nobby Stock. Dagenham's first reverse came the following week when it took on the strong Eastbourne team. Even Hodgson, for so long unbeatable on the Ripple Road circuit, met his match when, in the opening heat, he had to give best to the Eagles captain, Tiger Hart. Hart remained unbeaten throughout the match to give Eastbourne victory by the same score as Dagenham had won by the previous week. Romford's second match was against Smallford, who narrowly won the match by 42 points to 40. Jack Tidbury was the Rommers' star rider. Smallford's captain was Doug Wells. Wells had ridden for the 1937 Dagenham team.

Dagenham held a special evening meeting on Thursday 19 May with special events and a searchlight display. Unfortunately, the meeting was to end in tragedy as a young rider by the name of Harry Rogers died after crashing in a race.

Later in the year, Dagenham held a number of trophy meetings with the trophies donated by some of the top London riders. For example, on 12 June, New Cross star, Stan Greatrex presented his trophy and on 19 June, West Ham's Canadian rider, Eric Chitty presented his trophy. The Eric Chitty Trophy provided some of the best racing of the season. Hodgson was naturally favourite to win, but he had stiff opposition from Jim Baylais and Jack Tidbury. Hodgson and Baylais met in heat eight. Baylais shot off from the tapes and led for practically the whole of the four laps. Hodgson tried everything but Baylais hung on until the very last bend when Hodgson managed to shoot past him. The crowd was on its toes as the two riders tore down the finishing straight neck and neck with Hodgson just managing to hang on to win by less than the width of a wheel. When Hodgson met Tidbury in heat eleven, their last race, they both had 9 points. The race itself however was a bit of an anti-climax as Hodgson roared away from the start and won by a good 2 lengths to win the trophy. Tidbury was 2nd with Nobby Stock 3rd.

3 July saw the return of Eastbourne. The match was said to have been 'too boisterous' for Dagenham's second strings and the Eagles ran out the winners again, this time by 43 points to 39. The following week, Putt Mossman put in an appearance at the track during a match between Romford and The Rest.

On 3 September the *Speedway News* reported that Dagenham was in danger of closing and called on London promoters to rally round and save the track as it had produced more young riders for teams like Hackney, Harringay and West Ham than any of the other training tracks. At this point the clerk of the course, Les Thornton, stepped in and reorganised the whole management of the track. After a short closure, Dagenham reopened on 9 October with a re-laid track and a redecorated stadium. He had also managed to get support from a number of top riders who had agreed to help

The Dagenham team in 1936. From left to right: Snowy Blackman, Roy Duke, Frank Hodgson, A. Sawdy, Jim Boyd, Fred Quick.

him save the track. Danish rider Morian Hansen took over microphone duties for the evening, New Cross's Stan Greatrex and Ernie Evans became pits marshals, Wimbledon's Benny Kaufman and New Cross's Ron Johnson agreed to help out as stewards and the 1937 World Champion, Jack Milne, said he would present the trophy. During the season, West Ham Hawks had used the stadium for their National League Division Two fixtures. On 16 October, a special match was held between Dagenham and the Hawks, with Tiger Stevenson on the microphone. The season came to an end with a special Guy Fawkes night on 6 November. Although it had been the local north London tracks that had so far used the services of the Dagenham training track the most so far – both Hodgson and Stock had been signed up by Hackney for example – an announcement was made during the winter that New Cross had adopted Dagenham and that in future would have first call on any Dagenham riders.

In spite of the Sunday Dirt Track League no longer being in operation, Dagenham re-formed its team at the beginning of the 1939 season to race a series of challenge matches. The opening meeting was a Probables *v*. Possibles match. The two captains for the Probables and Possibles teams were Jim Baylais and Nobby Stock, with Frank Hodgson having finally decided to ride for Hackney Wick full time. Nobby Stock had been introduced to speedway by Frank Hodgson who lived near him in Rainham. At the age of eleven, Stock had bought a belt-driven Raleigh and, together with other local children, made a small track on the village green. By the age of fourteen, he was working on a milk round and Hodgson had become something of a hero to the young Stock who used to clean Hodgson's bike for him. In 1937, Hodgson encouraged him to go along to Arthur Warwick's training school. He spent all his savings, £70, on Eric Chitty's old speedway bike. By 1938 he had progressed so much that he had not only made the Dagenham team but had also been signed up by Hackney. After the war, he became a regular Harringay Racer, partnering the great Vic Duggan.

In keeping with the new regime at Dagenham, three of the best riders on view in the Probables *v*. Possibles match were New Cross juniors, Benny King, Alex Gray and George Craig, although it was Stock who took the second-half individual title after a hectic struggle with Baylais.

Frank Hodgson, Dagenham's captain in their one and only league season in 1938. Hodgson also rode for Hackney Wick and later went on to ride for Middlesbrough.

Nobby Stock also rode in the 1938 team. He later rode for Hackney Wick and Harringay, in whose colours he is seen here.

Jim Baylais captained the Daggers in 1939 in a series of challenge matches. He also rode for Hackney Wick.

A special trophy meeting was held on 16 April to celebrate Dagenham's 100th meeting. Jack Tidbury, Nobby Stock and Eric French joined the unbeaten Jim Baylais in the final. An untidy scramble for the first corner resulted in French falling and the race being re-run with all four riders. In the re-run, Baylais shot away from the tapes, with Stock being filled in by Tidbury and French, who finished 2nd and 3rd behind the deserved winner of the trophy, the still unbeaten Dagenham captain, Jim Baylais.

In the 13 May issue of the *Speedway News*, a correspondent, Mr W. Bridges, wrote to ask if everyone was fully appreciative of the beneficial effect that Dagenham Speedway had had on the sport as it 'must have produced more stars than any other one track.' He then went on to list the riders who had been discovered at Dagenham: Frank Hodgson, Doug Wells, Jim Baylais and Nobby Stock, now all with Hackney; Malcolm Craven at Wembley; Alan Smith, Norwich; Eric French, Bristol; Dick Harris and Crusty Pye, Harringay; Dick Geary and Aussie Powell, West Ham; Ernie Pawson, Crystal Palace; Fred Tuck, Stoke, Jim Boyd and Alf Kain, Southampton and Benny King, Alex Gray and George Craig, New Cross.

Jack Milne visited the track again on 4 June to present the Milne Cup. Apparently, the greatest race of the afternoon was by Milne himself as half-way through the meeting he suddenly remembered that the trophy he was supposed to be presenting was still on the sideboard of his home in Forest Hill. He rushed off, praying the traffic lights would be with him, and returned just in time to present it to the winner of the day's meeting, Gil Craven, Malcolm's brother.

Later in June, two more future top stars made their first appearances on the Dagenham speedway track when first Frank Lawrence and then Bill Gilbert appeared. Lawrence later went on to ride for New Cross while Gilbert went on to ride for the all-conquering Wembley Lions team of the immediate post-war years, and finish 4th in the 1948 British Riders' Championship final. About this time, contractual difficulties arose between the company holding the stadium lease and the speedway organisers. The consequence of this was that, for the time being, Arthur Warwick's training school suspended operations. To overcome this he began negotiating with the nearby Dagenham Greyhound Stadium to lease it for speedway in 1940. The proposal was that in the following season, the Ripple Road circuit would enter the Second Division and the new track would continue with the training school and the Sunday afternoon meetings. In the end however, the difficulties were resolved when a new promotion team of Arthur Warwick himself, Stan Greatrex and Alex Dovener took over the speedway organisation and the idea of moving to the greyhound track was dropped.

The new organisation set about improving both the training school and the Sunday afternoon meetings by once again re-laying the track, this time with decomposed granite, and putting more effort into the promotion of events generally. The changes were obviously successful as, on 23 July, a record crowd turned out to see Nobby Stock win the Wilson Cup.

Dagenham met West Ham Hawks on 7 August, Bank Holiday Monday, and was surprised when West Ham turned up with leading rider, Eric Chitty, as captain. Chitty

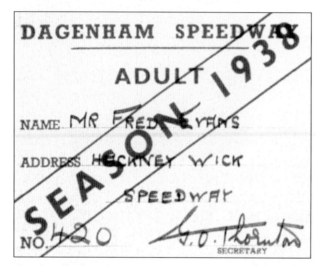

A 1938 Dagenham season ticket made out to Fred Evans, the Hackney Wick promoter.

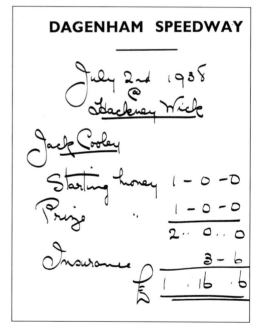

Dagenham rider Jack Cooley's payslip after a challenge match at Hackney Wick on 2 July 1938.

204

Hackney's Morian Hansen (right) and Wimbledon's Benny Kaufman (p.206) were two of the top stars who helped save Dagenham from closing in 1938 by offering their services to the track.

was, not surprisingly, unbeaten all afternoon, but it was a measure of the progress made by Bill Gilbert that he ran Chitty a close second in a couple of races. The Daggers won the match by 47 points to 36. The nineteen-year-old Gilbert had only been riding for three months but had already made such phenomenal progress that he was now Dagenham's best rider. Others in the team were captain Nobby Stock, Jack Cooley, Dave Anderson, Benny King and Roy Uden.

Although it had no flood lighting, Dagenham staged an evening meeting on Thursday 17 August. The track was lit by flares supplied by the British Oxygen Co. which stood on the grass verge. The feature of this meeting was a special match race between Tiger Stevenson and Colin Watson. The experiment turned out to be so successful that Dagenham decided to run Thursday night meetings in addition to its normal Sunday afternoon meetings for the rest of the season. The only difference was that electric lighting was to replace the flares, which did not prove too effective. Warwick and Greatrex had now dropped the idea of moving to Dagenham Greyhound Stadium, but they had not dropped the idea of entering the Second Division in 1940. Gates had increased to an average of 3,000 under their management – it had been as low as 300

Wimbledon's Benny Kaufman.

sometimes before they took over – and they felt the time was right to bring major league speedway to Ripple Road. They explained that that was the real purpose behind the experimental Thursday evening meetings as this would be the day they would run on. Their proposed team was Jack Cooley, Benny King, George Craig, Frank Lawrence, Paul Anderson, Bill Gilbert and yet another member of the Craven family, Stan.

It is not clear when the final meeting of the curtailed 1939 season took place. The last meeting for which a definite result is known took place on 27 August when a special challenge match between Arthur Warwick's Hawks, consisting of Nobby Stock, Charlie Spinks, Gil Craven, Bill Gilbert, Roy Uden and old favourite, Frank Hodgson, took on Stan Greatrex's Rangers, Ray Duggan, Bill Longley, Jack Cooley, Dave Anderson, George Craig and Benny King. The Rangers won the match 47-36. Another match was due to take place on 31 August, advertised as the 'Great Four-Team Match Race' with teams captained by Jack Cooley, Gil Craven, Bill Gilbert and Nobby Stock. There seems to be no record of the result of this encounter. Nevertheless, there is no reason to suppose that it did not take place as, although it was only three days before the outbreak of war, other meetings took place in London and elsewhere on that evening.

Speedway racing reappeared at the Ripple Road Stadium in 1946, but it was very much an amateur affair operated by the Barking Racing Club who ran a series of open meetings, but they did not really impinge on the mainstream of speedway in this country and on the whole, it was just local enthusiasts who took part. The track had become overgrown and was something like a cross between a grass track and a dirt track. The track remained open in 1947 for training purposes only, but at the end of that season it closed its doors to speedway forever. The site of the track later became a car park for the Dagenham Greyhound Stadium, and then all of it became part of a large cold store complex.

12

LUTON

Luton speedway operated for three years, 1934-1936, at Luton Greyhound Stadium. It was run mainly as a training track for Wembley with Jim Kempster and Don Durant as resident coaches. In 1935, the Lions' second team held its Junior League matches against the other London clubs. Members of the team included Mike Erskine, Jack Dalton, George Hannaford and Keith Harvey. The first match was on 6 May against Wimbledon and resulted in a 32-21 victory for the home side.

Not long after the start of the season, Hannaford was injured in a bad crash while road racing on the Isle of Man. His friend, Tommy Price, met him at Wimbledon just afterwards. Price thought he seemed a little strange and that perhaps he had been more seriously hurt than had first appeared. He took him home and called the doctor. The doctor confirmed there was something wrong. Hannaford had a fractured skull! As Hannaford was due to ride for Wembley Juniors at Luton the following day, Price telephoned the Wembley manager, Alec Jackson, and explained the situation. Jackson asked Price if he could deputise. Price did so and top-scored for Wembley. On the

strength of this, Jackson included Price in the second-half Novice's event, or 'Mugs' Race' as it was affectionately known, the following week at Wembley. Price won the race and continued winning the event for the next six weeks. This was Price's first major step on the road that was to take him to the World Championship in 1949.

Back at Luton, attendances were falling and running Reserve League meetings at the track was no longer a viable option, so the track closed for the season on 13 July. It reopened in 1936 for a series of open meetings, but an injunction was served over the noise levels and it closed down for good.

Future World Champion Tommy Price was discovered by Wembley promoter, Alec Jackson, while riding at Luton in 1935.

13

SMALLFORD

Smallford was another of the local training tracks like Dagenham and Rye House and run along the same lines. It opened in 1936 under the auspices of the Hertford and District Motorcycle and Car Club. It was unique in the fact that it was a drive-in speedway, where spectators could watch from their cars. A number of riders including Doug Wells, Dick Geary, Archie Windmill and the Brine brothers rode at Smallford for two shillings a point.

Percy and Cyril Brine's father, Ron, was in charge of the starting gate, while the Gearys, Len and Dick, and the Wells, 'Pop' and Doug, looked after the track. According to Dick Geary, this was, 'a fascinating procedure which involved a worn-out garden rake and a leaky watering can, which seemed to spread water everywhere but on the track!'

In 1938, Smallford entered the Sunday Dirt Track League along with Eastbourne, Rye House, Dagenham and Romford. The team, nicknamed the Stags, was captained by Doug Wells and included Archie Windmill, Ken Tidbury, Percy Brine, Dick Geary, Charlie Appleby, Steve Bullivant, Harry Bower, Bob Wells and Cyril Brine. Smallford's first match was on 15 May away to Romford. After an exciting match, the Stags managed to pull off

a surprise win by 42 points to 40. They returned to the Dagenham track a week later to take on the Daggers, but this time they were easily defeated 49-33.

A few days later, on 23 May, Smallford entertained Eastbourne at home and even without their captain and star rider, Doug Wells, managed to overwhelm Eastbourne, winning by 54 points to 27. Smallford's star rider on the day was Archie Windmill who took 11 points and won the Eastbourne Scratch Race. Tidbury also scored 11 and Percy Brine, 9.

On 12 June, Smallford took on Rye House in the first leg of the Herts Championship Cup presented by Dicky

Percy Brine, a leading rider at Smallford in the 1930s.

Case. The second leg at Rye House took place a week later on 19 June. The team continued its league programme throughout 1938. At the end of the season, the league was disbanded and in 1939, the teams returned to their former ways.

Smallford reopened on 30 April. The *Speedway News* reported that 'the track has been smoothed out, and that notorious bump which the riders loved (?) so well, will be missing. The bends have also been banked slightly more. The spectators have been catered for by the erection of a covered stand near the pits … Racing at Smallford is fast, and provides many thrills, and in the last three seasons Smallford has been running it has produced some fine young blood. The track is ideal for the training of youngsters.' Doug Wells, Percy and Cyril Brine and Dick Geary continued to appear in open meetings at the track along with George Gower and Bob Wells. Along with most other tracks in the country in 1939, speedway ceased before the season ended, but unlike most other tracks, speedway never returned after the war. The site is now a potato field.

OFFICIAL PROGRAMME
of the
SIXTH MEETING
OF THE SECOND SEASON
at
SMALLFORD SPEEDWAY

3D.   3D.

Hertford and District Motor Cycle & Car Club.
Winners of the A.C.U. Rally Trophy, 1933.

Sunday, 18th July
3.30 p.m.

Held under the General Competition Rules and Speedway Regulations of the AUTO CYCLE UNION and by special permit by the South Midland and South Eastern Centre A.C.U.

OFFICIALS:
Judge..A. E. BUGG.
Starter...W. STANLEY.
Chief Pit Marshal..............................B. WELCH.
Clerk of the Course...........................F. GOBBEE.
Track Marshals.............................CLUB MEMBERS.
Timekeeper....................................A. F. FURR.
Announcer.....................................B. WEBB.
Hon. Secretary of the Meeting—
    F. GOBBEE, 106, Railway St., Hertford,
                          Phone 371.

NOTICE. Should it be necessary, owing to weather, or any other cause, to abandon a Meeting before the sixth race, Re-Admission Tickets will be issued at the exits. These tickets will be available for any the following meeting. Under no circumstances will money be refunded.

BETTING PROHIBITED

A Smallford programme cover from the meeting on 18 July 1937.

PART III
OTHER TRACKS

14

GREENFORD

Following the success of High Beech's opening meeting, tracks began to open up all over the country. One of the first off the mark was another venue close to London at Greenford in Middlesex. Along with Mr R.G. Spikins and Gerald Garland, Frank Longman, a well-known TT racer, formed the Greenford Motor Cycle Racing Club in March 1928 and, together with the London Trotting Club Ltd, redeveloped the latter's track for dirt-track racing. Mr Longman felt that High Beech was too small for 'proper' speedway and that the half-mile track at Greenford was the most suitable length. This, he felt, would allow real broadsiding to take place.

The track had two straights 220 yards long, joined by bends of similar length, and was 35-40ft wide. The bends were slightly banked and a spring wire safety fence was erected. Later on in the season, sandbags were placed on the straight in an attempt to make the bends sharper. Mr Longman explained to potential riders and spectators that meetings would be held under Open Permit granted by the ACU who had licensed the track for eight solo riders or four sidecar machines in one race as there was sufficient width to ensure overtaking. He felt that, 'At quarter-mile and even smaller tracks, considerable difficulty is experienced by riders in overtaking, owing to the narrowness of the track.' Meetings were to be held every Saturday throughout the season and also on some mid-week evenings. There was an annual subscription to the club of £3 3s which allowed free admission to the track and private enclosures at all meetings and practice sessions. A 'handsome' badge was also provided.

The first meeting took place on Easter Saturday, 7 April 1928. It was literally a baptism of fire. On the very first lap of the very first race, A. Welston, riding a 346 Royal Enfield, hit the safety fence and crashed heavily. His machine immediately burst into flames and, to add to the spectacle, petrol from his tank ignited and blazed merrily in the centre of the track. Nowadays this might just cause the referee to stop the race, but not in those days! The other riders in the race had to dash past within a yard or so of the bonfire to finish the race. Apparently the fire took some time to burn itself out. Although the Royal Enfield was badly damaged, Mr Welston escaped with a cut to his knee.

After this start the rest of the meeting seemed comparatively tame. As at High Beech, all races were over five laps even though the track was much longer. The racing was dominated by the Australian Billy Galloway, who proved to be much faster than anybody else. His best speed of the day was 47.62mph He won both the Ealing Cup and the Greenford Cup. One young British novice who did show promise was Ivor Creek, who won the Middlesex Cup Race for Scratch Grade 'B' Riders. In spite of Frank Longman's assurances that the track was ideal for broadsiding nobody did, not even Galloway.

Greenford's first taste of 'real' speedway came at the next meeting on 14 April. Before the meeting all the talk was of a New Zealander called Stewie St George who was so keen to race at the half-mile circuit that he had cabled his entry and flown the last part of the journey. It was rumoured he could broadside in his sleep. He was also said to be so tough that he ate six-inch nails and spat out rust! St George proceeded to show the Greenford crowd that his reputation was justified as he laid his Duggie over at impossible angles with the rear wheel slewing right round. It didn't quite work out as planned for Stewie though as, in his first race, Alf Foulds fell off in front of him and, in avoiding him, the New Zealander injured his hand as he scraped the safety fence. He took no further part in the meeting. However, Galloway was back again and this time he also put on a display of broadsiding as did a young English rider called Les Blakeborough. The *Speedway News* was of the opinion that he 'might have been born to the game so quickly has he learnt the art of broadsiding.'

On 5 May, the Greenford crowd was treated to the best performance of racing it had yet seen when the legendary American Lloyd 'Sprouts' Elder made his first London appearance at the track and put on a display that eclipsed anything seen there before. He was followed in June by another American, Art Pechar, who recorded a speed of 52.94mph, lowering the track record by 1.81mph. Even better was to come from Pechar

A scene from a 1928 meeting at Greenford showing a sidecar and a midget car in the same race.

however when, on 18 August, he clocked 56mph, the fastest speed ever attained on a British speedway track.

July 1928 was a very dry month, which caused problems at Greenford. 'The dry weather has made the Greenford track almost unbearable from the point of view of dust. Every time a rider went into a bend last Saturday [21 July] he raised a sufficiently large cloud of dust to envelop himself and anyone else who happened to be near. Thus from some points of the track the entire field was completely hidden from view when it dived into a dense cloud at the beginning of a bend, and the riders could not again be seen until they emerged on to the following straight...' (*Speedway News*, 26 July 1928.)

During the season, a number of English riders continued to improve with regular rides at the track, particularly Les Blakeborough, Freddie Dobson, Les Dallimore and Jimmy Sloman who were soon able to match the best of the Australians and Americans. Dobson, for example, got the better of Pechar in a special match race on 30 June, while Blakeborough won the 'All Star' Scratch Race final on 1 September, beating Galloway. A week later, Dallimore, mounted on his brand new Duggie, won the *News of the World* Cup final at a speed of 49.5mph. Later in the meeting he recorded 52.94mph for one lap. One rider who had his first taste of speedway at Greenford, but who was not a success

GREENFORD MOTOR CYCLE RACING CLUB

PROGRAMME of the

First June Meeting

Saturday, June 2nd, 1928

at

GREENFORD DRIVING PARK

(Entrance in Birkbeck Avenue, close to Greenford G.W.R. Station), Middlesex.

Bus routes No. 247 and 97.

Racing commences at 3.15 p.m.

Official Programme Price 6d.

MOTOR CYCLING

The Journal with the Green Cover

WEDNESDAYS 3d.

FIRST OUT with all news of motor cycling TRACK EVENTS

Above: *Stewie St George (right) with Clem Beckett (left). St George, a New Zealander, was the first rider to demonstrate the art of broadsiding at Greenford.* **Right:** *A programme cover from a 1928 meeting at Greenford.*

The legendary American showman and speedway rider Lloyd 'Sprouts' Elder made his first London appearance at Greenford on 5 May 1928.

to start with, was future World Champion Tommy Price. The big half-mile circuit did not suit him at all.

At the beginning of 1929 it was announced that a new company known as Greenford Motor Tracks Ltd, had been registered to conduct motorcycle and car races at Greenford during the coming season and that although the Greenford Motor Cycle Racing Club would continue to exist the whole concern would be completely reorganised. The 1929 season commenced on 11 May and continued on Saturday afternoons until the end of July, when Greenford changed its race day to Monday. This was probably because of the competition from other London clubs on Saturday as Crystal Palace, Harringay, Lea Bridge and Stamford Bridge as well as High Beech all ran on that day. The popularity of Greenford declined sharply throughout 1929. The track was too long and completely unlike any other mainstream track so the top riders no longer wished to race there. At the end of the season speedway racing ceased at the track. A short revival took place in 1931 when once again the Greenford Club took over the running of the sport, but, as before, it was mainly local juniors and club members who raced there.

The end came on 10 October 1931. Complaints had been received from local residents about the noise and dust and the track was closed down. It was later redeveloped as a housing estate.

15

BRIGHTON

On 23 June 1928, Associated Southern Speedways (Brighton) Ltd, under the direction of Johnnie Hoskins, opened speedway at the Hove Stadium, Hove. The track was built inside the existing 525-yard greyhound circuit. When it opened to the public it was still unfinished and the local riders had had hardly any time to practice, but Charlie Datson and Ron Johnson put on a demonstration to give the crowd some idea of what speedway racing was all about. Lionel Wills also put in an appearance, driving down to the stadium in his Rolls-Royce, to 'ginger up the racing'. (*Speedway Star,* 28 June 1928) Unfortunately he fell and twisted his ankle but he still managed to complete his scheduled rides even though he was unable to walk properly. Datson won the Brighton Scratch race worth £40 while H. Miller won the Hove Handicap worth £50.

The next meeting was held on 6 July and was held under much better conditions as the track itself had been greatly improved and the local riders had had more time to practice. In fact, there was a surprise in the scratch-race final as local rider Reg Parker from Worthing took on and beat three of the biggest stars of the day, Datson, Johnson and Sig Schlam. However, the reason he won was because Datson's engine was playing up, Johnson shed his chain on the second lap and Schlam did exactly the same on the third, leaving Parker to finish the race alone. The main attraction at this meeting was the appearance of perhaps the greatest female rider of all time, Fay Taylour.

Two further open meetings were held that season, the fourth and final meeting taking place on 21 July. After that, mid-week practice sessions continued at the track until the end of August. It is unlikely that speedway ever took place again at the stadium. An application to run meetings there in 1947 was turned down by the local council as was a further request in 1948. Further rumours that speedway might be staged there surfaced in 1955, 1965 and 1966. In the summer of 1976, Bob Dugard confirmed that he had opened negotia-

Australian star, Ron Johnson, rode in the first meeting at Brighton on 23 June 1928.

Paul Hurry proved himself to be an expert on the tight indoor Brighton circuit, winning the Brighton Bonanza in 1997 and 1999.

tions with the stadium owner to bring speedway back to Brighton. The local council gave provisional approval for the scheme as long as they could be satisfied that restrictions over noise levels could be met. Dugard asked Sussex University to help him come up with a satisfactory answer to the noise problem, but they were unable to and in August 1977 Brighton Council finally refused permission for speedway to take place at the stadium.

Speedway did return to Brighton however, on Sunday 14 December 1997. Promoted by Jon Cook and Martin Dugard of Eastbourne, they used the Brighton Centre as the venue for 'real indoor speedway.' Eighty tonnes of shale was used to convert the indoor conference centre into a 130-metre speedway track for the 'Brighton Bonanza.' There were two meetings, one at 3 p.m., the other at 7.30 p.m. Either side of these two meetings there were two pop concerts on the Saturday and the Monday, so the whole track had to be laid and taken up again within that time restraint. It was an amazing achievement.

The afternoon event took the form of a team match between Brighton Tigers and Greg Hancock's World Select, with the Tigers running out winners by 62 points to 51. Paul Hurry won the evening Brighton Bonanza Individual Championship. Craig Boyce was banned from appearing again following a confrontation with Shane Parker.

Cook and Dugard returned again in 1998 when England beat the Rest of the World 70-42 and Brent Werner took the Bonanza Championship, although Joe Screen became the darling of the crowd with his all-action style. For the third running of the Bonanza in 1999, Cook and Dugard relented and allowed Boyce back in. Riding with Mark Loram, Boyce seized his chance to rehabilitate himself and together they won the Millennium Pairs Championship, which was this year taking the place of the team competition. Paul Hurry was again the victor of the Bonanza Championship. The Pairs competition remained for the 2000 staging. This time the winners were Shawn McConnell and Bobby Schwartz. Martin Dugard finished the main Bonanza event with an immaculate 15-point maximum. In the six laps final run-off he was up against the two previous winners, Hurry and Werner and the recently crowned World Champion, Mark Loram. Dugard and Loram clashed on the first bend and the race was stopped while Dugard received lengthy attention for what was thought to be a broken toe. Insisting that he be allowed to race in the re-run, he got away from the tapes first and held off a determined first-lap challenge from Hurry. Gradually he drew away from the others to deservedly take the chequered flag. It was a fitting reward for the co-promoter. McConnell and Schwartz retained their Pairs title in 2001, while another American, Ryan Fisher, won the Bonanza.

16

PORTSMOUTH

The first track to open in the Portsmouth area was at Chalton. A local man, Mr E.L. Jones, laid out a 440-yard track in a field, initially for training purposes to help local riders. Growing interest in the sport led to him organising an open meeting on 15 July, which attracted a number of riders from across the south of England. The second meeting, held two weeks later on 29 July, attracted a crowd of 2,000 people. After this apparently successful meeting however, nothing more was heard of the speedway track in a field at Chalton.

Speedway returned to Portsmouth the following year when the Wessex Stadium opened its doors to the sport. Although A.J. Hunting's International Speedway Ltd had planned to open the Wessex Stadium, Portsmouth for speedway racing in 1928 and had, in fact, built a dirt track, no racing actually took place at the stadium until 10 August 1929, when it was opened by Wessex Speedway Co. in conjunction with Dirt Track Speedways Ltd, the company behind West Ham and Southampton. The new organisation had to spend a lot of time repairing the 440-yard unbanked track which had become very bumpy and full of potholes. Prior to the opening, the promoters had spared no expense in publicising the event, even to the extent of parading a circus around the streets of Portsmouth. As a consequence, the first meeting was a huge success. Due to the tie-up with West Ham and Southampton, most of the riders appearing were contracted riders from those two clubs, with the major event, the Golden Gauntlet, being won by Sprouts Elder. Others to appear included Ivor Creek, Tiger Stevenson and Buzz Hibberd.

Although the track was still said to be bumpy, the next meeting was held a week later on 17 August. This meeting's main prize, the Silver Gauntlet, was won by another top star of the period, Frank Arthur, with Buzz Hibberd winning the open handicap. The third meeting featured a number of Australian stars, including Bluey Wilkinson, Jack Bishop, Col Stewart and Frank Duckett. Bishop won the scratch race event. The final meeting of 1929 took place on 31 August and saw the return of Elder, Arthur, Wilkinson and Hibberd. One of the reasons given for the early closure was the lack of covered accommodation, which had led to a marked decline in the number of spectators.

Over the close season, a new 382-yard track was laid in an effort to smooth out the bumps and covered stands were erected. The new track was tested out in trials on 5, 9 and 12 April and the track reopened to the public on Easter Monday, 21 April 1930. Cashing in on the success of team racing, Portsmouth formed its own team and ran a series of challenge matches. Two riders who appeared for the team during that year were two youngsters who had just arrived from Australia, Steve Langton and Phil 'Tiger' Hart. Others included Bill Clibbett, Ted Bravery and Jack Douglas.

Proposals to enter the Southern League in 1931 were aborted when the local council announced plans to build houses on the site. Even though the housing plans came to nothing, speedway never returned to the Wessex Stadium after 1930. The last meeting ever

Left: *The young Phil 'Tiger' Hart had his first rides in this country at Portsmouth in 1930. He later rode with great distinction at Birmingham and Hackney Wick.*
Right: *Programme cover from Portsmouth's second meeting held on 17 August 1929.*

PORTSMOUTH

Portsmouth (Dog Racing) Stadium
SPEEDWAY
Tram to Copnor Bridge.   'Bus to the Stadium.

PROGRAMME

OF THE **SECOND**

DIRT TRACK

MOTOR CYCLE MEETING

Organised by Dirt Track Speedways Ltd.
under the general Competition Rules of the
Auto. Cycle Union.
A.C.U. PERMIT (No. 306).

Saturday, Aug. 17th, at 2.45 p.m.

PORTSMOUTH SPEEDWAY.

DIRT TRACK RACE MEETINGS will be
held here every SATURDAY at
2.45 p.m. until further notice.
ADMISSION - 1/2 & 2/- (Spacious Car Park)

PRICE 4 PENCE

to be staged at the stadium therefore was on 2 October 1930, when a Portsmouth team took on a very strong West Ham team, which included Tiger Stevenson, Bluey Wilkinson, Reg Bounds and Allen Kilfoyle. It was a close match, with never more than four points in it. In the last heat, Bravery managed to beat Wilkinson to force a 26-26 draw.

In 1935, Harringay promoter Tom Bradbury-Pratt, built a 300-yard speedway track inside the greyhound circuit at Portsmouth Greyhound and Sports Stadium in Tipnor, near Portsmouth. Harringay had more fixtures than they could fit in at Green Lanes, so Bradbury-Pratt had the idea of building a track at Portsmouth to take the excess fixtures. In the event only one match was raced, a National League match against Hackney on 2 October, which Hackney won 35-32. A week later a challenge match was due to be held between Wembley and Wimbledon but it was rained off.

There were no further meetings at the stadium until 1937 when the Albatross Motorcycle Club promoted two matches. The first, on 14 July, saw a team called Portsmouth beat a team called Basingstoke 28-25, while on 29 September Portsmouth defeated Reading 36-26.

Two attempts were made to reintroduce speedway to the stadium soon after the Second World War with no success but then, in 1976, speedway supporters in the area organised a petition to bring back speedway to the stadium. They managed to collect over 1,300 signatures. Both the local radio station and the local newspaper took up the campaign and even Portsmouth's Lord Mayor offered his support. The G.R.A., the owners of the stadium, were also keen on reintroducing speedway. Everyone was very optimistic that speedway would be back in time for the 1977 season. But it was not to be. At the end of July, Portsmouth Council rejected the plan. It said that the increased volume of traffic in the area would be detrimental to local residents and that noise on race nights would be above acceptable limits. Although the G.R.A. disputed both reasons, arguing that there would be no traffic problem and that noise levels would fall within the legislative limits, the council would not reconsider the matter and that was the end of the prospect of speedway returning to Portsmouth.

17

BARNET

The track in Mays Lane, Barnet was opened on 17 August 1928. It started out as a grass track, but by 1929 the grass had been so worn away that it was, to all intents and purposes, a dirt track. The dirt-track element was further enhanced later on when cinders were put down round the bends. Racing was initially promoted by Messrs Banister, Botten and de Cort as Barnet Speedway Ltd and later by the North London Motor Club. The track was D-shaped with one long bend, one short bend and two sharp turns. The long bend had such a pronounced upward slope that it almost required the use of a gearbox.

By the early 1930s it had become a recognised training track putting on the normal fare common to the local training tracks of the day with individual events, scratch races, handicap races, match races and team matches against other training tracks in the area such as Rye House and Smallford. Many riders later to achieve National League status obtained some of their earliest experience at Barnet including Archie Windmill, Charlie Traynor, Bob Wells, the Brine brothers, Percy and Cyril, George Wilkes and the future World Champion, Tommy Price.

Many of the top stars of the day came to visit for a Sunday afternoon out. Ron Johnson, Roger and Buster Frogley and Wally Kilmister were regular visitors. In 1934, Frank Arthur was present when Tommy Price, George Wilkes and Charlie Traynor were

Archie Windmill, shown here in action for the North London Motor Club.

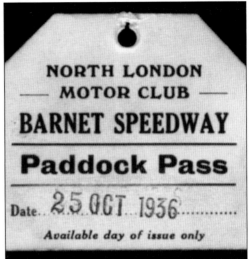

Left: *George Wilkes (the future Wembley star) was discovered by the Harringay promoter Tom-Bradbury-Pratt while riding for Barnet in 1934.*
Below: *A Barnet Speedway paddock pass valid for 25 October 1936.*

going through their paces. He was so impressed by all three of them that he spoke to the Harringay promoter, Tom Bradbury-Pratt, about them. On the strength of this, they were given a chance to show what they could do in a junior event at Harringay. When the tapes went up, Price shot away and led for three laps but then, in his over-eagerness to impress, he overslid and Wilkes sailed past to win. As a result, Wilkes was signed for Harringay and Price was politely thanked for coming along.

Lionel Van Praag, speedway's first World Champion, came to visit in 1936 on the occasion of the South Midlands Centre Championship. The prize for the young hopefuls who lined up for this event was a contract with Hackney Wick. Van Praag lent Windmill, who normally rode a Rudge, his JAP Engine. Windmill went on to win the event and to take his place in the Hackney Wick line-up the following year.

Barnet used to attract fairly large crowds, well over 5,000 on occasions, but not all of them paid to get in. As the track was in a rural setting, a number of the younger spectators used to climb the surrounding trees to watch from a rather precarious vantage point. In the mid-1930s, the manager, Arnold W. Day, later to become a well-known referee, concerned about the boys' safety and the fact that they were watching the racing for nothing, asked them if they would like to be rakers as that way they would still be able to see the racing for nothing but at least he would get something out of them. One young boy who had his first taste of the inside of speedway this way was future World Championship runner-up, Wally Green.

At the beginning of the 1937 season, the North London Motor Club decided to transfer its operations to High Beech and Barnet Speedway closed, never to reopen.

18

MISCELLANEOUS TRACKS

CATFORD

There are reports that speedway was tried out at Catford cricket ground in 1932 and that, on 1 September 1934, a 280-yard track was opened at the nearby Catford Greyhound Stadium. This speedway was promoted by Tom Bradbury-Pratt and several meetings were held, but, at the end of the season, the track closed. Further attempts to open it up were made in 1938 and 1949, but neither attempt was successful. The sound of speedway bikes was, however, heard again at the stadium at the beginning of 2000. A film called *Honest*, set in 1968 and directed by Dave Stewart of Eurythmics fame, called for a speedway scene. Catford Stadium was chosen as the location because it still looked like a stadium from the 1960s. Amongst the riders taking part were Barry Briggs, Jim McMillan, Nigel Harrhy, Mike Smart and Col Smith. The stunt co-ordinator was former Canterbury rider, Lex Milloy. The filming of speedway at the track started rumours that Catford might return to league racing, but so far no more has been heard of this proposition.

STAINES

Putt Mossman held one of his rodeo motorcycle meetings at Staines Greyhound Stadium in 1938. Several more amateur meetings were held at the stadium that year as well as a few in 1939. In 1947 an application to run speedway at the stadium was refused by the ACU and again in 1948, following an objection by the local Town Planning Committee. Even though an appeal against the refusal was successful in 1949, no further speedway ever took place, apart from some sidecar speedway in 1956.

ELSTREE

In 1947, nine meetings were held on a track in Elstree which had been prepared by a local farmer pouring oil onto a grassy field. The only covered accommodation was a canvas marquee which served as a dressing room, changing room and everything else.

Wembley's Roy Craighead was one of the riders who rode at Elstree in 1947.

The first meeting was held on 10 August and included riders such as Freddie Williams, Bill Kitchen, Cyril Brine, Tiger Hart, Bob Wells, and Roy Craighead. All nine meetings were refereed by Mr Arthur Humphrey. Although speedway did not return the following season, or ever again, the meetings were well attended and had sideshows such as beauty contests and knobbly knees competitions.

LYDD

In 1996 former rider Malcolm Smith built a 201-metre sandy-surfaced track on farmland in the Kent countryside. A demonstration meeting was held on 22 September that year for the benefit of the local council to show that speedway would not cause a nuisance. Seventeen riders took part in an individual trophy meeting with Ben Osborne winning the prize. In 1999, conventional shale replaced sand as the surface.

On 14 November 2000, Shepway District Council granted the track permanent planning permission for no more than 20 meetings between March and October with no more than one meeting per weekend. Meetings were allowed to take place on Saturday evenings between 5 p.m. and 8.30 p.m. or on Sunday afternoons between 12 noon and 5 p.m.

Since its opening in 1996, the track has continued to run as a training track under the guidance of Malcolm Smith with a series of individual meetings and team events for novices with a team called the Romney Falcons. In 2000, former World Champion Ivan Mauger was appointed president of the Falcons Amateur Speedway Club.

19

TRACKS WHICH NEVER QUITE MADE IT

CAMBERLEY

Camberley is one of the claimants to the title of the first speedway track in Great Britain as its first meeting was held on 7 May 1927, some nine months before the inaugural High Beech meeting. It is generally ruled out on the grounds that a) it was a sand track and not a dirt track, and b) the riders rode in a clockwise direction.

C. Harman was the leading rider at the opening meeting, and won the 350 cc and the 500 cc events as well as the sidecar race. Fay Taylour was one of the riders at that opening meeting. The track was 440 yards long but by the time of the second meeting in July, it had been lengthened to 1,056 yards, thus ruling it out for all time as a proper speedway track.

Fay Taylour, Britain's leading female rider, rode at Camberley in 1927.

CHARLTON

An application to run speedway at Charlton Greyhound Stadium was first proposed in 1938 and again in 1948 but on both occasions applications for a licence were turned down by the ACU. In 1965 another attempt was made by Wally Mawdsley, Pete Lansdale and Len Silver to enter a team in the newly-formed British League. Charlton Stadium was owned by London Stadiums Ltd and they were looking for someone to take over the stadium as greyhound racing had just ceased. Silver was confident that a Charlton team would be operating in the 1966 British League on Thursday evenings and even signed up the South African, Denis Newton, for the team as well as making several enquiries for other South African and Australian riders. He said that he intended to go to the BSPA Conference and 'name our team which will substantiate our claim for a place in the British League.' He added that the stadium was 'one of the finest in the country with seating for 2,000 spectators and covered accom-

Wally Mawdsley (left) and Pete Lansdale (right) successfully promoted at a number of tracks. However, their attempts to introduce speedway at Charlton and Edmonton were not so successful.

modation for a further 4,000.' The track was 300 yards long with wide well-banked corners and short straights. In the end the application came to nothing as the company found another greyhound promoter to take over at the stadium instead.

EDMONTON

The first attempt to open a speedway track in Edmonton came in 1938, but the organisers were unable to obtain an ACU licence. In 1961, Wally Mawdsley and Pete Lansdale proposed opening a new Provincial League track at Barras Sports Stadium in Edmonton, north London. The track was to be built on top of an existing 440-yard cinder athletics circuit. However, the local council refused planning permission so, although it is probable that some trials took place at the stadium, the public never saw speedway in Edmonton.

ERITH

The New Cross promoters, Johnnie Hoskins, Ken Brett and Nobby Atwell, proposed opening a 440-yard junior training track with boarded fence at Erith to run on Saturday afternoons. The local council felt that the current stadium would have to be altered too much and consequently refused permission.

MAIDSTONE

On 15 January 1968, Len Silver, on behalf of Allied Promotions Ltd, applied to Maidstone Council for permission to run speedway at Maidstone Greyhound Stadium, home of Maidstone Football Club. It was intended that the track would be of local ragstone dust similar to the one at Canterbury. The application was refused on 1 March on the grounds of noise, traffic congestion and insufficient parking facilities. Silver, supported by the football club, immediately lodged an appeal, which was heard in October. To facilitate the appeal, Silver arranged for Jack Biggs, Gary Everett, Malcolm Brown and Graeme Smith to give a demonstration at the track on 25 September. They ran the whole gamut of the different types of noise that could be heard during a meeting including warming up, clutch starts, first bend rushes and flat out racing. At the hearing, Mr Glover, an acoustics expert, said the noise from the warming up would not be a problem as this would be done in a sound-proofed area (the pits) and that therefore the crucial issue to resolve was how much noise the racing itself would make. Mr Glover's recommendation was that a 15-foot high

Hackney's Malcolm Brown, seen here between Prague's Antonin Kasper and Miloslav Verner in 1967, was one of the riders to give a demonstration at Maidstone in 1968.

acoustical screening wall should be built and this would mainly shield the residents in the nearby streets from excessive noise. Silver agreed to build the wall. As to problems with car parking, Silver said he was willing to run a shuttle bus to and from the nearest municipal car park.

In spite of these concessions made by the would-be promoters, the county planning inspector rejected the appeal and so, apart from the demonstration on 25 September, no speedway ever took place in Maidstone.

SLOUGH

In 1977, the Greyhound Racing Association, who owned Slough Stadium, submitted a planning application to the local council to run speedway in the New National League. But the application was turned down and no speedway took place at the stadium.